One little girl. Four tragic murders.
Her life ~~destroyed.~~ *reclaimed.*

I am
JESSICA

JAMIE COLLINS

Cover Design: Najdan Mancic, Iskon Design
Interior Design: Najdan Mancic, Iskon Design
Cover Photo: Joshua Humble

First Edition: April 2019
Library of Congress Control Number: 2019901978
ISBN: 978-0-9600867-9-5

Published by Bold Whisper Books, LLC

BOLD WHISPER BOOKS

Where stories breathe on paper.™

JESSICA'S DEDICATION:

To my husband and children,
The ones who gave me a family and a
place in this world.

JAMIE'S DEDICATION:

To my son Gavin,
Don't wait for life to come to you.
Go to it.
Be the light.

And lastly,
To the resilient ones living in the "after."
The ones we are.
The ones we know.
The ones we meet.
The ones we love.
And all those left behind.

We stand with you.
And we will not whisper any longer.

TRIGGER WARNING

*This book depicts real events that deal with violence,
trauma, and the difficult emotions experienced by a person
who survived a horrific tragedy. Parts may be triggering
for some trauma survivors.*

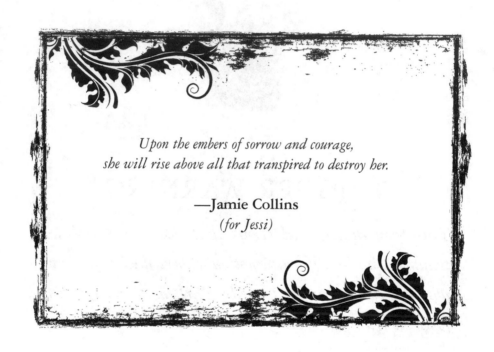

Upon the embers of sorrow and courage,
she will rise above all that transpired to destroy her.

—Jamie Collins
(for Jessi)

Each of us is born innocent; a clean slate, and a pure soul.
One that will later be etched, irrevocably,
by the things that happen to us along the way.
We each battle our own darkness.
We each seek our own light.
We each stand in the glory of our own truths.
And we speak the words of our own story.

Of these things, I am clear:

Where there is darkness, there is light.
Where there is evil, there is redemption.
Where there is despair, there is also hope.
Resilience grows steadfast through the cracks
we unwillingly possess.
It is shaped by the stories we'd rather not tell.
Where tragedy ends, a new beginning stands
at the end of a long, dark road.

Each of us has a different story to tell,
but our purpose remains:
To find our own way through the darkness.
To find our own way back to the light.

Even after our darkest days,
we may shine.

—Jamie Collins

A Note From The Author

O ne day during the spring of 2016, three months into our discussions about this book, I chatted with Jessi by phone. She and I had been talking for quite a while about various things, when I asked her a rather pointed question. "Jess, so let me ask you this. This is something people are going to want to know. *Why* are you stepping forward to tell your story now? *Why now*—why after all these years? You've been silent for almost three decades, and now you're telling this story. So, why now. Tell me why."

In the most sincere, compelling tone, she replied, "I guess the reason I'm doing this now is because I want people to SEE ME." The last two words left her lips with intense passion, saturated with yearning. I was captivated by her tone and I found her choice of words interesting. I knew this had to be significant, so I continued, "When you say that you want them to 'see you,' what do you mean by that? I remember you saying those exact same words to me once, but you didn't say them that way, it was in a normal, flat, matter-of-fact tone, like it was no big deal. I remember it clearly. But this time, when you said it to me, you really meant it. I could *feel* it, when you said those words—the 'see me' part—so help me understand what you mean when you say that."

In a serious tone, she said, "I want people to SEE ME. I want them to *know* that I *actually* exist. That I've been here *all these years*. Everyone else went on with their lives. I guess I did, too. But I'm still here."

I was intrigued by this statement. I knew there was something big hanging just beneath those words. I had to figure it out. I continued, "I can tell this means a lot to you. Do you think you can tell me a story or give me an example to help me understand? I can tell it means a lot to you when you said those words, but I need you to help me understand *what* it means *to you*." She replied, "Well, this tragedy changed every single part of my life. It was such a big deal at the time it happened that it made national news and was later featured on those shows {*Unsolved Mysteries and Dateline 20/20*}. Hell, my extended family has never really been around. They've barely interacted with me over the years, with the exception of a few Facebook likes. The people who knew my family, people who lived in Lakeville, Indiana, or read those news stories, or watched those TV shows seem to have no idea that I exist. It's like everyone seems to think that I died, too. But here I am, alive. I've struggled all these years to deal with this terrible thing that happened in my life. I lost everyone I loved. I lost everything I had. And people don't realize that I even exist. That I even lived through this shit. That I'm still here. That there was a survivor. And that survivor is me. *I feel like I'm suffocating in the middle of the street and no one can see me.* I want them to *SEE ME, to know that I exist.* I'm not sure why I survived, but I did. I always felt like my life had a purpose, that I was left here for a reason."

Mind. Blown. As Jessi spoke those words to me, my eyes pooled with tears, and a few slipped down my face. My breath caught in the back of my throat, and I took a hard swallow as I hung on her every word, trying to keep it together while fervently scribbling the words and the significance of them down on the page. Of all the words Jessi ever spoke to me, those words were the most powerful of them all. I'll never forget them. "I want them to SEE ME."

That moment hung between us. Those words. They mattered. It was the entire reason she was willing to lay her life bare, down to the bones, to allow others to take a hard, long look. It was so all of us could see her: the broken little girl *and* the resilient woman she had become

Her other words hadn't been lost on me, either, when she said she knew she "had a purpose for still being here, a reason for being alive." Jessi stepping forward to tell her story in an effort to help others out of their own personal darkness is a large part of that purpose.

For her, I would find the words. I would help the world to see her for the first time in three decades. The little girl whose childhood was annihilated at the age of nine. The rebellious teenager who would fight, claw, and crawl through all the years of her uprooted life in a swirl of instability and emotional chaos. And the beautiful woman now speaking on the phone with me: my resilient, awe-inspiring, fierce, bold, beautiful cousin. A survivor of tragedy who now stands on these pages, vulnerable. A survivor of tragedy who now stands on these pages, strong.

On this day, I saw the little girl Jessica clearly. And I saw the grown woman Jessi, too. I saw them both. And it became my sacred mission to find a way to share *both* of them with you. The vulnerable girl. And the strong one. They're one and the same. I see that now.

I've also learned that real life stories often don't end the way we *think* they will, tied up in shiny satin ribbons, without any flaws revealed in the packaging. Real life has a way of breaking our preconceived notions and, at times, annihilating this writer's carefully created plans for telling the story the way I initially thought it would end. That's something I learned the hard way while writing this book, in real time, as certain events transpired in our lives. I had no way to know what would happen eight months into our journey on this book. It was an ending I never saw coming and one I was not at all prepared to live out, much less write about. I had no way to know those hypothetical ribbons holding together a beautiful human package would fall undone in a heap of turmoil and memories, and that I would become the cousin, turned author, who would find herself bearing witness to the loudest silence almost *never* heard: the sound of the human soul splintering.

Be warned: This is one of the craziest true-crime-stories-turned-memoirs ever written. If you didn't know it was a true story, you'd probably never believe it to be one.

For those readers looking for one hell of a story, this is it. True crime junkies, buckle up. This is the untold story of my cousin, Jessica Pelley. And we don't sugarcoat a thing.

Olive Branch United Brethren Church

Lakeville, Indiana
May 3, 1989

*M*y name is Jamie Collins. I'm Jessica Pelley's cousin and the author of this book.

Back in May of 1989, three little girls found themselves seated in the wooden pews of a small white church in a small, rural farming community in Lakeville, Indiana. It was tragedy that put us there. On that day, that place of worship and spiritual light became a sanctuary where sadness dwelled.

The sobs in that room are something we will never forget. We were children surrounded by rows of wooden pews filled with adults, all of whom were deeply immersed in the soul-swallowing throes of grief, some crying, others sobbing. Audible gasps for breath punctuated the silence, bending our ears and breaking our hearts. Sorrow hung heavy in the air like a thick blanket of fog, enveloping us at every angle. The depth of grief around us was palpable. All at once, every person in the room began to sing along to the chords of a piano, in unison, the words: *"Amaziiiiiing Graaaaace, how sweeeeet the soooooound, that saaaaaaved a wretch liiiiiiike meeee . . ."* Hundreds of people sang the words. Sobs filled the air. Tears poured from our eyes, streamed in long, wet lines down the front of our faces, fell onto our laps, and clouded our vision. It was hard to breathe through the sobbing. The little girls were not singing. They couldn't. The words to this song would forever be burned into the soul of every person in this room, a religious sanctuary in which we would find no solace. An emotional scar etched permanently across our hearts like a scab waiting to be torn open again at any time. A song that would go on to haunt us for the next three decades. We will *never* forget this moment. Never.

There would be no closure. Not for us. Not for Jessica. Not for anyone. Closed caskets don't really afford a person the final formality of saying a proper goodbye to a person. Not even close. Just wooden caskets and flowers to serve as a placeholder for the people you loved, now lost. Our minds involuntarily flashed to vivid mental images of their final hellish moments here on earth . . . before the boxes. So young. So beautiful. So full of life.

Now gone.

And today, Jessica and those two little girls—me and her childhood best friend, Stephanie, who were both seated in that little white church with her nearly thirty years ago—are finally stepping forward to tell the story of an unfathomable tragedy. May her story cast a light into the darkness for those who need it most.

JESSI

(That's the name I go by now.)

April 29, 2016

April 29, 1989.
A date I cannot forget.
Numbers forever seared deep into my soul.

I t was 27 years ago, today. *Jesus. Get a grip, Jessi. They're just numbers. They don't mean anything. You're giving them power over you, again.* That's what I tell myself. But the numbers—those damn numbers—they haunt me. They always will. I cannot escape them. Not now. Not ever.

For most people, dates are just numbers on a calendar. No big deal. Random markers of time affixed to the top left corner of small, white squares on a page to depict days filled with choices, chances, and opportunities. At least that's what they are for the *normal* people. But I'm no longer one of them. For me, they serve as numeric reminders of the girl I used to be.

The 29th day of April: the date I will never have the luxury of forgetting. A tragedy that would irrevocably and mercilessly alter the life of a little girl wearing dark blue jeans, canvas lace-up sneakers, and a white tee shirt, accessorized by prominent coke-bottle glasses, her hair hanging in a messy bob. Her life would be forever dismantled. Gone. The moment they told me the words. The ones that I will never forget. At that moment, my life froze and shattered into pieces, splintering like bits of broken glass, dropping down onto the ground around me, like the remnants of a cracked windshield, falling fast before the spinning mind and tattered heart of a wide-eyed little girl.

Life, as I knew it, was over in that moment. What happened on that day has scarred me forever. A day that started out normally, before it became ensnared in marred memories, tucked between folds of tragedy and darkness. The lingering memories cut straight to the core of the hollow girl left behind.

The darkness delivers itself to me, every year, on schedule. Steadily. Greedily. Relentless. Haunting. It taunts the pieces of me that remain. *Every single year.*

I try to lift myself out of the darkness. I tell myself the numbers shouldn't matter. Not after 27 years have passed. *Jessi, It's just another day. You can do anything you want with it. Don't slip into the darkness.* But not even the voice in my head believes those bullshit lies I tell myself. Year after year, my happiness recoils, my thoughts run to a dark place filled with foggy memories and a void that swallows me whole. The door of despair opens and I'm trapped: alone, numb to the bone, emotionally deplete, devoid of all reality, space, and time. I hate the helplessness as I slip further into that dark place. A place that, long ago, was filled with light. A place where three little girls would sing happy songs, pick flowers, hold hands while skipping through tall blades of grass, and sit down at the dining room table, where they would bow their heads to pray before plates filled with food, in a home filled with laughter. Then it hits me—the life-defining, self-inflicted images of horror—of their final moments—screams, fear, blood everywhere, dragging me deep into the darkness. A place I would dwell for days, weeks, and months, turned into years.

Twenty-seven years ago . . . and I'm *still counting*. It's clear—I'm fucked. Forever damaged. There is no escape. There is only here. Only now. I hear the songs and laughter. I remember the little girls. The swinging, the playing, the happiness. And then I realize it's all gone.

But I'm still here . . .

JESSI

AGE 37
December 2016

I find myself seated on a twin bed in a stark hospital room in the psych ward a few weeks before Christmas. It's cold. It's lonely. I feel empty inside, like a shell of a person. And it sucks.

It's hard to imagine how a person ends up here with deep wounds in her heart, sad thoughts in her head, and a tattered soul. But this is precisely the type of place a person like me succumbs to after living through all that befell me, even if it is 27 years later. The load I was forced to carry in life became too great a burden; it nearly broke me. The sorrow within me runs so deep, it sits in my bones. I am too tired of silently struggling to keep my shit together for one more day. So, here I sit, "self-admitted patient, party of one."

They would allow me to leave this place if I wanted to. I'm past the initial holding period for psychiatric evaluation. But I'm staying here now because I want to. I choose to. Everyone around me can't wait to get out of this place. They hate it here. I hear them constantly complain about how much they hate the rules. Unlike me, they must not really need to be here. I'm staying because my life is spinning out of control. The routine fell apart. The habits and rituals could not protect me. I'm afraid to cry because I know once the tears begin to fall I will not be able to stop them.

I'm tired of fighting. I'm tired of feeling alone. I'm tired of running from my past. I'm tired of tucking it away and trying to forget about it, when I know I never will. Hell, at this point, I'm tired of being tired. I'm over all of it. I'm the girl who finally broke apart.

The breaking apart started following several major life "triggers." That's what the psychiatrists call them. The things, in the form of subtle reminders, that cause a person to recall things her mind (or body) has tried so damn hard to forget. In that moment, as the second hand makes it way around the clock, they catch you. You never see them coming. But they do. And once they do, they rob you of any progress you've made and steal your control. I would come to learn that, for me, my triggers were related to death, grief, and feelings of profound sadness.

I don't deal with death well, nor do I know how to cope with grief. I attempt to hide from both, until I cannot hide any longer. That's how I ended up here, in this hospital room. I'm here because I'm emotionally broken. I cannot pull myself out of the darkness this time. I've been pulled too low to find the light. The darkness looms and it consumes me. I'm stuck.

I want help. I know I need it. I realize that now. I need it bad. And that's why I'm staying here, in this hospital, during the most depressing time of year—the holiday season—somewhere that feels cold and institutional for an entire week, because it's a safe place.

I've always known I needed spiritual guidance. I bask in God's power regularly through prayer. I've always needed familial support, although I've never felt I had it. And I've always needed friends— real friends—but it's hard to keep them for long, or forge deeper connections with people, when I refuse to fully own or acknowledge what went down in my life before they met me. It allows the little broken girl in me to remain hidden in plain sight. It keeps people at a safe distance. My comfortable façade keeps me safe, but it also keeps me from existing as who I truly am in this world. It spares us all from the awkward words, uncomfortable exchanges, and deeply wounding looks laced with pity. But, in reality, all that distance is bullshit. And I'm over it.

I fought this battle by myself for a long damn time. I raged inside, cried internally, suffered alone, and tucked the brokenness away, but not without suffering the full wrath of trauma-induced consequences. Those consequences I know all too well as an adult. They are my constant companions.

Some of my habits are strange and some have become outright rituals. I like structure. I thrive on routine. I like things done a certain way. I don't like surprises. I get fearful in public places. I don't like guns. I hate crowds. The idea of touching soft fabric makes me want to hurl. I feel trapped in crowded buildings. I clean things in a specific way. I count stairs. The television volume must be on a number that ends in 5 or 0. I always grab the second items behind the first on a store's shelf. I drive the people around me a wee bit crazy with these idiosyncrasies, but it's not my fault I have them. For most of my life I just believed I was strange, different from other people. I didn't know these tendencies are a direct correlation to trauma.

You may think this sounds like a story of defeat, the story of a screwed-up person. In some moments, you would be right. But some of the best people this world has ever known have fought their way out of the darkness from here; it's a place called rock bottom. And it is the foundation upon which I would set myself free.

But before you find out how I ended up here, in this hospital room—the one where I just cleaned the entire floor of my gross room with wet paper towels because they refused to give me a sponge or mop when I politely asked—you'll have to revisit the past with me. Together, we will walk through the shadows of my past to say:

Goodbye to the little girl I used to be—Jessica.

And hello, to the woman I would ultimately become—Jessi.

But first, I'll introduce you to several people who played a significant role in my life. They're important to the story.

MONA

Jessica's mom's best friend

Back in the Day

My name is Mona. I grew up in Midland, Michigan, and was a student at Bullock Creek High School. That's where I first met Dawn Hayes—Jessica's mom, Hayes was her last name back then, before she married and had children. I was in the graduating class of 1976 and Dawn was one year ahead of me. When we met, I was a freshman and Dawn was a sophomore. She was one of those special people you instantly felt drawn to, almost like there's a magnetic pull that binds you. Dawn and I had a lot in common, shared many of the same interests, and quickly became inseparable. She became my best friend.

I'll never forget the year Dawn was named our Prom Queen. Winning that title seemed to shock the living daylights out of Dawn, but not anyone else. She was the type of person everyone liked; a person who had no enemies. Even if she wasn't someone you would label as being your "friend," she was a likeable person who didn't stir the pot and never got into trouble. She was a quiet person who never drew attention to herself, with the exception of the attention she garnered for her athletic prowess, positive spirit, and academic talents.

She and I both played clarinet in the high school marching band. Dawn sat second chair in the clarinet section. She was talented. Lord knows I always tried to beat Dawn for that coveted spot, but she beat me every single time. She was also quite athletic, and played volleyball, basketball, paddleton, wiffleton, softball, and bowled. In addition to being athletic, she was also extremely smart. She was a member of the National Honor Society, reserved only for people with exceptional GPAs. She was involved with the Pep Club and the Girls Athletic Association (G.A.A.) and was even named Best Girl Athlete of the 1974–75 school year. She was in G.A.A. her freshman through senior years and ended her senior year as its president. She was a teacher's aide her junior and senior years in high school. The word "active" doesn't even begin to cover it when speaking of Dawn Hayes.

What else can I tell you about my best friend? She loved to help people. Her gorgeous smile lit up a room any time she entered it. She had a quiet radiance about her. And she had the most beautiful big brown eyes, the type people typically refer to as "doe eyes." When Dawn looked at you it felt as though she was looking through you, to your soul. We always had so much fun together. I loved her laugh and she and I shared many bouts of giggles together over the years. I loved her faithfulness. I admired her loyalty toward those she loved. She always made time for everybody in her life. Those she loved became her priority above all else in life. She had a way of making you feel like you were the most important person in her world. She was meek and mild for the most part and, sometimes, even downright shy until she got to know you, but once she did, her companionship and loyalty were unparalleled.

I remember this one time when Dawn and I were at band practice. We were all marching across the football field in formation to practice our steps, when I somehow managed to clumsily trip over my own foot and fell. Let's just say my fall wasn't the epitome of grace. I went down more like an elephant on an ice rink, fast and hard. Dawn and I both began giggling, and once we started laughing, we couldn't stop. Trust me, we tried. Our laughter ultimately led me to snort aloud, and after that, we had the entire band cracking up with us, with the singular exception of one seriously pissed off band director. Through angry eyes he glared, as he pointed over at Dawn and me, and said, "BOTH OF YOU— OFF THE FIELD—NOW." I still can't stop laughing anytime I think about this. It is the only time I ever remember either one of us getting into trouble.

When we each exited the doors of Bullock Creek High School for the last time in 1975 and 1976, our friendship remained intact. We remained best friends over the years, and shared each other's dreams and secrets. We shared our victories and sorrows, our laughter and tears. She was the ultimate confidante for me, as I was for her. Eventually, we went on to become wives and mothers and raised our own families. We always remained in touch, even when the hectic busyness of our family lives consumed more of our daily time and attention—the way it typically did for most people. Regardless of how much we spoke, what about, when, or how often, we remained close.

Dawn was my best friend in life. She always will be.

I never realized her loyalty to others would become her greatest fault; an attribute which would one day cause her to pay the ultimate price for her gratuitous trust and unintended naiveté.

And it would happen on April 29, 1989 . . .

DAWN HUBER

(née Hayes)

Jessica's mom

I'm Jessica's mom. I'm here to tell you a little bit about her dad. Edward Huber was a handsome, funny, charming young man. But if I'm being entirely honest, he wasn't one I had any intention of dating, at least not in the beginning anyway. I was far more shy and reserved than Ed. I guess you could say he was outspoken, even slightly rambunctious. He was more of a "life of the party" type of guy. Everyone loved him, especially the ladies. But date him? Me? No way! Then one night at a high school dance I found myself in his arms dancing to Roberta Flack's melodic voice. The song was *Killing Me Softly*. I'm pretty sure it was his humor and good looks that eventually overtook my trepidation in the romance department. I put up a good fight while it lasted. Not only would I dance with Ed that night, but we would fall in love and marry two years after my graduation from Bullock Creek High School. It was on November 7, 1977, that we sealed our love for one another with formal vows.

Growing up, Ed had seven drop dead gorgeous sisters: Marla, Cheryl, Paula, Brenda, Mary, Marilyn, and Maureen. The last two were twins, one of whom, Maureen, died at age nine, when she was tragically struck by a car while riding her bicycle. Ed somehow managed to survive growing up as the lone male sibling. Perhaps that's where he inherited his charm—if you can survive living in a household with six sisters adamantly vying for outfits, attention, and a coveted spot in the bathroom—you apparently learn a thing or twenty about how to interact with women.

After high school Eddie enlisted in the military. At one point he was stationed in Alaska. Eventually, we decided to start a family together. We had three beautiful girls: Jessica, Janel, and Jolene. Once again, Eddie found himself the lone male, in a house full of women. (The irony was not lost on him, me, or anyone else who knew him. But it's a genetic curse he happily bore.) Our first two girls were a year apart, and Jolene was a few years behind them.

After serving time in the military, Eddie worked at various odd jobs over the years to provide for our family. He was a handy guy who loved working on cars. While we didn't necessarily have a lot financially, what we did have was a vibrant, beautiful family, and a house to call our own in Toledo, Ohio. We were happy there. Sure, the house could get a little loud and crazy with three little ones running around, but we loved it. Eddie and me. The girls. It was the family we always wanted, and it was ours. Perfect? No way. Like any married couple, we were far from it.

We had disagreements, and quarreled often. There were times when our marriage was placed under a great deal of strain due to financial reasons, daily living strife, or those dreaded circle arguments married people have, the ones where you discuss the same issues repeatedly. We had our fair share of problems. We were a normal, young married couple. At times, we wanted to leave one another and threats of divorce were slung both ways. Our closest family and friends were aware of our struggles. But above all else, we loved our girls. We were a family.

That all came to a sudden end when Ed unexpectedly passed away. One day he was there with us. The next, he was gone. As the girls' mother, I felt it was my duty to pick up the broken pieces and fill the void. To support the girls. To be there for them. To listen to them. To comfort them. To nurture them. And, of course, to love them. Unwaveringly. I was their mother. They had lost enough already. We would carry on. Somehow. Some way. I would always be there for them. Always.

I loved my girls. They were my world.

And I would do anything for them.

Anything.

JESSICA

AGE 5

I love my daddy. He loves me back. I can feel it. He is nice. He makes me laugh. We laugh together. We play games. We tell stories. We do fun things. He always makes time for me. We leave the house, just daddy and me. We go places. We like to fish. When I'm with daddy, I feel like I belong. He tells jokes and makes me laugh. He acts silly. I get to act silly, too. I don't have to worry about being quiet and acting good all the time. I can act like me.

I am five. My birthday is in June. I have blond hair the color of wet sand, just like my daddy's. My eyes are blue, kind of like the ocean. My eyes don't work right, so I have to wear these stupid glasses. I live in a yellow house. It's yellow like the sun. I live there with daddy, my mom, and my two sisters, Janel and Jolene. They are littler than me. We live in a place called Ohio. People also say we live in Toledo. We live in the United States of America. We have a garage, but it's in our backyard, not on the front of our house like other people's. We have a porch. I like to sit out there. There's a big bench and it swings.

My sisters and me like to sing. We sing a lot. We sing songs all the time. I fight with Janel sometimes. She's only four. I love her, but she bugs me. She gets on my nerves. I think she tries to. I get on her nerves, too. I think it's fun to make her mad. My little sister is named Jolene. She is only two. My mom calls her "the baby." I am the big girl. Janel is in the middle of us. I am the oldest, but I'm also the baddest. Mommy thinks so for sure.

I have a lot of energy. I get in trouble a lot. Like all the time. Like every single day. I don't mean to. I just don't like to be all perfect and quiet. Daddy seems to be okay with the way I am. Mommy seems annoyed. I think I get on her nerves. "Don't do that, Jessica." "Sit down, Jessica." "Please be quiet, Jessica." "Get over here, Jessica." "What are you doing, Jessica?" "Stop bugging your sister, Jessica." "Stop touching that, Jessica." "Just come stand over here by me, Jessica." I know my mommy loves me, but she gets tired of the way I act.

I really don't mean to be bad. But I can't help it. I don't want to sit still. I don't want to be quiet. I want to bug Janel, run around, be loud, and play! It's not like I don't want to be a good girl. I just don't want to sit down and be quiet. That is no fun at all. And that makes me a bad girl . . . a lot.

This one time, I asked mom if I could ride my tricycle upstairs. She said "yes." I was so excited! She even carried it up the stairs for me. Then my mom went back downstairs to what she was doing before I bugged her. I decided I wanted to ride my tricycle down the big, wood stairs like Wonder Woman. I love Wonder Woman! I have her underwear and everything. Mom even made me a costume, so I could dress up like her for Halloween. It was so cool! But I fell *all* the way down the big, wood stairs on my tricycle and a nail scraped the skin under my left eye. It hurt. A lot. There was blood and everything. I cried. Mom was angry. She said, "Jessica, why would you do that? This is going to leave a scar." I don't think I'll get to ride my tricycle upstairs again.

Once I ate a whole stick of butter off the white butter holder thingy that was sitting on the table. I picked it up and ate it, just chomped it down. Mom was really angry. She told me "It's butter, not a candy bar, Jessica. Why would you do that?!" I don't know why. I guess I just really like butter, or I was bored. It seemed like a good idea at the time.

One time I heard daddy say "shit." I decided I wanted to say it, too. I don't know what the word "shit" means, but, now I know it means you get your mouth washed out with soap. And soap tastes yucky. Like really, really gross. Shit is a bad word. I don't think I'll say it anymore.

My daddy doesn't look at me like I'm a bad girl. He loves me. When I'm bad, he punishes me. Sometimes he spanks me, but he loves me even when I'm bad. My sisters are calm and quiet. They aren't like me. I am different. Daddy doesn't seem to mind that I'm different. He makes me feel like it's okay to be different. Maybe that's why I can't be quiet. Maybe that's why I don't want to sit down and be still. I don't want to. It's boring and hard to be good.

My mom likes to cook. She cooks a lot. She washes all our clothes in a washing machine. It has lots of knobs and buttons on it. I want to push them. I don't think my mom likes to clean our house. My sisters and me mess it up a lot, like every single day. Sometimes, we mean to make a mess and sometimes we don't. I love my mom's meatloaf. It tastes so yummy. She likes to make me and my sisters wear dresses that match when we go places. That makes my mom happy. We go to places, like the store or church and people say they like our dresses. They tell us we're cute little girls. My mom always smiles when they do that. I smile, too. I like to feel pretty.

My mom works inside our house at daytime and at nighttime, she works at a place called "AT&T." Daddy says she works "second shift." She takes naps with us sometimes. When she goes away to work, we stay at our babysitter's house. She's the lady who makes mashed potatoes that taste like dog food.

Daddy works outside of the house, too. He has a job where he gets paid to go do things for a man called a "boss." I wonder if he's rich from working all the time? He works a lot. Wow, he must have a lot of money. Mommy took me to visit him at the gas station where he worked once. I like going to visit him. I always like to see daddy.

Mom takes care of me. She makes me behave. But when I'm around my mom, I don't always feel like I belong. Not the same way I do when I'm with my daddy. I've heard people say something about a "daddy's girl." I'm not sure what that means. But he's my daddy and I'm a girl, so . . . I'm pretty sure that makes me one. I am a bad girl, a girl trying to be a good girl, a girl who can't be good, and a daddy's girl, so I'm a lot of different types of girls.

JESSI

AGE 37
2016

*L*ooking back, the following is what I remember about my dad:

ONE: He was a handsome, kind, fun-loving man with a warm smile and a gentle touch; a man who lit up a room by being in it. I loved him.

TWO: We enjoyed fishing together.

THREE: He was once featured on a television program about deer hunting. He was all decked out in his finest hunting attire while attempting to hunt a deer on the show. I remember my sisters, mom, and me all eagerly clamoring around the television set in the living room with anticipation to see daddy on TV.

FOUR: He is dead.

At five-years-old, this is all I was left knowing about Edward J. Huber, more fondly known to me as daddy. Not much, I know. He became a gaping hole in my life. A void. Someone I barely got to know, but whom I loved deeply. I always felt cheated. Cursed. Ripped off. But at least I still had my mom and sisters to cling to. (I was five, my sister Jolene was four, and my baby sister Janel was only two at the time. My mom unexpectedly became a widow at age 28.)

Back in 1985, at age 27, my dad was found unconscious beneath a car he was working on in our garage in the back yard of our house. It would become the place where he would draw his last breath: one filled with carbon monoxide fumes, and fatal. Since he was a mechanically handy type of guy who worked on cars frequently throughout his life, this seemed highly suspicious to our family. Something seemed off. Not quite right. It is a point that would never be reconciled. We would be left with no answers. No closure. The cause of death was simply listed by the family in his obituary as "unknown." Unknown: a word that would become true in more ways than one. My daddy. My rock. My protector. Now unknown. The advice my dad would give me throughout my childhood, teenage, and adolescent years: Unknown. The way my dad would look dressed in his military blues to give me away on my wedding day: Unknown. The way my dad's smile would radiate with happiness on the day my own children, his grandchildren, were born: Unknown. Unknown. One little word with a hell of a lot of meaning.

His death would mark the first blank page within the chapter labeled "after" in my life. You know, the whole "before and after" thing. My life before. My life after. I now had two of them—two completely different lives, that is—or at least that's how it felt to me. And it all began on the day of his passing: January 2, 1985. What a terrible way to start a new year.

In an instant, it became one square on the calendar that suddenly had a more profound meaning. The date of my daddy's death. Then add one more forever changed square for his birthday; that gets us to two. Two dates of remembrance. Two dates to serve as formal reminders.

For me, my dad became an angel who would look down on me from heaven over the years. That's what I told myself, growing up as a little girl. That is what I continue to tell myself today. I hope we are one day reunited in heaven. It's a thought I will always cling to. I used to be daddy's girl. Now, I'm what's left of her.

JESSICA

AGE 5

My daddy is dead. I'll never see him again. I can't talk to him anymore. At all. Ever again. Mommy said it's okay to be sad, but we have to try to learn to move on. That daddy wouldn't want us to be sad.

I miss him so much. He's the only person who made me feel okay, and now he's gone. I am soooo sad. I cry all the time. I cry a lot. My mom cries sometimes, too. She looks sad all the time. Her eyes get red or puffy. We are all sad. We all miss daddy. Me and Janel, and Jolene and my mom. Sometimes, I forget he died. But my mom cooks us food and we sit down to eat, but daddy isn't there at the table anymore. I miss him. I miss him so much. I'll never get to go fishing with him ever again. I won't get to hear his funny jokes. I won't get to sit on his lap or laugh with him. I won't get to see him smile. I won't get to hear his voice. I won't get to feel like I'm okay just being me. I would even let him spank me if he came back. I wouldn't even care. But he is gone. He's not coming back. He's just dead. He's gone forever.

I'm just supposed to never see him again. I'm supposed to be okay with it. I'm not okay with it. I'm not okay with it at all! I am angry. And sad. And my stomach hurts. And my heart hurts. It isn't fair that I don't get to have a dad anymore. Everybody else still gets to have a dad. Every single other person gets to. But I don't. Now I just have a mom and two little sisters. I am the saddest girl ever. The saddest girl in the whole wide world. *Why* did my daddy have to die? *Why?*

JESSICA

AGE 6

My daddy died eight months ago. My mom told us we "get to" live with Bob now. His real name is "Robert," but he goes by "Bob." She likes Bob. Bob is her "boyfriend." He has brown hair, and brown eyes, and wears glasses. She met him at a family get-together the summer after my daddy died. I wish she never did meet him. He lives in a place called Florida. I don't want to move to Florida. I don't want to move into Bob's stupid house. I don't even want to *see* his house. I don't want to have a new sister and brother. I don't. It's not fair! I want my dad back. I miss my dad. Bob is NOT my dad. He will *never* be my dad. They can't make him be my dad. They can't. I don't care what my mom says. He's not!

None of this is fair. I will *not* move to Florida. And I do *not* want a new house, or a new dad, or a new family, or a stupid new sister and brother, or to move away. I'm staying here. In Toledo. In Ohio. In the United States of America. In the house that is yellow like the sun. In the house where I lived with my daddy. My sisters are staying with me. I am not moving. My mom can try to tell me Bob is nice. She can try to make me like him. It's not going to work. He is not my dad and there isn't anything anybody can do about it. I am not going to like him. I'm not.

JESSICA

AGE 6

*A*fter my mom and Bob got married in November of 1985, eleven months after my daddy died, we moved to Florida. It's the place where Bob lives with his two *real* kids, Jeff and Jacque (pronounced like "Jackie"). Jeff's real first name is Robert, just like his dad, but he doesn't go by that. We call him "Jeff." Jeff and Jacque are older than us. Jeff is eight years older than me and Jacque is five years older. Bob has a job here. I'm not sure what he does. He goes to work every day. I think he works at a bank and uses a computer a lot. I know he is going to school to be something called a "minister." I think he wants to work at a church or something.

My mom stays home with us. Florida is nice. It's warm here. I kinda like Florida. I don't hate it as much as I thought I would. I'm mad I had to leave all my friends behind in Ohio. In Toledo. In the United States of America. I had to say goodbye to the yellow house. The house that looked like the sun. My daddy's house. The place I loved. But it's warm here. It's okay.

There are palm trees here. Lots of them. They are all around our house. Palm trees are everywhere in Florida. Our house has one floor with a living room, and a kitchen, and four bedrooms. It feels a lot more like "Bob's house" than our house, but we still get to live here. We only brought our clothes and some of our stuff. We didn't bring all our furniture from the yellow house. And guess what? There is a pool! I thought only rich people get to have their own pool at their own house, but we get to have a pool! Another thing about Florida is there are these little lizards here that run around everywhere. If you do catch one, then guess what? Their tails fall off. It's kinda freaky. Gross, really. But they are still neat looking.

I may like it here, but I still don't like Bob. I really like the beach. It's my new favorite place. I get to go with my mom and my sisters. We bring our towels and mom makes us put on this stuff called "sunscreen." It smells kinda like coconuts and is kinda grody and sticky. My sisters like the beach and Florida. It is kinda cool here, I guess.

Florida is still in the United States of America, but it's really, really far away from my yellow house in Toledo, where we used to live: Me, my dad, my mom, Janel, and Jolene. Now it's just Bob, my mom, Janel, Jolene, and Bob's kids: Jeff and Jacque. They keep saying this is our "new family." I didn't ask for a new family. I want my old one back! But daddy is dead. He's not coming back. I begged God, and prayed all the time, and cried a lot. He'll be gone forever. Now I just get to have Bob. I don't want Bob. They can't make me change my mind about him. He's not ever gonna be my dad. They can't make him my dad, and that's not gonna change. Not ever!

Jeff and Jacque have their own rooms. I share a room with my sisters now. We have a bunk bed. It's pretty cool. Me and Janel still fight sometimes. She gets on my nerves. We do like to play together though. We like the same things since we're only one year apart in age. I'm still the oldest! Jolene is only three. She's funny. She tries to do the same things we, "the big girls," do, but since she's so little, she can't always do them. She's starting to talk more. I like Jolene. She thinks I'm really cool because I'm her older sister. I'm pretty sure she looks up to me because I'm the oldest. She thinks I'm the coolest. I wonder if she thinks I'm fun? I think she does! She follows me everywhere. I like that. It gets on my nerves sometimes, but I still like it. I like being around my baby sister, Jolene.

Janel and Jolene don't seem to miss daddy the same way I do. They don't seem to miss the yellow house, like me. If they're sad inside, like me, they don't show it. I do feel really sad inside, deep down. I mean *really* sad. Sometimes, it feels like I'm the only one who misses our old family. Like I'm the only one who still thinks about my daddy. It seems like everyone else can just pretend this is our real family now, like we never even had a different family. But

I know we did. I remember. I don't know why my dad had to die. It ruined everything. Maybe one day I'll make some friends here. Then I'll be in the second grade here, and then the third grade. Elementary goes to like the fifth grade, I think. Because I get to live in Florida at the beach! Maybe I'll build the world's tallest sandcastle. I'll let Janel and Jolene help me with it. I don't like my new family, but Florida is pretty okay. At least I get to live here with my sisters and my mom. It's warm and nice. We get to play, and laugh, and have fun together.

JESSICA

AGE 8

*I*n the fall of 1986, my mom and Bob got all of us together in the living room one day: Jeff, Jacque, Janel, Jolene, and me. That's when they told us their "big news." Hah. More like "bad news." We are moving to Indiana. Bob got a job as a minister at a church there. He got a job and they said it's a big deal that he gets to be the minister at his own church. Some place called Lakeville— Lakeville, Indiana.

I was starting to like Florida. And now we're moving *again*. We just moved here. I am tired of moving!

Indiana . . . who wants to live there, anyways? Not me. Not Jeff. Jeff is the only one who is as mad as me about this big, dumb move. He doesn't want to leave Florida, either. His friends. His school. The place where they lived with their mom, before she died of breast cancer. She died one month before my daddy. Jeff was 13 and Jacque was 11. They lost their mom just like I lost my dad.

But we are leaving. They don't care that we don't want to go. We are going anyway. We're just kids and they don't care what we think. They don't care what we want. They want us to just be happy about it. But I am *not* going to be happy about it. No way. They can't make me be.

Indiana. What do they have there anyway? Probably nothing. Definitely not palm trees. Not a beach. I bet we won't have a pool at our house anymore. What a dumb idea. This idea is even stupider than moving to Florida. I'm tired of switching schools! I'm tired of trying to make new friends! I'm tired of feeling like all we do is keep moving to new places! I'm tired of moving. I don't want to move anymore . . . ever again. This isn't fair. *It's not fair at all.* I really thought this was going to be our new house, and we would live here forever, or at least until I'm a grown-up who goes to college. I finally like it here. But we are moving . . . again. What a bad idea. Jeff thinks so, too. He is really mad about it. We are both mad. I'm pretty sure Jacque isn't too happy about moving to stupid Indiana, either, but she's a lot quieter about it. My sisters just go along with whatever. They're too little to care. They act happy about it. Why are they doing this to us? Don't my mom and Bob know we *don't want to* go there? Don't they care?

Why does Bob want to work at a church anyway? I know he went to school for that, but still, why can't he just find a job at a church in Florida if he wants to work at a church? Where we live? The place where we're all happy? Because they are grown-ups and they get to do whatever they want—that's why. They don't care if we hate it.

Well, they can *make* me move to Indiana, but they *can't* make me like it. I don't think they can make Jeff like it, either. *I don't care what they say.* What a dumb place to live. *What a dumb idea. Dumb. Dumb. Dumb.*

Goodbye beach.

Goodbye swimming pool.

Goodbye sand.

Goodbye seagulls.

Goodbye friends.

Goodbye school.

Goodbye "new" home.

Goodbye Florida and everything I like here. Goodbye.

JESSICA

AGE 8

*M*y mom sat us down and asked if Bob can adopt us: me, Janel, and Jolene. I don't even know what that means, to adopt someone, but I don't want to be adopted. I don't like Bob. I don't like him at all. Why does he think he gets to be our new dad? He's not. He doesn't get to be. Not now. Not ever! He will NOT be my dad. My mom said our new last name will be "Pelley." I don't want to be a Pelley. That's a dumb name and I do not want it. My name is Jessica Huber. Huber was my daddy's last name—Ed Huber. I'm Jessica Huber. That's who I am. I don't want Bob's last name. I am so angry. I will not change my name to Pelley. I won't. They can't make me. I am Jessica Huber. I am not Jessica Pelley. I don't even like that name. They can forget it. I'm not doing it.

So . . . both of my sisters just agreed to be Pelley people. I guess I have to become a Pelley person, too. Even if I *really* don't want to be. I'll just say I'm okay with it, since my sisters said "yes," and I'll tell them it's okay, since my mom wants me to, but I am *so* not okay with it. I will never be Jessica Pelley, not really. Because I am totally Jessica Huber. That is who I am. Forever.

They *can* call me what they want, but they *can't* make me like it.

STEPHANIE

AGE 9

Jessica's Childhood Best Friend

Fall 1986

I cannot even begin to tell you how excited I was when the Pelley girls moved into town. It's not that I didn't have any friends. I had some. But Lakeville, Indiana, is a small farming community. You won't find a lot of friends in the corn and bean fields, that's for sure. The moment I first met the three Pelley girls—Jessica, Janel, and Jolene, ages six, five, and three—we clicked right away. I was nine years old. I guess you could say we became "fast friends."

My dad works as the Trustee for Olive Branch Church. It's next to "the parsonage"—that's what my dad always calls it—the house where the girls moved in with our new minister, Bob, his wife, Dawn, and Bob's two kids from his past marriage, Jeff and Jacque. Any time my dad is at the church, I'm at the parsonage. The girls and I love to play outside. We are tomboys all the way. Our parents make us put on dresses every Sunday mornin' for church, so we look the way they think we should look. But when we aren't wearin' those church dresses, our feet are dirty, our hair is slightly messy, and there is a glimmer of fun hiding behind our eyes. There isn't an inch of that property we haven't explored, includin' the small woods next to the parsonage. We love to ride our bikes, play tag, and run through the cornfield that sits behind the house. And if we aren't doin' one of those things, you can find us on the swing set. Yep. That's where we'll be.

Like most little girls, we also like to play those "pretend" games—you know the ones—I'm the cashier and you're the customer; I'm the teacher and you're the student; I'm the waitress and you're a hungry person. We also like to play dress up. The funkier, the better. Dresses, shoes, hairdos, you name it. I guess it's the one time we get girlie.

Dawn is a good mom. One thing I noticed about her right away is she never—and I mean never, ever—gets mad or annoyed, when one of the girls tries to tell her somethin' while she's talkin' (you know, the thing most grown-ups refer to as "interrupting"). Not Dawn. She is always happy to stop talkin', so she can hear what one of the girls has to say. I was kinda jealous of that, in a way. You don't meet many parents like that, the never annoyed type. It never seemed to bother her when the girls, especially the littlest one, Jolene, constantly clung to her. (And I mean Jolene hung *all over* Dawn: on her legs, clutched around her waist, hangin' on her hip. All. The. Time.) She is more patient than any grown-up I ever met. She is gentle. Soft-spoken. Kind. She never wears any makeup, but she's still really pretty. One of the first things I noticed about Dawn is her smile. Not only did it light up her face, it lit up the room when you saw it. I guess you could say she's one of the nicest grown-ups I ever met.

Bob seems like a nice guy. He's funny. Outgoing. I swear he could strike up a conversation with anyone, anywhere, at any time. He really could. I think that's one of the things all the church members like about him. The door to their house is always open to anyone, at any time. If the family is home and awake, the doors are unlocked, the garage door is up, and you are welcome there.

As a couple, I think Bob and Dawn seem happy. As an outsider lookin' in, I think it looks like a happy family. I can't really tell you much about Jeff and Jacque though. I don't see them much. They are older than us, so they're either in their rooms or hangin' out with their friends. Jessica, Janel, and Jolene sleep in the basement in one room, so we hang out down there a lot. Jeff and Jacque's rooms are upstairs. Even when they are home, we don't really see them. We pretty much stick to our own groups around the Pelley household. Given the difference in ages and interests, it isn't too surprising. It's Jeff and Jacque. And then Jessica, Janel, Jolene, and me. Two different circles of kids livin' under one roof. One thing I do notice is that Jeff picks fights with Dawn a lot.

And I mean a lot. I don't think he likes her. He refuses to call her mom and anytime she talks to him, he snaps at her. He looks at her like he can't stand her. He argues with his dad quite a bit, too. Jacque is pretty quiet. From what I know of her, she is nice. She seems kind of shy, but like she never seems to get upset about anything. Her and Jeff seem different in that way. But I'm not around either one of them much.

My life is a lot more fun since the Pelleys moved to town. I feel kind of like another one of their girls when I'm at their house. Any time the Pelley family sits down for a meal when I'm there, Dawn always tells me I can eat with them. In fact, I eat breakfast with them every Sunday before church. Dad goes to unlock the church and I run over and pull myself up to a plate of pancakes at the parsonage. Anytime the girls are home, I'm welcome here. It's nice. It feels a bit like a home away from home. It feels like havin' a second family.

At least it did . . .

JESSICA

AGES 6 TO 9

I'm stepping in as my adult self right now to tell you what life was like for me between the ages of six to nine. I need to do so to give you some insight.

Living together, as far as us kids went, sucked for all of us. Jacque, Janel, and Jolene seemed to blend into the new family fairly well. Jeff and I, uh, not so much. Not because we couldn't have, if we tried, but because we didn't want to. He and I each made that clear in different ways.

When I first met Jacque—my "new" sister—I remember thinking she had the world's greatest hair. It was back in the 1980's, so the big, tall hair that was curled and teased to perfection and held in place by half a can of hairspray was all the rage. At that time, girls seemed to vie for the biggest, coolest hair on the block, and in my eyes, Jacque's took the prize. Back then, my hair was cut into a shorter, jagged style bob that feathered away from my face. Pretty plain and pretty boring. In contrast, Jacque's dark brown hair was longer and always looked perfect with not a strand out of place. I have no idea how much time or gravity-defying hairspray it took her to get it that way, but it was impressive. If there was an award for "Most Perfect Hair," she had a lock on the sash and roses. No need to enter the contest, people. It was Jacque Pelley—hands down.

Jacque was never anything less than cordial and decent to my sisters and me. Looking back, she treated us pretty much the same way a person would treat a coworker in passing, with civility. We didn't spend much time together over the years. Jeff and Jacque were older than my sisters and me, so the gap in ages, interests, and desired pastime activities was real. To them, we were just little girls. We probably got on their nerves. I'm sure we did. To us, they were just distant older kids in their preteen and teenage years. With them being five to eight years older than me and even further apart in age with my little sisters, I guess you could say there wasn't much overlap in our social circles. Nor was there much commonality in our activities. But over the years, I cannot remember one single time when Jacque was ever anything less than kind to us. Not one.

Jeff was a skinny kid. He had dark brown hair and eyes to match. His hair was cut shorter on the top and sides than it was in the back, where it was longer and extended down the back of his neck. That was the style back then. It was the hair cut all the cool guys had, a mullet. I remember from the first time I saw him. There was something about his eyes that struck me. It's hard to explain, really. It's like you couldn't get a read on him. Like there was more going on behind his eyes than you saw. Jeff was the one, despite his voiced assertions to the contrary, who was dubbed our stand-in babysitter when the need arose. That meant anytime our parents needed a babysitter of convenience, it was Jeff. I'm sure that annoyed the living hell out of him, as a teenage boy more interested in friends, free time, and girls, like most teenagers that age would be. Getting stuck in a house full of little girls you didn't ask to live with, much less be around, then being forced to watch them every time your dad needed you to? Good times. Probably not so much. But that's the way it was.

One time, I remember all of us girls decided to camp outside in our yard in a tent. We hauled our stuff out and had it all set up in the tent. We were lying down in the tent. Suddenly, someone unzipped the entrance/exit on the side of the tent. He was wearing a black ski mask; the type that only has holes cut out for the person's eyes. I was terrified. Absolutely terrified. He grabbed me by my feet and pulled me out of the tent so fast, I couldn't even react. Then he slung me over his shoulder and took off running into our house. I started screaming. I was crying hysterically. I seriously thought I was going to die. This was it. My final moment here on earth. Some man in a black ski mask was going to kill me, right here, right now, in our house. I remember the masked man plopping me down kinda hard onto our kitchen counter. By this time, I was in a full-on frenzy of kicking, crying, pleading, and screaming. When my butt hit the counter, my glasses fell off my face, so I couldn't see a thing. It was in that moment that Jeff pulled the mask up off his face and had it bunched up on top of his head, so I could see it was him. He tried to calm me down by telling me, "It's just me. It's okay." Then he picked my eyeglasses up off the counter and placed them back onto my face. I was so relieved that it was Jeff, and not a killer. I remember thinking it was nice that he picked up my glasses and put them back on my face, so I could see again. I remember being so glad I wasn't going to die, that it was just a prank. Looking back, I honestly believe it was a prank from Jeff's teenage perspective. From mine, it was more like a terrifying, near-death experience, at least up until the moment he unmasked himself to me. It was the stuff little girls' nightmares are made of.

I remember Jeff taught me how to play poker when I was young, probably seven years old. One time, we were playing a hand of poker, and Jeff decided to put his new pick-up truck in as the ante. Proudly, my nine-year-old self won that hand of cards, but he obviously didn't give me the truck. It was fun. It was one of the few times I remember Jeff and me doing something together and having a good time. One of the only moments we each let our guard down, dropped the invisible wall of separation, and weren't individually embroiled in a small-scale social turf war within the Pelley household. This is my best memory of Jeff.

Jeff was eight years older than I was, and I was the eldest Huber girl. For some reason, which I still don't know to this day, Jeff always treated me differently than he did my sisters or his real sister, Jacque. I became the target of his aggression during the babysitting hours. One time, I remember he threatened to throw my little sister into the swimming pool if I didn't do what he said. He followed it up with . . . " 'Cause I know she doesn't know how to swim." Of course, I did what he asked me to. I don't even remember what it was now. I just remember knowing she really couldn't swim, and not wanting my little sister to drown. One time he threw ice cubes into the bathtub with me because he thought it was funny to make me take an ice-cold bath. Another time, he threw a blow dryer, which he told me was plugged into the outlet—although it wasn't—into the bathtub with me. To say I was terrified in that moment is entirely accurate. I thought I was going to be electrocuted.

One last memory that comes to mind during the babysitting years is Jeff locking me out of the house naked. I had just taken a bath and was getting dressed, when Jeff told me I needed to go check something outside. I thought he was crazy. I wasn't even dressed. But he convinced me to do it. I was young and naive. I went to check on whatever it was, stark naked, and he started chasing me. I ran through a bur field, buck naked, with him chasing after me. Eventually, I hid behind the garbage cans beside our fence. Jeff went back into the house. I checked the door several times and it was locked, so I couldn't get back in. At some point, Jeff knew our parents would be coming home, so he finally unlocked the door, and I was able to get back in to clothe myself and end my stint as the Terrified Naked Running Girl, now complete with thorns in the soles of my feet. Jeff and I sat together pulling the burs out of the bottoms of my feet. Again, I'm pretty sure he found this funny. To me, as a little girl, I found it terrifying. It seemed so wrong to me at the time. But there wasn't anything I could do about it. I never knew what to expect. I wasn't sure what he would do next. These incidents weren't isolated but just the ones I remember most vividly. (Read: the ones that scared the living hell out of me.)

I never saw Jeff treat my sisters the way he treated me. When these types of things occurred while he babysat us, Jacque may have been home at the time, but I *know* she was never actually around to witness it. She was probably in her room, talking on the phone, or gone hanging out with her friends. I think he chose me because I was the easiest target. I was the bad one. I was the one always in trouble. I was the rebellious one who acted out. I was the one our parents would not believe. It was brilliant on his part, intentional or otherwise; a great formula for years of mean-spirited manipulation of me with no parental repercussions. All I know is I feared my parents leaving me alone at the house with him. Between the ages of six and nine, these events felt monumentally significant, terrifying, and utterly unescapable. As a young girl, it felt a bit like emotional torture. What I do know is that I loathed every single second of the babysitting hours, and the hours or days leading up to them. I was gripped in terror.

Did my parents believe me about any of these things? No. They did not. Did they happen? Yes. They did. I always told my mom and Bob about what transpired while they were gone, when they left us with Jeff, but they did not believe me. They thought I was making it up. It was clear they thought I just didn't want them to go out and was trying to get them to change their plans and stay home. It got to the point that I would enter a state of total panic and cry any time I knew they were going to leave us with Jeff. Leave *me* with Jeff. I felt scared and helpless. Once they got home, Jeff would sometimes overhear me telling my mom and Bob about what happened while they were gone, and he'd chime in to say, "She's making that up. That never happened." I guess the truth doesn't always set you free.

To this day, I'm not sure if he disliked me, or simply viewed these as harmless pranks. All I know is that they happened. I hated every second of it.

And Jeff Pelley still owes me a truck.

JESSICA

AGES 5 TO 9

*I*t all seems so obvious to me today, when I look back at the scattered pieces of my Pelley upbringing through adult eyes. You can call a cardboard box a car, but that doesn't mean you can drive it. Not any more than you could call us a family and actually make us become one. Ridiculous. Laughable. Improbable. Just some of the words you could use to describe the concept. We were a family brought together by two unfathomable deaths, the three of us girls forced together with Jeff and Jacque. This anything-but-Brady-Bunch-blended-family was laced with feelings of resentment, sadness, anger, and betrayal.

Our parents had the best of intentions when they decided to merge our fragmented families. That's not to say they didn't realize there would be difficulties, but they clearly viewed them as surmountable. My mom and Bob each suffered their own personal loss of a beloved spouse, who died suddenly and unexpectedly. Each was left behind with children, to carry on. They loved one another, perhaps not as much as they loved the spouses who came before, but they did love one another. They didn't want to be alone and they wanted to move forward in their lives. To know some happiness. But their attempts at a "new" family would ultimately fail. As would their attempts at a happy, new normal. For their choice in blending us as a family, we each would pay a different price.

Jeff and I were the eldest siblings in our respective families and would bear these emotions far more deeply than the others. The others actually had a chance at happiness.

Jeff and I were emotional gladiators fighting for our lost parent, at least that's how I see it today. My sisters were younger and able to blend in. The memories of my father were less vibrant for Janel at four, and nonexistent for my little sister Jolene at two. They accepted Bob. They liked Bob. My sisters were happy at the parsonage for the most part. I was left floating in the wind after daddy died. I didn't fit in to begin with, and certainly didn't fit in after he departed.

I'm not saying Jacque didn't miss her mom. I know she did. Deeply. But her demeanor and personality allowed her to better assimilate into the new household. She wasn't rebellious. She didn't seem to be at odds with her dad. She didn't cause any trouble. She was quiet and kept to herself. She was more adaptable. I'm not saying she didn't prefer Florida over Indiana, and I'm not saying she was excited about her dad starting a new family, but she seemed to find a space that worked for her. Any angst she felt seemed to stay tucked below the surface.

Jeff seemed to take his mother's loss the hardest, just as I did with my dad. Losing her to cancer at age 34, when he was only 13-years-old, had to be nothing short of a child's version of hell. We were left with gaping holes in our lives. A loss of significant depth that the others didn't seem to fully comprehend. That isn't to say Jacque, Janel, and Jolene didn't experience a significant loss when they lost a parent—they did. It's just that Jeff and I seemed to carry the torches of our deceased parents like they were embers of loyalty embedded in our flesh. That any act to immerse ourselves into the new family was an act of betrayal, an acceptance of something we did not want. A flame we didn't allow others to attempt to extinguish that made it far more difficult to blend in, if not impossible. It was not going to happen, not for us. It seems Jeff and I had a few things in common, yet we found no kinship in our suffering. We remained incidental tourists wandering through our new, unwanted lives in the same household, a million miles apart.

Jeff and I were the ones in individual counseling for our anger and behavioral issues, in addition to the group counseling we attended as a family unit. We were the "bad" ones. We were the ones who talked back and rebelled. We were the ones who couldn't just do what we were told to do and behave as expected. We were the ones who didn't understand how everyone else could just forget the loss we experienced and move forward as though it never even happened. Dawn would *never* be his mom. And Bob would *never* be my dad. We would *never* like them. We would *never* accept them. We weren't going to let anyone forget about it, either.

Jeff and I were the ones spanked with a belt by Bob as a means of discipline. I know Janel and Jolene were never spanked with a belt. To my knowledge, Jacque never was either, at least not when I was around. I held a grudge toward Bob. You bet I did. He would take me in his bedroom and shut the door. Each smack across my backside with that leather strap placed me miles further away from him. I'm not sure if he hoped to strip the rebellion from me with the lashes, but what he did was drive it further into my core. Harsh punishment, delivered by the hands of someone I deeply resented. And Jeff was the consummate host of hostility toward my mother. She couldn't do anything to win his respect, affection, or even his decency. Jeff being snippy to my mom was the norm. It was apparent he hated her.

We were two angry children forced to pretend all was well, when it was far from it. Two lost kids, searching for something that didn't exist anymore beneath the roof of a parsonage full of people, all expecting more from us than we had to give, and also expecting us to forget something we swore we never would.

On a day not too far off, we would lose more than we already had, individually and collectively. Our worst days laid ahead of us. And they were not too far off. Not too far off at all.

MONA

Dawn's best friend

The Visit

About three weeks before April 29, 1989, my best friend, Dawn, traveled to Michigan to visit her former mother-in-law, Gayle—that's Jessica's "gammy," her dad's mom—and I drove over to Gayle's house to see Dawn and the girls: Jessica, Janel, and her youngest, Jolene. Those little girls were all Gayle had left to cling to of her son Ed. I hadn't seen Dawn in a while and I always loved seeing the girls. They were growing up so fast.

At this point, Dawn and the girls were living in Lakeville, Indiana, with Bob, her new husband, the minister, and his two older children from a former marriage—Jeff and Jacque—who were teenagers. I knew there was some strife in the family. Their perfect Brady Bunch family, a blended merger, was a charade from the beginning, from the vantage point where I stand today. I wouldn't have told you that back then, though.

From my many conversations with Dawn over the years, I knew there was a lot of tension in the household. Dawn didn't like the way Bob disciplined the girls. He was always on them about one thing or another. He was strict, way more of a disciplinarian than she was. Dawn felt he was too tough on them. That he expected too much from them as little girls. I remember her telling me once, "It's just not how Ed and I raised the girls, Mona. But Bob is their father now and the head of our house . . ." I could sense her inner struggle. It was palpable. I knew how uncomfortable it made her to balance this new life she had with her internal barometer going off about what she felt was right or wrong in certain situations. She and Bob found themselves entrenched in this blended family of theirs, where they pretended they could make it work out exactly like they had it pictured in their heads before the merger, with Bob raising Dawn's and Ed's girls and Dawn taking the reins as woman of the house. It wasn't easy by any means. It was tattered at the seams. It wasn't easy to make the transition from becoming a young widow to living in a new household with Bob and his two kids, but they were trying to make it work.

I could also tell it wasn't easy on Dawn being a minister's wife. A lot of pressure came with that role. I could see she always felt she needed to convey the proper image, look and act a certain way, carry herself as a good, upstanding Christian woman, and have her children viewed in a light favorable as being the "minister's children." I'm not sure if this pressure was exerted by expectations set by Bob—intentionally or otherwise—those who attended their church, societal suppositions, or something created from Dawn's own internal thought process and personal expectations of what it meant to be a minister's wife, but I could tell she felt as though she and her girls needed to carry themselves in a particular way.

The girls were to behave in church. They expected them to sit in the church and act like little adults, to stay quiet, not talk or interact with one another, kick the pew, or do anything that could draw unnecessary attention to them as Bob's (seemingly perfect) kids. Dawn also focused a great deal of effort on the appearance of the girls. She liked to dress them alike frequently for social outings, and even when the girls were wearing play clothes, they needed to look a certain way. She also seemed to feel as though her house was never clean enough. And cleaning isn't something she liked to do. At all. It's like she felt like she and her girls were constantly being judged. She grew up in a household with what I would describe to be a domineering father and a soft-spoken mother who had a personality much like Dawn's. As a people pleaser, Dawn always seemed to try to fill the role, as expected. It's just one of those things I took notice of over the years during our regular telephone calls and my occasional visits with her.

Sitting in Gayle's house that day, we began by talking about normal things, kind of just making small talk and catching up on what was new in our lives since the last time we'd spoken. The girls must've been playing in another part of the house or outside, I cannot specifically recall now, but the conversation turned serious between Dawn, Gayle, and me.

Dawn told us she was unhappy. That things weren't going well at home. There was a lot of strain between her and Bob and all of them as a family unit. She went on to say they'd been attending counseling as a family to try to work out their issues, but it didn't really seem to be helping. The blending of their two families wasn't working out as they had hoped it would.

Dawn also raised concerns about Jeff's anger, his outright hatred toward her and resentment toward the girls, and the way he treated her. There were two extremes. Jeff either ignored Dawn completely or would snap at her. When his dad was around, Jeff interacted with her as little as possible and kept his negative interactions to a minimum.

Jeff's hatred of Dawn was something I'd known about from the beginning. On some level, I wasn't surprised by it. He'd lost his mom to cancer as a boy and resented Dawn trying to take his mom's place, the same way Jessica resented Bob trying to take the place of her beloved daddy. The fact that Dawn was only 13 years older than Jeff certainly didn't help things. Jeff and Jessica were two young children at war with themselves, after being placed into an environment that included a new step-parent they never asked for and did not want. I remember Dawn saying there were times when Jeff would look at her when he was angry and that "he had fire coming from his eyes." I'd asked if Jeff had ever threatened her or hit her and she said he hadn't. That he was just an angry person.

She tried to be kind, washed his laundry, cooked him food. But even when she did something nice for him, it didn't help. He would snap off a few clipped, bitter words in her direction. He would walk past her bearing a look of disdain. Their relationship became one of avoidance, awkwardness, and forced tolerance.

Dawn went on to tell us she had concerns about there being guns present in the house. She said she'd told Bob she wanted the guns gone on several occasions, even as late as the prior week, but Bob hadn't gotten rid of them. There was even a gun rack which hung above their bed that held a bow and arrow and a hunting rifle. Based on our past conversations, I wasn't entirely surprised to hear any of this. I'd heard it all before. I chalked it up to her being concerned about having a moody teenager in the house who could potentially harm himself. After all, he had once threatened to commit suicide after he had gotten into some trouble.

When listening to my best friend, I could tell she was uncertain about how things were going in her marriage and her life. She voiced her concerns to us one minute with information that supported her concerns, but in the next, would do an about-face and speak of her hope that things could work out. She still seemed to love Bob, couldn't imagine how she could raise three little girls as a single mom with some type of a menial job. She also likely didn't want the stigma of being divorced—a marriage failed with a minister, no less—after already losing one husband to death. What would that say about her as a dedicated wife, a caring mother, and a Christian person? The world truly was a different place back then. The three of us talked through the scenario at length. Dawn went back and forth with her decision. One minute she wanted to leave. She felt she would be better off. The next minute, she was staying. It was one of those times when you hear someone say all the reasons they shouldn't stay in a particular situation, but in the end, not actually possessing the ability to walk away.

After listening to Dawn pour out her feelings, Gayle looked at Dawn and said in a serious tone, "Then why don't you leave? You and the girls can stay with me, until we can get you situated." Dawn responded, "I don't want to give up. I love him. But I don't know how much more we can endure." Gayle replied, "Why don't you leave the girls here with me and you go back to try to work things out with Bob?" Dawn flashed a weak smile and said, "Bob would be mad . . ."

In that moment, I realized my best friend's marriage was in trouble. Her family life was fraying at the seams. As a woman, I think we've all felt that way or had those types of thoughts at one point or another. Her thoughts seemed to ping pong back and forth between staying and leaving. It was clear she harbored doubts and had a fear of making the wrong choice. Lord knows blending two families certainly isn't the easiest thing to do, and especially not when each set of children and each new parent is entering the equation precipitated by the death of a parent or spouse.

After that conversation, I was concerned Dawn was headed for potential heartache and a future filled with uncertainty, potential financial difficulty, struggle, and emotional strife, depending how things unfolded for her. My heart went out to her. She had already been through so much with Ed's death four years prior.

Following this visit with me and Gayle, Dawn and the girls resumed their lives in Lakeville, Indiana, with Bob and his two children. She wanted to try to make things work. She wasn't ready to walk away. She was loyal. Maybe if she tried a little harder. Maybe if she didn't give up. Maybe they could find a way to be a happy family.

Maybe.

JESSI

AGE 37

S unday, April 30, 1989, began like any other day of my life,
but ultimately became so life-altering that its traumatic
magnitude hit the scale at 10.0, the earth as I knew it shifting like
sand beneath my sneakers. It's not easy to explain things when you
have a fucked-up past, like mine.

That day was so unimaginably horrific and emotionally
crippling that my nine-year-old mind shut down. It had to block
some of the memories I should have from that time as a means of
self-preservation. It was far too much for me to emotionally process.
Most adults could not have fared any better. If I had a good therapist
over the past three decades, I'd ask her to explain it to you. But she
can't, because she never existed. There was no good therapist. There
was no real help.

A lot of my would-be-memories from my darkest day are now
gone. Irretrievably. Permanently, or so it seems. They're tucked
away so deeply in my subconscious that I cannot retrieve them.
Psychologists refer to these memory gaps surrounding traumatic
events in a person's life as "repressed memories." These are
memories we push way below the surface into our subconscious
mind. We don't even know we're doing it. We only know that
we cannot recall something we should be able to and it's directly
tied to our trauma. You don't understand now, but you will.
I was friends with a girl from my school, who lived down the street
in LaPaz, which is not far from where we lived in Lakeville. She's
a girl I hung around regularly. We were good friends. I spent the
night at her house frequently. I liked her a lot. I was fond of her
mom, too. She was a nice lady. This family is one I spent a great
deal of time with. My friend had a younger sister who was friends
with my sister, Janel.

I saw these people all the time, was in their home often, and knew them well. But I cannot—for the life of me—tell you their names today. Not my friend's, nor the mom's, nor the sister's. Their names, first or last, the color of my friend's hair, the color of her eyes, the way they probably lit up when she laughed with me, the color of her bedroom, how it was decorated, and many other details I did (and should still) totally know are apparently now tucked deep in the folds of my mind, somewhere between the depths of grief and time. I cannot access them. So, the little girl, once a dear friend, is now "The Nameless Girl" to me. Nameless. Faceless. As is her mom. A generic placeholder where my friend formerly held a place in my past. What I do remember, I remember all too vividly, but the names and faces are buried, irretrievable. Some of the parts that I do remember, I wish I could forget. They were with me when the sun stopped shining. They were with me the day my world stopped spinning. The day the ground beneath my feet buckled and nearly gave way, my lungs searching for air to breathe, my heart nearly forgetting to beat in my darkest hour. They were the ones with the broken little girl.

I could have done research to try to track down my friend's name to share it with you here, but I felt it important to tell this story authentically. Accurately. And the truth is, the past broke me, scattering all the pieces of what I had and who I used to be to the point that I cannot tell you the name of The Nameless Girl, my childhood friend. The girl I adored. The one I spent time with and remember fondly. I cannot tell you her name. Not anymore.

JESSICA

AGE 9
Friday, April 28, 1989

I'm going to tell you what occurred on April 29, 1989, and in the days leading up to it. We'll start one day prior, on the 28th of April.

I am so excited when the bell rings at school today, Friday, because I have big plans to spend the night at The Nameless Girl's house down the street in LaPaz. Janel is friends with her little sister. She is supposed to go with me. Not just for one night, but two! It'll be an all weekend sleepover for us. Since my sister Janel and I are so close in age, we have a lot of friends in common, The Nameless Girl being one of them.

My stepsister Jacque is going away for a weekend sleepover, too. She's going to stay with one of her friends at Huntington College. I think it's some type of a church thing. We'll both be gone for two nights and come back home on Sunday.

Janel and I rush home from school to pack our bags. I'm downstairs in the basement, when Janel comes down to tell me, "Mom said I can't go." "What do you mean you can't go?" I reply. I stand up, make my way around the corner, and run up the stairs one-by-one to ask my mom why Janel can't go now. We already had this planned. It was supposed to be me and Janel at the sleepover, not just me.

I make my way down the hall, past the kitchen, and walk into my mom's bedroom at the end of the hallway. She is in her bathroom, which is connected to her bedroom. That's when the words leave my mouth, "Janel is supposed to go, mom. Why can't she go now?" My mom replies, "You're just going to go tonight. Just you." To say I was upset about this last second change of plans—my fun plans, and

Janel's—would be an understatement. I went from super happy and excited to totally mad in three seconds flat. I try again, "But Janel is supposed to go, too, mom. Why can't she go?" My mom's reply is fast and serious, "Just YOU are going to go tonight, Jessica." That's when I got "the look." The one she pops her head out the bathroom doorway to give me. And what that look means is this: Jessica, you should just stop talking right now, because nothing good will come of it if you don't. Learned that one, having talked myself down off the side of Mount Mad Mom on many occasions when I continued to run my mouth after the look was sent my way. I decide, for once, to take her warning and say nothing further. But I'm not happy about it. I'm mad, but quiet about it. After the death stare, I knew there was no point in arguing with her. None at all. I huff a bit, turn on my heels, walk out of her room, go to grab my overnight bag, and walk out to the van, where The Nameless Girl and her mom are waiting for me. Before pulling the door to the parsonage shut, I say goodbye. I just kind of shout it out into the air, as I walk out. The way people often do. "Bye."

We had two fun days together, The Nameless Girl and me. She had a set of bunk beds that was cooler than mine. That much I do remember. We spent a lot of time outside playing in her yard. We climbed trees, ran around, and played freeze tag. We talked until we finally fell asleep on Saturday night. It would be my last peaceful night of sleep—on Saturday, April 29, 1989—and I don't mean for a while, either. I mean forever.

STEPHANIE

AGE 11
Saturday, April 29, 1989

*M*y dad came to work at the church today, so I stopped by the parsonage to play with the girls. As it turns out, just Janel and Jolene are home today, because Jessica went to spend the weekend with a friend she knows from school. A girl from LaPaz. She left yesterday, on Friday night. I'm friends with all the girls though, so her not being home doesn't faze me. I'll just play with Janel instead.

Janel is happy to see me. She and I walk over to the church. We run up and down the concrete ramp that's attached to the church to entertain ourselves for a while, until we grow bored of it. At one point, Janel turns to me and says, "Hey, do you want to spend the night?" "Of course, I do!" I tell her, "Sure! I'll go ask my dad." We both turn and make our way into the church to seek permission.

My dad is working downstairs in the church, so from the top of the stairs, I call down, "Hey Dad, can I spend the night with Janel tonight?" He replies, "No." And it was a stern no. The type of no uttered in a tone that said, "don't ask me again." Left unspoken, yet known. Janel and I are so disappointed. I had spent the night at the parsonage with Jessica, Janel, and Jolene many times over the years. They were like a second family. I don't know why he said no so fast tonight.

After all, this was the minister's family. If you could bet on one thing, it was that I'd be at church on time the next day. This wasn't the night for a sleepover in my dad's mind. That much was clear.

Janel and I decide to take a bike ride down the road to explore. Janel is riding her own bike. I have to borrow Jolene's bike, since mine isn't here at the parsonage. Our feet hit the pedals and we make our way down Osborne road, pedaling fast as heck toward the bridge. We aren't supposed to go to the bridge. We know that. Our parents don't like us riding on the road you gotta take to get there, but for some reason, today, we don't care. We are just two little girls breaking rules in the name of fun and freedom.

We begin to throw rocks across the empty street for a while—not at cars or anything—kind of like skipping stones, but across the concrete, instead of water. We're talking and looking around to see what we find around us in nature today. After a while, we decide we should probably head home. After all, we don't want to get caught down here on our bikes. It's a total violation of our parents' rules that keep the universe aligned, or something annoying like that. So, we ride back to the parsonage. As it turns out, nobody missed us. "Operation Hanging out at the Bridge We Aren't Supposed to Ride to" was a success. We pull into the driveway, hopping off our bikes once we're halfway up it. We walk up to the garage, pushing the bikes along beside us the whole way to put them away where they go. Before I even step out of the garage, my dad walks up to me and says, "Let's go." The intent was clear, we're leaving right now.

I turn and say, "goodbye" to Janel. A regular goodbye, like I'll see you later.

STEPHANIE

AGE 11
Sunday, April 30, 1989

*A*s usual, dad and I got up this morning, got dressed for church, and hopped into his green pickup truck to head over to the church early, like we always do on Sunday mornings. Every Sunday my dad is usually the first one to unlock the church, get things prepared, and wait for Minister Bob and all the other church members to arrive for the Sunday service. My plan, as soon as those tires landed in the church parking lot, was to immediately run over to the parsonage, like I do every Sunday, to pull myself up to a plate of whatever it is Dawn is cooking. Pancakes, eggs, bacon, sausage, toast. I love eating breakfast with the girls on Sunday mornings. Dawn cooks to order. I mean, she goes all out with it. If you want your eggs scrambled, they will be. If you prefer them fried hard, she'll do that, too. Of all the days that I enjoy eating at the parsonage, Sundays are, far and away, my favorite. It's the best breakfast ever.

I'm not sure if Jessica is back from the slumber party with her friend yet, but I know Janel and Jolene will be there! I take off running across the grass toward the parsonage. I see Bob's car and Dawn's car parked outside where they always are. Jeff's Mustang isn't there.

I see that the garage door is down, which is unusual, so I go try the other door, the sliding door located next to the kitchen. It's locked, too. *Huh. That's weird. Where are they? Why are the doors locked? That's odd. Whatever. No big deal. I'll just go to the other door.* I walk around to the sliding glass door near the kitchen. It won't open. It's locked, too. This has never happened before. *Well, maybe I can just go knock on one of those little windows that looks down on the basement, so Janel and Jolene will see that I'm here.* The curtains are pulled across all the windows, so I can't see in at all. *I wonder why? Huh. That's weird.* Those curtains prevent me from getting a look at much of anything, besides fabric. Trust me, I'm looking. I'm trying to see in. *Where are they?* It's a total no go.

Maybe they are still asleep or something. Maybe they're still getting ready for church. I don't know where they are. I don't see them anywhere. *It's weird that the doors are locked. Are they still sleeping? They can't be! It's Sunday. We have church. And I've been knocking. No one is coming to the door.* The garage door is down. The cars are still parked outside. *That means they have to be here! I'm not sure why the doors are locked and the curtains are all pulled shut. They never have the doors locked when they're home—ever. Why are the curtains pulled closed? This is weird.* I don't know what to make of this. But something doesn't feel right.

Not knowing what else to do with all the doors locked and no one answering, I run back over to the church, run downstairs to find my dad, and exclaim, "They must still be asleep. No one is there. They aren't answering the door. The doors are all locked. I couldn't get in." It doesn't make sense, not to me, or to my dad and the other church elder. It was Sunday. Bob had a church sermon to preach. The girls needed to eat breakfast, get dressed, and make their way over to the church with their mother, like they always do. But there were no girls. There was no breakfast. There was no Bob Pelley. There was no Dawn Pelley. Just a bunch of closed curtains and locked doors. Even more oddly, Bob's car and Dawn's car are both sitting in the driveway. Yet, it seems they aren't home.

My dad seems concerned. He doesn't look outright scared when I tell him, but he seems to feel the same way I do. "What is going on?" seems to be the general consensus. Some elders of the church decide to walk over to the parsonage to check it out for themselves. They see the curtains drawn shut, just as I did. (I didn't go back over to the parsonage with them. I'm just telling you what happened.) They knock on the doors, just as I did. They confirm the doors are locked, just as I did. There is still no answer. Their level of concern now seems to have taken a hard right along the ditch of dread, just like mine did the moment I found myself running away from the parsonage, sans breakfast and friends, a few moments earlier.

Still no pancakes. Still no girls. Still no Pelleys. Nothing.

The other church elders decide to go retrieve the key to the parsonage that was kept at the church to check things out. They have access to it in case it's ever needed and this seems like as good a reason as any to use the key to the minister's parsonage.

The key does not fit the lock. After searching for and trying a few different keys, a lady from the church finally arrives to the parsonage with the real key. They put the key into the knob. The lock clicks unlocked. *Yes!* They turn the knob and walk into the house, toward the kitchen. At first, nothing seems out of place. But then they see Bob's glasses lying on the floor. They see a man's shoes. They realize they are Bob Pelley's shoes, attached to Bob Pelley's feet, attached to Bob Pelley's body, which is now lying on the floor in the hallway near the kitchen, soaked in blood. He is dead. No need to check for vitals. It is clear no one could survive the gunshot blasts to his chest and neck/chin areas. There are some papers and a pen lying near his body, along with a pool of blood: Bob's blood. Bob is dead. Our beloved minister: dead. He is lying on the floor, with the doors locked, and the curtains drawn shut all around him.

The church members immediately call 9-1-1, then realize they are standing in the middle of a crime scene, so they step outside of the parsonage, pull the door shut, and wait on the police to show up. Someone came back over to the church, where I was still waiting, to tell the members of the church that Bob Pelley had been found dead. By this time, some church members had gathered inside the church, wondering what was going on as they waited for the Sunday sermon to begin. Others stood outside of the parsonage, waiting, wondering, and worrying. I was sitting inside the church, waiting and wondering what was going on because Bob still wasn't here. All at once, one of the church members shouts, "EVERYONE

TO THE ALTER TO PRAY." I have no idea what is going on. And that's when I overhear one of the church members by me telling another lady that Bob is dead. That they had found him inside of the house. That he had been shot. *Bob is dead. Oh my God. Oh My God. Oh my God. Nooooo. Why? How?* I am kneeling on the steps by the altar. Some of the ladies around me are sobbing. Other people are praying aloud. I can't even believe this is happening. *How is this possible?* My throat begins to feel thick and closed, making it hard to swallow. My lungs feel heavy. The thoughts won't stop and salty tears of sadness spill down my cheeks, like rain. I can't even believe this is happening. It feels like a dream. No, more like a nightmare. It almost feels like none of this is real right now. It can't be. And the thoughts raced through my mind over and over again.

Where is Dawn? Where is Janel? Where is Jolene? Where are they? I can't believe Bob is dead. Who killed him? Are my friends okay? Oh, my gosh, please let them be okay, God. Please. I can't imagine something bad happening to them. Not them. Not the girls. Not my friends. Not Dawn. Please God, please tell me nothing bad happened to them. Pleeeease. I am begging you. Please . . .

JOLENE

Jessica's youngest sister

AGE 6

One day prior:

Saturday, April 29, 1989

We helped Jeff wash his car today. It was fun! He lets us help him wash it sometimes. I like to help. You get all wet, and you get to play with bubbles, and you get to rub them all over the car. Your feet get all wet and bubbly, too. And sometimes, me and Janel try to get each other really, really wet. It is so much fun!

Jeff is going to the prom tonight. What's a prom? I think mommy said that it's a dance. People in high school get to go to it. Me and Jessica and Janel will get to go to prom one day! Some day when we grow up and we get to be teenagers. We'll get to wear pretty dresses and curl our hair all fancy, and wear makeup, and get those neat flower things that a boy brings you, and my boyfriend (I wonder if I'll have a boyfriend?) will pick me up in a car that he just washed. Maybe his little sisters will get to help him wash it, just like we're helping Jeff wash his car right now. I can't wait to be a teenager! It is going to be so much fun. I think I want a light purple dress, with ruffles everywhere, that sparkles, with jewelry.

My big sister, Jessica, isn't home right now. She got to spend the night with her friend on Friday. They picked her up from our house in their white van after school. Janel was supposed to go, but mom said no. That's how come Janel is home with me right now. I like spending the night at a friend's house. It's fun! You get to do things together, and talk, and laugh, and sleep in your friend's room, and eat with them, and play with their toys. I think Jessica comes back home tomorrow. We have to go to church tomorrow, because it's Sunday. We always go to church on Sunday. Bob is the one who teaches it. But right now, I'm home with my other big sister, Janel. She's eight. Both of my sisters are older than me. I'm only six. Jessica is the oldest. She's nine. My mom and Bob are home with us today. It's Saturday. I like Saturdays, because we get to play outside and have fun with each other! We get to stay up a little bit later, since it's the weekend and we don't have to go to school. I like weekends!

Earlier today, Bob went to visit the church people. He goes to their houses and talks to them and stuff. I don't know what they talk about. I think they like to talk to him though, because he is the boss of the church. All I know is, people like to talk to Bob. They talk to him a lot. They stop by our house all the time and talk to Bob and my mom. A lady from the church stopped by earlier, when we were washing Jeff's car in our yard. Me and Janel wanted to spend the night at her house, because we get to do that sometimes. We get to play with her kids, our friends. Her mom was at our house talking to Bob, but when we asked, she told us, "No, not tonight. Maybe some other time . . ." She was talking to Bob. People stop by here all the time. They go to our church. It's right over there, right next to our white house. Our house is right next door to it, like the church is our neighbor. I like to wash cars. I'm glad we got to do that. I think it's so fun!

A girl stopped by our house today with her boyfriend to show Bob her dress for the prom thing. I think she used to be Jeff's girlfriend before, but she's not anymore. Bob wanted her to come over to show her dress to him. So, she did. I love her pretty dress! She must feel like a princess. I want to dress like a princess, just like her. To wear makeup and fancy shoes one day, when I'm older. Another boy stopped by our house, too. I think he's one of Jeff's friends. Prom means you get to dress up and go to a dance. Prom sounds so cool!

Mommy went to a Girl Scout meeting earlier today. I don't get to be a Girl Scout yet, because I'm not old enough. But I do get to be a Daisy! I love wearing the cool dress you get to wear if you are one, and you get to earn cool patches that you get to stick on it. We eat cookies and cupcakes, and sing songs, and learn about neat things. Lots of stuff about nature and helping people and stuff. Right now, mommy and me and Janel are in the basement. That's where we sleep. We hang out down here a lot, too. There is a living room with a couch, and a TV, and Bob's office is down here, too.

BANG. *Oh, my gosh—that was sooo loud—what was that?* Mommy heard it, too. BANG. *Oh, my gosh. I heard it again. What was that sound?* It is super loud and scary. Like the loudest thing I ever heard. *What made that sound? Is it in our house? It sounded like it came from upstairs.* All I know is, all of a sudden, mommy's eyes got all big like she's freaked out. Mommy never looks scared. But she is talking really fast and is shaking a little bit. I can tell how scared she is by her eyes. They look all big and worried. She is trying really hard not to let us know she is scared, but she is. I can see it. I can feel it. I know it. Janel does, too. *What was that sound? That really, really, scary, loud sound? The BANG, BANG sounds, and then the thump.* Now it's just quiet. I hear walking. I hear footsteps.

Mommy just told me and Janel to come over to where she was standing in front of the coffee table, near the bottom of the stairs. She kind of rushed us over by her and pulled us next to her. *Oh, my gosh, something is wrong. Something is really bad wrong. Mommy looks so scared. I can tell she doesn't want us to be scared though.* She keeps trying to tell us "it's okay, everything is okay," and trying to make us feel okay. That it is going to be okay. *But I know my mommy is really, really scared right now. Like I've never seen mommy look like this, ever, and it's making me even more scared than I already am from hearing that loud sound. That really, really, scary loud sound.*

Mommy is standing in the middle of us. Janel is standing on one side of mommy and I am standing on the other. We both have our arms wrapped around our mommy. Around her waist. We are holding her, and she is holding us back. She has her arms around us. Both of us. Holding us to her. We are hugging our arms around her and mommy has her arms over the top of us, wrapped around us, pulling us into her. *She is so scared. So scared.* I can tell. She is shaking. Mommy is shaking. I feel her arms shaking around me. When she talks to us, it's a whisper, real quiet, and real serious. *I'm not sure what's happening. It's so scary right now. So scary. All I know is I'm so scared. So scared. Something is wrong. Something is really bad wrong.*

I hear footsteps. They are coming down the steps to the basement. That's where we are. They are getting louder. I hear each one. Footsteps. More footsteps. They are getting closer now. They are coming to where we are now. They are louder. *Oh, no—they are coming to where we are! Oh, my gosh. No. Don't come down here. Please don't come down here. It can't be good. I am so scared right now. I am so, so scared. Is there a bad man in our house? Is he coming to get us, too? To hurt us? Is that what that loud sound was upstairs? No, no no . . . please, no. Please leave us alone. Please just go away. Please don't come to where we are. Please don't.*

My mommy is so scared right now. I am so scared, too. Janel is scared. We are all scared.

I am holding onto mommy so tight now. Me and Janel are both scared. We are really, really scared. We are all standing together, bundled together, like when you're really cold, with our arms all around each other. I can feel my mommy's heart beating really, really fast, it seems like she's holding her breath, and her arms are shaking. I can feel them shaking over the top of me. She has them around us still—me and Janel—she is holding us tight. She is holding us. I just keep my head tucked into her because I don't want to look. It feels safer tucked into my mommy. I will not look. *Please don't come down here. Please don't find us. Please just go away.*

And that's when the footsteps get louder. They are really close to us now. I mean really close. You can hear each one making its way closer to us. They are almost all the way to us. *Here they come.*

They are almost all the way here. They are here. I see a gun. It's a big, long gun. A really, really, big, long, scary looking gun. The next thing I hear is Clack, Clack—BOOOOOOM. It's loud, like thunder. The loudest thing I ever heard. My ears are ringing. Ringing loud. Ringing. It's so loud that I can't hear anymore. I can't hear anything. All I hear is a ringing sound. And my mommy is bleeding now. She fell over on the carpet. She is hurt. She is really, really, bad hurt. But I'm still holding her. I'm holding her tighter. I won't let go. I felt it hit her. I felt it. Her head— It's messed up. It's so messed up. *Her head. It's gone. She doesn't look like mommy anymore. Oh, my gosh—mommy!!!!! No, mommy!!!! Please don't hurt us! Please don't hurt us! Please don't. Pleeeease. Please don't. Please don't. Please, no. Whyyyyyyy did you hurt my mommy? Whhhhhyyy.*

Me and Janel are both crying now. We are crying really hard. And begging. We are begging. And we are still holding onto mommy, and mommy's arms are still around me, but mommy isn't moving anymore. Her arm feels heavy. There is blood now. Blood is everywhere. It is all over the wall, and on the floor, and all around us. Mommy is bleeding all over us. She is bleeding. On us and on the floor, on everything around her. It's my mommy's blood. It is on my shorts and my t-shirt. My mommy's blood is on me now. It's on everything. *Oh, no. It's bright red blood.* It feels wet, and warm, and sticky. It's my mommy's. I see blood. I see blood. I still hear a ringing sound. Mommy! Mommy! She is still here in between us, but I think my mommy is dead! I know she is. She isn't really here anymore. *She is dead. Oh, my gosh, my mommy is dead! Oh no, oh no, oh no. Please don't be dead, mommy. Please don't be. Please not us, too. Please don't shoot us. Please no. Why did you hurt my mommy? Leave us alone! Pleeeeease don't hurt us. Pleeeease . . . Please don't hurt us. Leave us alooooone! Go away. Just go away!*

Clack, Clack—Oh no, please don't shoot us. BOOOOOM. Loud like thunder. *It didn't hit me. It didn't hit me. It didn't hit Janel.* It hit the book that is sitting on the coffee table in front of us. It didn't hit us. *Thank God—it didn't hurt us. We're still okay. Me and*

Janel. We are okay. We are still alive. We are still here. We are okay. Please don't shoot us. Please, nooooo. Please don't shoot my sister. Not Janel. Don't shoot us. Please no. Please don't. Pleeease. The gun is pointed again, this time at Janel. At my sister, Janel. *Please not Janel. Please don't. Pleeeeease.* Clack, Clack—BOOOOOOM. She is bad hurt like mommy. There is blood. More blood. So much blood. I know she is dead. Bad hurt. She has to be dead. They are both dead. My ears are still ringing. They are ringing loud. I can't hear anything. *Everyone is bleeding. Mommy and Janel. Oh, my gosh . . . they are both dead. They are dead. They are dead. They are dead. Please don't be dead. Please don't be dead. Please don't be dead. Pleeeeease.*

Now it's just me. I am on my knees beside my mom. I'm still hugging mommy. *Please don't hurt me. Please don't shoot me. Please don't. Pleeeease don't. Pleeeeease.* I know what's coming. I know what is going to happen next. *It's my turn. I don't want it to be my turn. I don't want to have a turn at all. I don't want to die. I don't want to die. I don't want to get shot. Please don't shoot me. Noooooo. Pleeeease don't. I'll do anything. Anything. Please . . .* The gun is so close to me now, so close. It is so close I can almost touch the end of it with my hand. That's how close it is. Too close. *Oh no. Not me. Please. Pleeeeease.* Clack, Clack—and in that moment I know what is coming, I know I am next. And I raise my little hand because I know what is about to happen. Clack, Clack—BOOOOOOM. My hand is gone. Clack, Clack, BOOOOOOOM.

THE INVESTIGATION
(Based on the evidence)

Sunday, April 30, 1989

The investigation would reveal that Bob Pelley was the first person killed. He suffered two massive gunshots: one to the neck/chin area and the other to the chest, deer slugs fired from a 20-gauge shotgun. The first blow likely struck 38-year-old Bob in the chest, knocking him off his feet and onto the floor in the hallway of his home. Blood spatter located on a baseboard near his fallen body indicated the killer then stood over Bob Pelley's badly wounded body and fired a second shot, fatally wounding him in the neck and chin area, from close range. He had, undoubtedly, looked upon the face of his killer. A small notebook, and some rolled-up papers were found near his head, as were his eyeglasses, which were knocked off his face. A pen remained propped against Bob's head, likely tucked behind his ear at the time of the shooting. Bob was found lying on his back with his feet pointed toward Jeff Pelley's bedroom. His left arm was extended all the way down his side and his right arm was curled up halfway. It appeared that he had dropped the items he was clutching at the time he was shot, leaving traces of an otherwise normal day surrounding his body.

In the master bedroom, at the end of the hall, not far from Bob's fatally-wounded body, a gun rack hung above the bed, holding a bow and a few arrows. The drawer of a nightstand in the master bedroom was pulled open and left ajar, appearing as thought someone had shuffled through it. In it sat a single buckshot shotgun shell and two tarnished rifle cartridges. Normal personal items you would expect to find in someone's home were lying on a nearby dresser and in other areas of the home.

A book entitled *Our Baby's First Seven Years* was found lying on Jeff Pelley's bed. In Jacque's bedroom, a camera, still in its case, sat on her bed.

In the bathroom three washcloths neatly hung over the edge of the tub, each at a varying stage of wetness. One was wet, but not dripping, another was slightly damp, and the third was dry. Water droplets were found on the bathmat near the tub.

Moving downstairs to the basement of the home, where the three little girls, Jessica, Janel, and Jolene always slept, lay the bodies of Dawn Pelly, age 31, Janel Pelley, age eight, and Jolene Pelley, age six. A slain mother whose body met its final resting place in between her two young children; a scene described by some as "a circle of feet." They were closely huddled together into a protective, unified configuration. Dawn was lying on her right side, wearing jeans and a "Chicago" sweater covered in her own blood, a fatal wound to her temple, now disfigured. Janel's body lay next to her mother with her legs near Dawn's face, which was turned to the left, with a massive gunshot wound to the forehead. Unfathomably, Janel's head was found off to the side, lying near the west wall. The body of little Jolene Pelley, who was shot below her right eye from a distance of about a foot away, was lying to the left of her mother, with her little arm still clutching her mother's dead body.

Both little girls were dressed in regular clothes consisting of shorts and plain t-shirts. Each executed in their own home, shot at close range, lying in the futile circle formation where they each drew their last breath. Little Jolene was missing one of her hands, which was apparently blown off as she attempted to block the shot intended to take her life. The little girls had kneeled over the body of their fatally wounded, disfigured mother, at the time each of them was shot at a close range of one to two feet away. A stray bullet was lodged in one of the books which sat atop a nearby coffee table, where one misfired shotgun shell was lodged. A rolled-up newspaper was found beneath the coffee table, which sat in front of the Pelleys' plaid couch. On top of a coffee table was an empty Tupperware bowl holding a spoon, as well as a single white "church" sock which likely belonged to one of the little girls, along with a white lace top.

Blood spackled the basement, saturated the carpet around the three bodies, the walls and ceiling encrusted by spatters of crimson. Brain matter was found on the northwest wall. It was the site of an execution. A family slaughtered in their little white home on an otherwise normal day.

Every window of the parsonage was pulled shut. All the curtains were drawn. All doors to the residence pulled shut and securely locked confining the horror contained within the house. There were no signs of forced entry. Nothing appeared to be missing. Robbery was quickly ruled out as a motive. In a laundry room located at the bottom of the basement stairs, off to the right, the washer contained a small load of clothing that had been washed and left with the laundered pieces, still clinging to the side of the drum. The load consisted of a pair of jeans, a pink and blue shirt, and two white socks. In the corner of the basement on Bob's desk sat a plastic container filled with popcorn. A nylon case for a shotgun was found behind a pile of rolled up sleeping bags in a corner of the basement.

At least six shots were fired inside the home, deer slugs, possibly as many as seven. The time of death for Bob, Dawn, Janel, and Jolene was never determined. A battery of tests that could have narrowed the time frame for their deaths were never conducted. The temperatures of their bodies were not checked. The condition of their eyes was not studied. A rigor mortis (body stiffness) test was not conducted. The lividity (pooling) of blood to various portions of their bodies could also have narrowed down the time of death. Their deaths were simply listed by the coroner as occurring "late Saturday afternoon or early Sunday." The lack of an official time of death would become a major point of speculation and contention as time drew on.

A local forensic pathologist who worked for the state happened to drive by the parsonage that evening and decided to stop by, after seeing a multitude of police cruisers and yellow crime tape surrounding the perimeter of the property. He was informed about the murders by police officers located outside the home and entered the parsonage to study the state of the bodies, generally, as well as any blood evidence present at the crime scene, consisting of blood spatters and blood droplets throughout the home. His findings were documented, but still, no time of death tests were conducted.

At a little round table in the kitchen of the parsonage sat three detectives, their supervisor, and a criminologist, consumed by profound sadness and a deep sense of duty. They had spent the day surrounded by unimaginable images of horror and puzzled as to who could have murdered the Pelley family—an upstanding minister and his lovely wife, pillars of the church and good people—and two precious, innocent little children in such a gruesome manner. The imagery told them how each little girl had undoubtedly clung, likely while weeping and praying, to the body of their mortally wounded and lifeless mother, as each begged for her own life, while looking in to the sadistic eyes of their killer, before falling to the carpet in a circle of feet.

STEPHANIE

Jessica's Best Friend

Present Day—2018

I knew when I walked around the parsonage and saw the curtains all drawn over the windows. I knew. When I saw all the doors were locked and I couldn't get in, like I usually do. I knew somethin' was wrong. Deep down in my soul, I knew it. That feelin' I had in my gut was right. That bad feelin' you feel deep down that tells you that somethin' is wrong. And never in all my life had I ever wanted to be *more wrong* about somethin'. This dark, ugly, horrible thing. But I wasn't wrong. And they were gone. Just like that. An entire family, gone.

How? *Why?* Why would someone do somethin' so terrible to them? In that moment that I learned what had happened, the depths of truth set in for me, much like a fast setting cement weighin' down upon my disbelievin' soul. There would be no more pancake breakfasts on Sunday morning with the Pelleys, ever again. There would be no more wrestlin' with Bob in the living room, while us girls tried to jump on his back to take him down. There would be no more sleepovers. No more bike rides down to the creek. No more freeze tag. No more runnin' through the cornfield or into the woods with my friends. No more skippin' rocks or runnin' around the house. No more playing dress up, no more games, no more fun, no more anything. They were gone.

Jessica survived because she wasn't home, thank Jesus for that. I still had her, my best friend. But Dawn, Bob, Janel, and Jolene, they were gone. As an 11-year-old girl, I would watch as their bodies left the parsonage for the last time, on wheeled gurneys covered by white body bags, one by one. That last image seared into my soul, a part of me forever.

To others, the Pelleys would become the family who was massacred in their own home, in that little parsonage that sat beside the little white church in that small Indiana town where I grew up. But not to me. To me, they were people I knew. People I loved. People I would miss, dearly. People I would think of often. They became people whose names would twist my heart, with a simple thought, the smallest reminder, or a flicker of a memory. They were a second family to me. I loved them dearly.

And that is something that time, distance, and death would not change.

JESSICA

AGE 9
April 30, 1989

*T*he Nameless Girl and I wake up, eat breakfast, and get dressed. We then shuffle our way down the driveway and into the van: The Nameless Girl, The Nameless Girl's Mom, and me, to take me back home. As we drive the familiar stretch of road from LaPaz back to the parsonage in Lakeville—the place I called home—I did not know that this would be my last few fleeting moments of a normal life. The trees pass by our windows. Birds flit across the sky and land on utility lines. People step out of their homes and clamor down their driveways to fetch the Sunday papers from their mailboxes. We continue to drive down the road.

We pull onto my street, before pulling into the gravel driveway. The first thing I notice is bright yellow crime scene tape stretched around my house. There are police cars—a lot of them. There are people from our church standing in our yard. There are police men walking around in their uniforms and other men dressed in street clothes who I would later learn were detectives. The Nameless Girl's mom stops the van in my driveway, in the middle of this chaos. At this point, I'm in the backseat sitting next to The Nameless Girl. The first thing I think to myself is, *"Oh no, my dog must have died."* I was referring to my dog, Major. He was a big, gray husky with black tipped fur and a white belly. He always sleeps outside in the kennel in our backyard at night. We got him when we moved here to Indiana. I love him. *What in the world could have happened to him?*

As I look further, I see that the yellow tape appears to go all the way around my house, extending around the front side, wrapping around the garage, and stretched toward the back of our house. The words on the tape are upside down. That strikes me as odd. *What are all these people doing here? Did my dog die?*

It's then that a uniformed police officer walks up to the van. The Nameless Girl's mom rolls down her window. "Ma'am, who are you?" She replies, "I am [whatever her real name is, again, I cannot tell you what that is]. I have Jessica in the back." In response, he says, "Okay. Ma'am, could you please step outside of the vehicle? There is something I need to tell you." She opens her door and steps out of the van. I see the officer talking to her beside it. I see her begin to cry. I see her wiping away tears as they stream down her face.

She walks around to the side of the van, slides the door open, and looks at me. In a kind, gentle voice, she says, "Jessica, I need you to get out of the van. I need to tell you something." She then places me in the front seat of the van. I feel a warm sensation flash through my entire body. It feels like I'm about to overheat, all of a sudden. My heart is beating rapidly in my chest, so fast it almost hurts. I'm not sure if I'm breathing faster or holding my breath in this moment, but my breathing feels different.

Looking at The Nameless Girl's mom, I see nothing but sadness. Deep sadness and a look of panic. Internally, I'm chanting: *Please be my dog. Please be my dog. Please be my dog.* At this point, no one in my family is standing outside. There are certainly plenty of *other* people standing outside of our house. *But not them.* Her eyes brim with tears, although she wills them not to fall in front of me. They fill the bottom of her eyelids and sit there, waiting, just like me in this moment in time. While I have no idea what she is about to tell me, I know it isn't good. It is really, really bad. *Where is everybody? Where is my mom? Where are Janel and Jolene? Where is Bob? Why aren't they out here to tell me about this—whatever it is? All of this is so weird.*

I'm going to have to paraphrase what she said next. It was the words—the ones no person ever wants to hear, the words I felt, staking me through the heart—the words I blocked. But it was something along the lines of, "I have to tell you something." She looks visibly shaken. *How could she be so upset, when she didn't even know my dog? She never even met Major.* Grown-ups are always able to hold their emotions together. They keep it together. Always. They don't lose it in front of kids. Not like this. They don't break down. But she is on the verge of losing it, in this van, right in front of me, right now. Whatever she is about to tell me, it is *bad, and I mean really bad*, to cause this type of a reaction from an adult. My heart is beating so fast in my chest. I feel it rise and fall. My pulse is racing. Breathing is no longer easy for me. It is a silent struggle. She has a hard time getting out the words, that I remember clearly. "Jessica, your mom, your stepdad, and your sisters are not here anymore . . ." The words, I hear the words, her carefully selected words, the ones to tell me they are dead. Gone. My family is gone. My mom. Janel. Jolene. Even Bob. All of them. I'm not going to see them anymore.

She may still be talking to me right now, but if she is, I'm no longer listening. I am dwelling on the words—the ones that left her mouth a moment ago—what it is those words mean; the reality of them crashing into me, sinking deep into my bones. *What does she mean "gone"? Why are they gone? They died? Why did they die? How did they die? My entire family? How is that even possible?* I begin to cry. The type of cry that The Nameless Girl's mom was trying so hard to hold back. An ugly cry that rips through your soul and pours out in the form of unfiltered agony. Pain. Hurt. Longing. Disbelief. It was the worst kind of pain imaginable. Actually—forget that—this kind of pain was *unimaginable*, completely unimaginable, as were the words to tell me what had happened to my mom, Janel, Jolene, and Bob.

At one point, one of the police men asked me if I knew where Jeff and Jacque might be. I knew Jacque had spent the night with a friend at Huntington College for a church thing and I assumed Jeff was probably at Great America with everyone else from prom. I didn't know.

It was on a Sunday, in the gravel driveway of the little white parsonage on Osborne Road, on April 30, 1989. It was the Lord's Day. It certainly wasn't *my day*. It was anything but. She pulled the van back down the driveway of my home, the one I had up until 10 minutes ago, and drove us back to The Nameless Girl's house.

The world kept spinning, people kept moving, kept talking, the sun continued to shine, and I wept as the deaths of my family were laid at my feet.

I just want to be with them.
Why did they have to die?
Why couldn't I just die with them?
Why am I left behind, all alone?
Why am I still here?
Why me?
Why be alive? What's the point?
The questions to which I would spend years upon years of my life seeking the answers.

MONA

Jessica's mom's best friend

The Call

I was standing in the kitchen when the phone rang. I picked it up. It was one of Jessica's aunts, who was a friend of mine. (One of Jessica's dad's sisters.)

"Hello."

"Mona, it's me. I'm calling to tell you there's been an accident." I could tell she'd been crying.

"An accident? What do you mean an accident? What kind of accident—a car accident?"

"Dawn, Bob, and the girls are gone."

"Gone? What do you mean gone?"

"They died. Dawn and Bob and the girls were shot and killed yesterday."

"All of them?"

"No, Jessica wasn't home. Jeff and Jacque weren't there either . . ."

At this point, I threw down the phone and began screaming hysterically, as I sunk down onto the floor, "No, no, no, no, no." "No, no, no, no. . ." My husband immediately came running into the house because he heard primal screams. I'm not sure how long I screamed my denials into the air around me. And I'm also not sure if I formally ended the call or how long I cried. Perhaps sobbed would be a better word to describe it. I was a hysterical mess, sitting on that kitchen floor for what seemed like an eternity.

I did not eat or sleep for an entire week following that call. I couldn't. Any time I tried to sleep, I would wake to hellish nightmares where I relived their final moments here on earth. It was unparalleled mental horror. There was no way to imagine their last moments not being filled with the worst type of personal terror, as they stood gripped and clinging to one another, in fear of dying. And the little girls. *Oh why, oh why, God? Why would you allow this to happen? Why would you take the little girls?* I knew exactly what Dawn felt in that last moment, when she had her arms protectively laced around her little girls. I knew. Her mind raced to thoughts of this being the end, that this was it for them, this hellish, tragic, terrible way to die, and her having absolutely no way to protect them—her children—her babies. And I would resume sobbing again.

I cried almost nonstop. Any time I had a moment when I thought I could pull myself together, I realized I couldn't and would begin sobbing again. After about seven days of this, my husband became concerned that I might not be able to pull myself out of this, could have a legitimate mental breakdown, and at the rate I was going, would not be able to get it together to be able to care for our own children and household as I needed to. He was right. I was struggling. I was falling apart. I was probably pretty darn close to breaking. I definitely felt that way. I just couldn't stop the thoughts from racing through my mind. I kept coming back to their final moments, and the visit with Dawn not even a month before; how I should have known, or that I could have tried to change things. It was on an endless, soul-suffering loop in my mind. My husband was beginning to think I needed to see the doctor about getting a prescription for tranquilizers, so I could try to sleep. Any time I did fall asleep, the nightmares came. I was tortured. That's the best way to put it. Completely and utterly tortured.

Dawn was gone. Those precious little girls, they were gone, too.

That was it. That's all there was for them. We were still here. And they weren't.

It was so sudden. So terrible. And so incredibly tragic. Pure evil. That's all I could think.

Who would hurt them? Who would hurt little girls?

Tears upon tears were shed. I cried until I didn't think I possibly had any tears left to cry. I always found more. I had no idea how I was ever going to get over this, or if I even should. How could anyone get over this? It was such an evil act.

I eventually began to pull myself together during the day to care for the kids, but at night, when I was all alone in my bed, I would fall apart. My soul was in a state of perpetual suffering. My heart, broken. My best friend, gone.

That last visit I had with Dawn at Gayle's house ate at me. It chiseled away at me, bit by bit. I carried guilt in such abundance, my mind became its harbor following her death. I should have said more, tried to help her more, encouraged her to leave more strongly, or even yelled at her, if I had to, in order to get her to leave. I could have kept this from happening. If I'd just been more passionate or presented my views in a more animated way. But I didn't. And because of that, *she is gone.* That guilt gnawed at me in the minutes and hours of each passing day.

I wasn't sure I would ever be able to pull myself together. I was having a hard time taking care of my own children, two little boys, ages three and six; the youngest of whom was born severely mentally and physically handicapped and had special needs that required my constant attention 24 hours a day. I was also running a daycare for six children out of my home. The idea of caring for little children only further reminded me of the loss of Janel and Jolene, so innocent, so precious, so young.

Then one night, as I lay in my bed, trying to relax and praying for sleep to overtake me, the smell of Dawn's favorite perfume, Avon's "Sweet Honesty," began to waft through my room. Upon smelling that fragrance, I immediately thought of her. And a mere moment later, at the foot of my bed, stood Dawn. I swear to you, she was right there. Not faded out, partially transparent, nor basked in light. She looked so vivid and real, a mere bed length between us. She was literally standing there, at the foot of the bed. I saw her whole, beautiful and alive, just how she was, even bearing a smile. It was Dawn, in my bedroom, right there, with me.

And then, she spoke:

"I don't want you to cry anymore, Mona."

"We're okay."

"You need to take care of Jessica."

And then, just as quickly as she came, she was gone. Those would become her final parting words to me from beyond the grave. Trust me, I know this sounds completely crazy. I felt crazy telling my husband about this experience after it occurred. I felt crazy telling Jamie about it when we discussed my chapter for this book. But it was as real as rain. It's something I cannot possibly explain, but will never, ever forget. And I'm telling you, it happened.

Following the encounter, I felt a sense of calm wash over me. I felt different, like I could try to move on. I knew that's what Dawn wanted for me.

Dawn's last words from the grave continued to play in my mind: "Take care of Jessica." That's what she told me. Those were her final words. I didn't even know where Jessica was living at this point. But I would try to find her.

MONA

Jessica's Mom's Best Friend

(As told present day, 2018)

*W*hile I did try to move on with my life following the tragic loss of my dear friend Dawn and her children, the guilt never left me. In difficult times, I was a person who turned to God. I entrusted my faith in Him to help me through the bad times. The problem was that I found myself questioning God about *why* he would allow something as horrific as this to happen to such good people, whom I loved. It was such an act of evil. They didn't deserve for this to happen; no one does. Why did He let this happen? Why the girls? What good could possibly come from it? How could this be a part of God's master plan? What could be the purpose? My faith was truly tested in the weeks and months that followed the murders. I tried to make sense of it all in a spiritual manner, to no logical end. But still, I tried. I found myself grappling with my own faith. Attempting to come to terms with the how and why of something so terrible it held no logic.

Every morning while the house was quiet and everyone else was still asleep in their beds, I would sit at the kitchen table to read my Bible to try to make sense of things for which sense could not be made. To find some comfort or explanation. There was many a day that I found neither comfort, nor explanation. Those days turned into weeks. Those weeks turned into months. Then gradually, the months turned into years, but I kept reading verses of scripture in search of something, anything that would help me: maybe a deeper level of understanding, some small sliver of personal healing, or some answer for it all. I don't know. I felt like I was in search of something that I knew may not exist.

I found myself questioning God, pondering the purpose of life, and wondering why in the world their lives would be cut so short in such a terribly violent manner. There would be no formal answers to my questions. But I guess, that's why they call it "faith." You either have it or you don't. Over time, I did discover certain Bible verses that seemed to help me. I cleaved to them. I read them over and over again to try to make my mind understand what my heart never would be able to. If I'm being entirely honest, I was angry at God. You bet I questioned his will in allowing this to happen. I could not see any possible purpose in their deaths. But still, I clung to the scriptures to find a way through the suffering.

Each morning, I would open my Bible and read these scriptures:

Romans 8:28 *And to know that in all things God works for the good of those who love him, who have been called according to his purpose.*

2 Corinthians 4:7 *But we have this treasure in jars of clay to show that this all-surpassing power is from God and not from us. We are hard pressed on every side, but not crushed; perplexed, but not in despair; persecuted, but not abandoned; struck down, but not destroyed.*

Genesis 50:20 *As for you, you meant evil against me, but God meant it for good in order to bring about the present result, the saving of many lives.*

And this one, that reminded me of Jessica:

Jeremiah 29:11 *"For I know the plans I have for you," declares the LORD, "plans to prosper you and not to harm you, plans to give you hope and a future. Then you will call on me and come and pray to me and I will listen to you. You will seek me and find me. When you seek me with all your heart."*

"I will be found by you," declares the LORD, "and will bring you back from captivity. I will gather you from all the nations and places where I have banished you," declares the LORD, "and will bring you back to the place from which I carried you into exile."

For years, I read the verses. I still do. In the end, what I kept circling back to is this: We are God's and to God we will return. But that doesn't make it any easier.

As children of God, all our days are planned. All our days are numbered. They are God's, and, to God, they did return.

JAMIE

AGE 12

Jessica's cousin

May 3, 1989

I'm Jessica's eldest cousin, but we're only three years apart in age. My mom, Marla, was one of eight siblings on that side of the family, consisting of seven girls and one boy. Jessica's dad, Eddie, known to those outside the family more formally as Edward and casually as Ed, was my mom's younger brother. She was the oldest of the brood. The two held a special bond and were close. That is how Jessica and I are related.

Jessica's dad's funeral was the first one I ever attended. I was only seven years old at the time. I remember looking down at my Uncle Eddie, lying in that casket, and thinking two things. First, that he was so handsome. And second, that it looked like his face was made of wax. I ran my little hand along his cheek to see what it felt like. I had never seen a dead person before. Nor had I ever heard the 21-gun salute. Each shot fired from the rifles of the soldiers standing in a line at his funeral jarred me, emotionally. Watching one of the soldiers hand my Aunt Dawn a folded American flag left a permanent imprint across my heart. Jessica would have been four at the time of his death. I don't remember her being there, but I'm sure she was. The little Huber girls—my cousins—were there with my Aunt Dawn.

Jessica and I never got to see one another too often. Having military dads and living in different parts of the country certainly doesn't help. If you imagine this side of our family as a slice of Swiss cheese, Jessica's dad and my mom are the holes. Each for differing reasons: Eddie's early death in 1985 at the age of 27, and my mom's alcoholic-induced absence, coupled with my parents' divorce when I was five, and me living with my dad since that time. There were years when my mom was a part of my life and I visited her during the summer. And then there were several years when we didn't even know where she was, so my dad would take me to visit my grandma (her mom) and aunts (my mom's sisters) instead. Our link to the family chain was a bit broken. Our spots no longer quite so clear. Besides that, when Jessica and I actually found ourselves in the same room over the years as children, as introverts, we often found ourselves cloaked in silence with not many words passing between us. Don't get me wrong, we love each other, but just don't know each other too well. She is my cousin, as I am hers. We are family. Forever. Holes and all. (A point we would come to remember many years down the road.)

And that brings us to today. I'm riding in the passenger seat of my dad's car: a pale blue, four-door Mercedes he bought while stationed as a helicopter pilot on an army base in Stuttgart, Germany. The place we would call home for several years when I was a toddler, and again from fourth through seventh grade. I'm now in the eighth grade and attend junior high where we live in Indianapolis.

Right now, we are driving north toward Lakeville, Indiana. It's a long drive. I'm trying to keep my mind busy wandering to aimless thoughts. The billowy clouds in sky. The black bird sitting in a nearby tree before taking flight. That, or faintly mumbling along to the voices of Bruce Springsteen, Neil Diamond, Abba, or Fleetwood Mac—dad's choice tunes—playing on the radio to avoid the thoughts I'd rather not think. My only distraction from the nerves slicing through my stomach, like tiny jolts of electric current, are the rows and rows of winter wheat standing on the tan and green fields quickly passing by my window. It's just me, my dad, and the farmland of rural Indiana, as we make our way toward a place I loathe going, on a day that I will never forget.

This morning I woke up nervous. My stomach flitting between anxiety and sorrow. The dark gray skirt I'm wearing right now is causing the back of my legs to stick to the leather seat. The clip I used to pull half of my hair up is digging into the back of my head when I press it back against the headrest. I look down and twirl my finger around the thin layer of black tulle that lays beneath the dark gray cotton fabric of my skirt to further distract myself. We drive for what seems like a long time, but, in reality, was just a few hours. We finally arrive at our destination in northern Indiana: 22750 Osborne Road, and pull into the parking lot, where my grandma (my mom's mom, also Jessica's gammy) stands, awaiting our arrival.

I see the church. It's a fairly large structure covered in bright white siding, with a tall steeple peaking at the front of it, a rounded window of reddish glass below it, accented by beautiful, vividly colored stained glass windows decorating the side of the church. There are people everywhere. My Grandma King is dressed in black. The sadness in her glossy eyes is evident, like sorrow is hiding behind them. I can't help but think of how she had already lost two of her own children. I can tell she's been crying. But in her face, I see strength. She stands straight and tall, with her head held high, in a situation where I'm not sure how anyone could. It takes me back to Uncle Eddie's funeral four years ago. She's now lost two more small pieces of him. We all have. There is no escaping the dread I feel. The nervousness climbs up my spine.

We exit the car and walk up to her and she pulls me into a tight embrace. It's not the typical hug you'd expect when seeing a relative after many months apart, but the type that conveys so much more—hurt, deep longing, a small dose of comfort, and unwavering love. We both linger there for a moment, between the folds of reality and time, before pulling away to face what awaits us.

Together, we begin to walk toward the church. As my grandma takes a step forward, she leans over to pull me in close, intentionally tucking me into the crook of space at the side of her body—the one perfectly made to comfort 12-year-old girls on days like this—her left arm wrapped, tightly clutching around my waist, pulling me into the protective space. It's as though she's trying to shield me from something. But from what, I don't know. In the moment, I'm not sure why.

We begin to stride up the grassy hill toward the white building. With each step I take, the stubby heel on the back of my little black pumps defiantly digs down into the dirt, sinking into the earth a bit. With my next step forward, the first one is released, allowing me to step forward onto the other one. As we near the top of the hill, I feel her left arm grip my waist a little tighter. She quickens our pace. It's as though she's now ushering me up the hill in a more formal fashion. As we take our last few steps to crest the top of the hill, I see why.

There are reporters. They are everywhere. And I mean, everywhere. We don't stop. We begin to walk at a brisk pace, my grandma's arm still gripped tightly around me. Anxiety begins to rise in my belly. Right about then, the nerves hit full force. My heart begins to beat faster in my chest and my legs begin to tremble. I've never walked with more intention in all my life.

The place is swarming with people from the media. It's mayhem. There are news vans surrounding the perimeter of the property. Lots of them. I'm not sure what I expected . . . but this isn't it. News anchors are running around outside of Olive Branch United Brethren Church in a frantic effort to obtain the best photo and video footage to capture what would, unquestionably, become one of our darkest days. I see a flash of movement to my left as a lady wearing a black suit jacket, matching pencil skirt, and black heels rushes up to my side, eager, almost in a state of professional frenzy. Her mouth turned down into the top of a microphone to give a sound bite, she calls out to the cameraman, "Be sure to get a shot of this." *This* being my grandma and me, during the last few steps we would take in to the depths of emotional hell that awaited us. Featured on the evening news? That would be a yes.

God, I dread going into the church. I have no idea what to expect.

We enter the protective doors of the white church. It. Is. Packed. I've never seen so many people. The pews are filled to capacity and others stand to fill all available space along the perimeter of the room. I can't even begin to count them. It's almost overwhelming, really. I know why they're all here. I know why I'm here. It's the same reason Jessica is here today. How awful.

There is a special row reserved near the front of the church for us—the one for family. I take a seat beside Grandma on the wooden pew. I'm not sure what I expected this to be like. The anxiety is unshakable. The sadness and sobbing all around cuts me to the core. I know the next hour will be one of the longest of my life.

And then I see them—four wooden boxes filling the space in the front of the church. Caskets. Two regular ones. Two tiny ones in white. I see flowers decorating the top of them. I know what's in those boxes. My stomach drops, right along with my heart.

Today there would be no closure. Not for me. Not for Jessica. Not for anyone. Closed caskets don't really afford a person the final formality of saying a proper goodbye. Not even close. Just wooden boxes and flowers to serve as a placeholder for the people you loved, now lost. Our minds involuntarily flashed to vivid mental images of their final hellish moments here on earth . . . before the boxes. So young. So beautiful. So full of life. Throw in the fact that we are now seated in a church where Robert Pelley was the minister and maybe, just maybe, you get some small sliver of understanding of how utterly devastating and hellish this was—for anyone. This room was the type of place that would bring a stranger to his knees. There would be no comfort here. Just a cold, hard, unexpected goodbye; one that came far too soon for all of us.

The sobs are something I will never forget. Sorrow hangs heavy in the air. The depth of grief around me is palpable. It is a room full of grown-ups attempting to hold it together while falling apart. I can hear it in their wailing sobs. I see it in their tear-stained, grief-stricken faces. I hear a pipe organ playing in the background. All at once, every person in the room begins to sing along with the chords, in unison, the words: *"Amaziiiiiing Graaaaace, how sweeeeet the soooooound, that saaaaaaved a wretch liiiiiiike meeee . . ."* It sounds like hundreds of people singing the words. Sobs ringing through the air. Tears are pouring from my eyes, streaming in long, wet lines down the front of my face, falling onto my lap, and clouding my vision. It's hard to breathe through the sobbing. I am not singing. I can't. The words to this song will forever be burned into my soul. An emotional scar etched permanently across my heart, like a scab waiting to be torn open again at any time. A song that would go on to haunt me for the next three decades. I will never forget this moment. *Never.*

I will try hard *not* to return to this place, on this day, in this moment, ever again. It's too painful. It's too hard. I will run from it. I will forget it. I will tuck it away.

And then . . . there is Jessica.

JESSICA

AGE 9

The Church Service

*L*ooking back, I don't remember much from the church service portion of my family's funeral. I'm glad my cousin, Jamie, was there that day to paint the details. This is another one of the significant memories my mind has blocked and one of the traumatic memories I am grateful not to have.

I'm pretty sure I sat with Ed 2 (my grandpa from my mom's side of the family) and his wife, Lara, at the service. But I could not tell you, in this moment, who I sat alongside in that pew from my own recollection. I remember hearing people sing the song "Amazing Grace." No one in that church will ever forget it. Given the intensity of grief and soul-swallowing sorrow that filled that room, it's not too surprising my mind would block the details from those emotionally raw moments.

After the service was over, I remember whomever I was with instructing me to put on what equated to a makeshift disguise for nine-year-old-little-girls-who-needed-to-flee-churches with some modicum of privacy. That turned out to be a joke.

"Here—put this on, Jessica." They handed me a ball cap and big sunglasses.

"Why?"

"You just need to put these on."

So, I put them on. Not because I wanted to, but because they told me to. As soon as the church door swung open and we walked through it, the reason for me sporting this garb became apparent. It was a media swarm. There were frenzied reporters pointing video cameras, shouting out questions to us, taking into microphones, and people running alongside us.

It's then that I hear the words, "Just put your head down, Jessica. Don't look up. Just keep walking," as I was ushered by my family members toward the car.

And with that climactic, highly-anticipated exit that seemed to be the focus for the clamoring throngs of reporters, we made our way to the burial. The place where I would see them place my family, now in wooden coffins, into the cold, hard ground. Dead. Gone. Remembered. But still gone forever.

Most people want to know what I was thinking during the funeral and how I felt. My answer is probably not what most would expect. Was I drowning in sadness? Absolutely. I could barely breathe through the pain. It flowed from my pores. But I was also filled with anger; more anger than any 9-year-old child should ever have to discover. The honest answer is: I was angry at my mom. Furious. Of course, I grieved the loss of her, but a red-hot anger surged through my veins on the heels of her entirely unexpected departure. At age nine, children are fairly self-absorbed. I was no exception. You think about *your own* wants. *Your own* needs. How things affect *you*. What happened to *you*. How it changes *your* life. Every thought I had reverberated inward. So, was I angry with my mom? Yeah, you bet I was. For so many reasons.

I was angry we moved out of that yellow house I shared with my daddy.

I was angry she met Bob.

I was angry she married Bob.

I was angry she moved us to Florida.

I was angry she moved us to Indiana.

I was angry she allowed Bob to adopt my sisters and me.

I was angry she allowed Bob to beat me with a belt.

And more than any other thing, I was angry she didn't let Janel go with me to the Nameless Girl's House to spend the night with me on that fateful Friday.

I was angry they were all dead.

You bet I was angry. Mad as hell is just stepping into the ballpark.

I'm pretty sure therapists would tell you anger is a stage of grief. For me, it became a way of life, a stage that stretched out and consumed me at every turn for years and years and years.

I know that my mom—age 32 at the time of her death—did the best that she could, given the circumstances. She was left a widow far too young, at 27-years-old, with three little girls to raise alone. The way Bob punished me did not sit well with her. I realize that now. I would learn that many years later it is a point she discussed in great detail with her best friend, Mona, and her late mother-in-law (my "gammy"), Gayle. It only made me all the angrier that she didn't actually do something about it. Then, it was too late. Too late for her. Too late for my sisters. Too late for all of us.

As a nine-year-old who resented the choices my mother made following my father's death, that anger ran deep after this tragedy. That isn't to say I didn't love her. I did, still do, and always will, until the day I draw my last breath. But my mother became the primary focus of my angry thoughts after she passed. In reality, she was appointed some of them before she ever left. We had the typical spats a mother and daughter have. But she became a departed host of aggression beyond the grave for me in the years that would follow her death. Let's be real—I couldn't even bear to hear her name spoken aloud. Not that *anyone ever* spoke about my family to me after they died. Their names became one of the things that people buried on their tongues. Raw memories of loved ones lingered around me, along with the air I breathed, completely unacknowledged by those around me.

When I thought about my sisters, the predominant emotion was, and continues to be, an intense and irrevocable sadness. One that knows no end. One I cannot camouflage. A hurt I hide in the depths of my soul. Sadness at the loss of my life-long companions now flows through my bones and sits in them, like marrow.

I miss them all. I still mourn them. I wish for them. I long for them. And most of all, I remember them. Vividly. In a never-ending way.

But if you want to know how I felt at the funeral, I was angry as hell. Angrier than any little girl should ever be. Yet, there I was. So little. So alone. So angry. So very, very angry.

JAMIE

The Burial

(As told present day, 2018)

ollowing the church service, only one word could describe how I felt: numb. Completely and totally numb, and glad for it, although the remnants of my bloodshot eyes gave me away. To be in one place filled with so much suffering and sorrow really took it out of a person, and I, as a 12-year-old girl, was no exception. The funeral was so much worse than anything I had expected or prepared myself to face. Humans weren't built to live inside that type of grief. It was all-consuming, almost paralyzing. It was, far and away, one of the worst places I have ever been, in that little white church on that dark day.

Our next stop was the burial. It couldn't be any more emotionally jarring than the church service. Nope. It couldn't be. The numbness clung to the fabric of my gray skirt ensemble much like an invisible blanket, a coat of protective armor, and Lord, did I need it.

We arrived at the graveyard. There was a large white tent set up outside. The four caskets containing our loved ones were lined in a row at the front of it. I took my seat under the tent, next to my grandma. She had pointed them out to me at the burial before we sat down and explained to me who they were: "Those are Bob's kids, Jeff and Jacque." They were in front of me and a little to my right. This gave me the perfect view of the two of them, peripherally. I remember sitting there and studying them. Feeling sad for them. I'd never met them, and yet, I felt so much grief for the two of them, as total strangers who had lost their dad, and (nearly) the remainder of their stepfamily, in such a horrific way.

It was a normal response, I think. The same empathy I felt toward Jessica also extended to them, albeit internal and left unspoken. I was blending into the background, just one small body among a sea of several close friends and family members, seated beneath that white tent on a fairly chilly Indiana day. I sat, as we all did, at the final place where the four beloved Pelleys would be laid to rest.

My grandma had told my dad and me that the detectives considered Jeff a suspect. I know it may seem odd that I would be told this as a preteen girl, but as the eldest grandchild on that side of the family, and a mature kid, my grandma always treated me more like an adult where meaningful discussions were concerned. I can honestly say I found the news shocking. The stepbrother? Really? It sounded crazy. Unfathomable. She also told us the detectives planned to take Jeff Pelley aside following the funeral service to check his body for "kickback" marks made by a shotgun, based on statements he'd made during an interview he'd given to police about having fired a shotgun with a friend once that "knocked him on his ass."

While some may choose to believe that I showed up at the funeral that day with preconceived notions regarding Jeff Pelley—whom I'd never met before and still never officially met that day—what I hoped, deep down inside, was to depart there feeling there was no way my cousin Jessica's stepbrother could be the killer. No way. After all, this was the late '80s. Teenagers didn't kill people. Gun violence wasn't commonplace, like it is today. Mass shootings in schools, shopping malls, movie theatres, and workplaces weren't something you heard about on the evening news, especially not murders like this, in a rural town like Lakeville, Indiana. Grown-ups committed crimes. Bad, evil adults, typically men. They were the ones who killed people. Not teenage boys who were related to the people who died.

I wanted to look at Jeff Pelley and see a young, normal, all-American boy, likely consumed by grief. I wanted to see him and think there was no way he could have committed a horrific crime such as this. They had to be wrong. They wanted to believe it was him, but it wasn't. It couldn't be. I hoped to see him and leave there that day believing the police suspected the wrong guy—no way did Jessica's stepbrother do it—that's just plain crazy. How could he? Why would he? He was just a 17-year-old boy! But there I sat. Just as we all did. Watching. Grieving. Observing.

As I said, I had a good view of Jeff and Jacque throughout the entire service. It was clear Jacque was distraught. She was trying adamantly to be strong and hold it together; that much was clear, her grief was palpable. That is what I expected to see when I looked at Jeff. But throughout the entire burial, as I sat there watching him, I couldn't help but feel something was off—and I mean *way* off—the kind of "off" any reasonable, normal person just can't rightfully ignore. The longer I watched him, the more I felt a nagging, sinking, sick feeling in my gut.

His eyes were striking, so dark brown they were nearly black. Empty, cold, and flat. Emotionless. The visceral reaction to his intense gaze damn near put a deep crease in my soul. I didn't want to feel that way when I looked at Jeff Pelley, I really didn't. Yet, when I looked at him, that's what I felt. He had a distant gaze that wouldn't allow people to see what was truly going on behind his eyes, almost as though I was looking at someone hidden deep beneath a barrier of obsidian colored glass. His face was expressionless. It made the hairs on my arms stand on end. As a 12-year-old girl looking at him that day, it's not something I could miss.

I wanted to feel something when I looked at Jeff Pelley. Anything. Sadness. Grief. Anger. Shock. The stoic storage of emotions being held inward by a teenage boy in the throes of deep grief, who was implored by his father never to cry. A boy trying to hold it together. A boy trying not to fall apart. A boy feeling empathy for the emotionally distraught tears of his sister. Anything at all. But Jeff never shed a single tear. *Not one.* There was no gaze of empathy. He never proffered any emotion. He was there, *but he wasn't.* What I felt when looking at him was almost a lack of regard, a lack of presence, and a lack of humanity. A lack of anything you would expect to see or feel when looking upon the face of a teenage boy there to bury his family.

Jeff's demeanor that day was noticed by many. His behavior would become a topic of discussion, speculation, controversy, and whispers for the investigating detectives, our family, the church's congregation, and those who lived in that small Indiana town. Speculation based upon observation. That's all it was. Conjecture for the lay people. But it was there. We saw it. We felt it. And it's something none of us wanted to see, or feel, when we looked at him. Yet we did.

When the burial portion of the service concluded, I moved to a seat on the far right side of the white tent, where I sat patiently waiting for the relatives on my mom's side of the family to pay their social respects to other people at the burial. Jessica stood maybe 10 feet away from me, to my right. She was wearing the thick glasses she always wore. She looked so young standing there in a dress. So innocent. So utterly undeserving of this. It hurt my heart to see her and realize what all of this meant for her. The finality of what we had just done continued to linger at the graveside around us.

One by one, I watched as each of our aunts filed toward Jessica in a small procession to shower her with affection and bestow their kind, beautiful, heartfelt words upon her, each taking a moment to pull her in for a tight, emotion-laced embrace. It was one of those moments where grown-ups try to be strong for the kids. They try to hold their own broken pieces together and say just the right words, when deep down inside, what they want is nothing more than to drop the fraying pieces and fall apart. I remember them being kind to Jessica. Loving. Supportive. I heard each of them say things like, "We're here for you, Jessica." "We love you so much, Jessica." "We're here if you need anything at all, Jessica—you just let us know." "It's going to be okay, Jess. Your family loves you so much and we're here for you. We always will be." "You call us if you need anything at all, okay, sweetie?" I sat there feeling so much pity for Jessica. *So* much pity. An imperfect blend of sadness and sorrow.

I knew we would all leave there that day to resume our normal lives. Yes, our *normal* lives. The ones we still had. Me and the aunts. Me and the church members. Me and the investigators. Me and everyone else. But not Jeff and Jacque. And certainly, not my younger cousin, Jessica. This moment at a graveyard was destined to become a defining moment in her life. One of an uncountable many that would shape the ensuing years of trials and tribulations she would crawl, fight, or claw her way through.

I still see her standing there, beside the little white tent.

The chilly air around us.

The little girl in glasses.

Off to my right.

The one who didn't realize how broken this would make her.

I would leave Jessica behind that day.

I would fail her, in my own way.

We all would . . .

THE INVESTIGATION

April and May, 1989

The detectives working the case viewed Jeff Pelley as the prime suspect fairly early on. They suspected he had murdered his own father, stepmom, and two young stepsisters in an enraged act of rebellion against his dad's recent grounding. Bob had grounded Jeff, forbade him from driving his own car to the prom or the trip to Great America afterward, and had cancelled the insurance on Jeff's Mustang for a period of six months. The car insurance was still cancelled at the time of the murders. Bob was planning to drive Jeff and his date to the prom that Saturday night because he wasn't allowed to drive himself. While it may be perplexing to fathom prom attendance as the motive for murder, it was Jeff's odd behavior, his own words spoken to detectives and others around him, flat affect and lack of emotion, and also his own inconsistent retelling of the facts and events that had transpired leading up to the murders that affixed their eyes upon him initially.

A look at Jeff's background revealed he had a few bouts of criminal conduct in the past, mostly petty crimes, but nothing of a violent nature.

A year earlier, Jeff had been caught breaking into cars at the mall, shoplifting, and smoking pot. At one point, he had also stolen and forged a check that was in the possession of Dawn Pelley, which belonged to the ladies' church group which was administered by Dawn. It was known that Dawn had made Jeff stand up in front of the assembled group of ladies at the church to personally apologize to them for his transgression. While Jeff did do so, this only served to deepen the disdain he held toward his stepmother.

He got caught shoplifting. And in mid-March of 1989—about one month prior to the murders—Jeff had committed theft. He had robbed a home on Osborn Road and stolen some items, which included: 40 CDs, some coins, and some cash totaling less than $100.00. Bob knew one of the police detectives, who had contacted Bob to advise him that his son was suspected in the robbery. Apparently, the detective who contacted Bob had a younger brother who was friends with Jeff. Upon learning of this criminal conduct, Bob drove Jeff to the police station in Bremen, Indiana. When questioned about the theft, Jeff admitted to being in the house at the time the items were stolen. To avoid the criminal charges, Jeff had to repay the victim. Bob promised to keep a closer eye on Jeff in the future. As punishment, Bob took Jeff's Mustang away from him, barring him from driving it for a period of six months. Bob even went so far as to formally cancel the insurance policy on the Mustang and all other vehicles on the family's insurance policy that Jeff had access to for that six-month period.

At one point, Jeff Pelley had threatened to commit suicide. It was believed by his father and Dawn to be a ploy for attention, since Jeff had committed robbery and had his car taken away.

Detectives learned that Jeff and his dad were frequently at odds with each other and often argued. There were a few occasions when members of the church and family friends reported observing Jeff and his father raising their voices to each other or engaging in heated disagreements. There was at least one witness account, by Jeff's then-girlfriend, of Bob physically shoving Jeff down onto the ground during a heated altercation in front of her.

By Jeff's own admission, he resented his father's marriage to Dawn after his mother's death from breast cancer in 1985. Bob and Dawn had married just nine months afterwards. Jeff resented Dawn's age: she was only 13 years older than he was. He did not like her as a person, resented her presence in his life and in their home, merely "tolerated her" (his own words during a police interview), and refused to ever call her mom. It was noted that Jeff felt as though his dad's personality had morphed after he married Dawn and that his dad acted like a completely different person. Bob had even gone so far as to change his family's religious denomination when they moved to his new church job in Indiana. A disparity between the way Bob raised Jeff and Jacque and the way the girls were being raised by Bob and Dawn was also a point of contention. Dawn's parenting style was far different than how Bob had raised his own children. Jeff also resented being forced to leave his home, school, and all his friends back in Florida, to move to Lakeville, Indiana, with his "new" family.

The Pelleys had attended family counseling in 1988 and 1989 in an effort to resolve their familial conflicts stemming from the merger of two families into one. Jeff and Jessica also attended individual counseling.

Did Jeff really commit the murders to go to the prom?

Did a son really kill his own family?

The questions began to swirl.

Minds began to race.

Whispers carried on the wind.

Detectives continued to investigate. They wanted to find the murder weapon.

And a local community, still in mourning, wondered, watched, and waited.

THE INVESTIGATION
1989

On that sorrow-filled Sunday when the Pelleys' bodies were found, at around 11:00 A.M., Jeff Pelley arrived at Great America with his girlfriend and a group of friends. At around 11:30 A.M., Jeff's demeanor changed. His girlfriend noticed he was being quiet. When she asked him what was wrong, Jeff turned to her and said, "I've got a bad feeling." She replied, "Like what?" He responded, "I don't know. I can't explain it. It's like something is wrong." His girlfriend tried to inquire further about what could be wrong and Jeff dropped the subject.

Upon being located at the park by a security officer and escorted to the park's security office by a police detective from a local police precinct in Ohio, Jeff was told that his father, stepmother, and two stepsisters were dead, but no other details were given. Jeff said nothing in response. He did not ask any questions at all. Per the local detective, Jeff showed no emotion upon hearing the news. Not a single tear was shed. However, when Jeff was later asked by the Indiana detectives during a formal interview what his reaction was upon being told of the news, Jeff stated, " . . . (I) started crying . . . I mean . . . It stunned me, I didn't know how it could happen, I didn't know why it would happen." Yet he had shed no tears and had shown no emotional reaction.

In addition to cancelling the insurance on Jeff's car, Bob had also advised a church elder that he had removed the distributor cap from the engine of Jeff's Mustang, along with a few fuses to effectively disable his vehicle. Notably, on the way to pick up his date on the evening of prom, Jeff Pelley stopped at not one, but *two* different gas stations. At one of them, an Amoco, he borrowed a screwdriver because his car "wasn't running right." During questioning, he initially only mentioned stopping at one of the gas stations—Casey's—until detectives made it clear that they knew about the second stop at an Amoco, at which point Jeff claimed he had "stopped to get a pop."

Early that evening Jeff showed up at his girlfriend's house to change into his tux. That last part never made a lot of sense to anyone who heard this story. No pictures taken by Bob of his son Jeff in his tuxedo for his senior prom? He didn't even get to see him in it? Was it because they were no longer alive? This was odd, even to Jeff's girlfriend at the time, who was surprised when Jeff arrived at her house 20 minutes late, wearing street clothes, with his tux in hand, rather than on his body.

During questioning, Jeff's departure time from the parsonage didn't match up with the testimony of an independent witness, someone who was familiar with Jeff Pelley's Mustang, who testified that Jeff's car was still sitting outside the parsonage, when Jeff had stated to detectives that he had left his home 15 to 20 minutes earlier.

The outfit Jeff was last seen wearing by the account of one female witness, a prom goer and family friend, who had stopped by the parsonage to show Bob her dress—back when Bob, Dawn, and the girls were last seen alive—was the one lone outfit left clinging to the inside of the Pelleys' washer in the laundry room in the basement of their home. This was the outfit Jeff was last seen wearing by that same female friend, while she was standing in their home: a pair of jeans, a pink striped shirt, and a pair of white socks.

The doors of the parsonage were locked, shell casings picked up off the floor, and there were no signs of forced entry. Nothing was stolen. Detectives viewed it to be an inside job.

The week prior to prom, Jeff was telling his friends he was going to be able to drive to the prom and to the amusement park with everyone after all, because Bob had changed his mind. This is refuted by a church member who heard Bob telling Jeff on the afternoon of the day of the prom that Jeff would not be driving the Mustang, so Bob had no idea why he was washing it. Yet, Jeff did wash, and later drive, his Mustang, with no insurance, still partially disabled, but able to run.

Jeff drew the attention and suspicion of investigators through his own statements, inconsistencies, demeanor, and actions. Our entire family knew the detectives viewed Jeff as the primary suspect.

My cousin, Jessica Pelley, would know *none of this*. Not a single detail. She wasn't told the specifics of how they died. She didn't know whom the detectives suspected for the murders, nor any speculated motives. She didn't know any of it. She was left to draw her own conclusions as a nine-year-old child.

JESSICA

AGE 9

$\mathcal{I}$'m stepping in again as my adult self to tell you about the days that followed my darkest day. After leaving the place I used to call home, I cried for three straight days at The Nameless Girl's house. And I don't mean I cried sometimes, or every now and again, or only when I thought about certain things, I mean I cried for three solid days straight. From sunup to sundown. I cried through every tear I blinked away, every beat my heart took, and every breath I drew. The only time I wasn't crying—big wet lines of tears streaming down my face and audibly sobbing like the world's most broken little girl—was when I *somehow* managed to fall asleep, despite my intense grief and soul-swallowing sorrow. It was only a moment here or there when sleep overtook me, against my will. And when I did fall into a brief slumber, I'd awaken to my own voice, screaming out into the darkness, terrified, with yet another round of crying, due to hellish nightmares I had. Every dream I had was about death. I was one moment away from dying in every single one of them. Sometimes, I dreamt I was being pulled down into the drain of a pool and sharks were circling around below with gnashing teeth, waiting to kill me. Other times, I dreamt someone was chasing me or that someone was about to kill me. Just like my family. It felt like every person and everything I ever had that mattered to me was gone. Permanently. I was afraid to be alone. And alone, I was.

Home, for me, my honest-to-God-true-home was a little yellow house long ago left behind in Toledo, Ohio. My version of home died right along with my daddy. The parsonage was simply a place where I lived for several years of my life, but it never felt like home, not to me. It was too messed up of a situation to ever be that to me.

I guess home wasn't so much a place anymore, it was the people. And those people, they were now gone.

It felt like every single moment of peace I would ever know was gone, right along with my family. This was my new normal. This was far, far worse than being a Pelley. This was far, far worse than moving to Florida. This was *even* worse than losing my dad or pretending Bob Pelley could ever fill a single eyelet of his shoes in my young, daddy-adoring eyes. This marked the beginning of my darkest days. Day one, day two, and day three of my "new" life.

I never liked my stepdad, Bob, and was under the mistaken assumption that he had shot my mom and little sisters, then turned the gun on himself. From the evidence, which I knew absolutely nothing about after the tragedy occurred, that theory held no credibility whatsoever. But it's the theory I formed in my own detail-deprived nine-year-old mind as to how this all went down. When people will no longer utter the names of your loved ones and pretty much pretend they never even existed, they sure as heck aren't telling you the details surrounding their manner of death. They never told me a single thing about it. All I knew was the things I began to tell myself. Bob did it. I didn't like him. He did it. That's the story I wrote about the tragedy in my own mind. He killed them all and then killed himself. And I hated him even more because of it. Misplaced assumptions were all I had to go on. The resentment toward Bob Pelley—and my mother for choosing to marry Bob Pelley—ran deep.

After those three days of constant sobbing, I went to live with Ed 2 and his wife, Lara, in Michigan. I remember Ed 2 and Lara telling me they were going have a meeting with my aunts—my mom's sisters—to "talk about what to do" with me. Despite their pure intentions to help me, I now felt more like a piece of baggage waiting to be claimed than a child. I had nothing and no one. I was all alone, even when people were around me in the most crowded of rooms, and even when they tried to comfort me. Their words rang hollow. There would be no comfort here. Nothing would ever be okay again. I knew this is all I was left with: a life filled with an intense heartache that pierced me to the core, right down to the depths of my soul. Couple that with feelings of overwhelming uncertainty and you were in the running for the next Great Depression: mine. I didn't even care about the future anymore. What future? I didn't care about what I was going to do anymore. Why would I? It all seemed so trivial and pointless. I wanted to die. I was so mad that I didn't die right along with my family. Everyone who truly mattered to me was left lying on that parsonage floor that day and now they're lying in a cold graveyard. I would have been better off there, on the floor with them. Better off in a grave plot beside them. That's the way I felt. That was it. I wanted to be a joiner. And that's one hell of a thing to want to join. Believe me, I know it. But, there I was.

It felt like me against the world now. I was on a team of one — me, Jessica Huber, the one they all call Jessica Pelley now—the sole survivor of the Eddie and Dawn Huber clan. Jacque and Jeff still had each other. I know that their aunt, Bob's sister, was appointed as legal guardian, but whether they actually went to live with her or stayed with their grandparents, or someone else, I didn't know. But what I did know is that I was alone. I would have to learn to survive. Or would I? What was the point?

This is when the dark thoughts first began. I no longer wanted to live. Things that reminded me of the past made me sad. People intentionally not speaking about my family made me sad. Being around people who reminded me of the family I lost made me sad. My new normal would put down deep roots along the edges of sadness, despair, and self-pity. This was my new life, one filled with tragedy, death, and darkness. That's one hell of a combination for a little girl to sustain herself against.

They still called me Jessica Pelley at this point, and "Pelley" was the name being splashed through the media with a wide array of graphic, attention-grabbing headlines. The name would serve as a constant reminder of who I was before April 29, 1989. That is what age nine marked for me: my first steps into this darker version of my new life. Forget birthday parties, new dresses, the picking of wildflowers, and singing of songs. Forget first boyfriend stories, prom dresses, and wedding gowns. Forget everything. Everything . . . but this. I cried every moment, of every single hour, of every day for three days straight, then downshifted to crying most of the time, but not every waking second. The darkness wasn't making its way to me. It was already here. It came so quickly, I never saw the approach. I was left alone. Sad. Unloved. Unwanted. Perhaps that's not what anyone around me wanted for me—I know it's not, but that *is* how I felt. I'd like to tell you I was wrong, that I wasn't alone, sad, unloved, and unwanted—but it was more like a premonition of what was to come. I knew it in my heart, long before I ever really saw it in reality.

Goodbye again, daddy.

Goodbye, mom.

Goodbye, Janel.

Goodbye, Jolene.

Even you're gone, too, Bob.

Goodbye.

I cried until I didn't think I had any tears left to cry, and then I'd find some more. Day after day. Tear after tear. Thought after thought. Still here. The depression wrapped itself around every nerve, every fiber, every piece of cartilage, every bone. It ran through my blood. I couldn't escape it if I tried. And I didn't try. I watched it roll over me like thick rain clouds over a prairie, and breathed it in deeply, filling every part of my soul. I wasn't sure I would ever leave the darkness. And it would be a really, really, long time before I even tried. For now, I tucked myself between the folds of darkness to stay awhile. I made myself at home. It was my new life. The start of before and after. And this, my friends, was after. *It was, most definitely, after.*

JESSICA

AGE 9

I'll never forget the day I first returned to school. I was in the fourth grade. I was nervous. I didn't know how other people would react to me. From the moment I stepped through the doors of the single-story, brown brick building of Laville Elementary in Lakeville, Indiana, I immediately felt out of place. Different. Disconnected. Seated in my classroom at my small, wooden desk, I tried to act normal. I had no idea what that was anymore. I could feel eyes on me. I tried to ignore them. I fidgeted a bit, picking at the pink eraser on the end of my pencil. I was shaking my foot up and down in an effort to channel my nerves. I so badly wanted to fit in with my classmates again. I really did. But that moment of pretending to be normal was brief and fleeting, interrupted by the principal's voice which came echoing through the loudspeakers overhead with that morning's announcements.

"Today, we would like to extend our deepest sympathies to Jessica Pelley, whose family passed away over the weekend . . ."

Some children wept. Others stared. I cannot even begin to tell you how badly I wanted to run away and hide from it all. My immediate reaction was to flee, and fast. So much for going back to school to be normal. All I can tell you is in that moment I realized there would be no going back. I could not escape these truths:

ONE: I am Jessica Pelley.

TWO: My family was murdered.

THREE: I am still here.

FOUR: Life as I knew it is over.

Please explain to me how any nine-year-old girl could possibly act *normal* given the circumstances. In my presence, the children around me now typically acted one of three ways: scared, uncomfortable, or completely freaked out. And the grown-ups weren't much better. Anything Jessica Pelley could have been just a week prior was out. Gone. Now, Jessica Pelley was simply a girl who lost everything. The one spoken of in whispers. The one people only saw through sad eyes. The one other people's parents felt weird about letting their daughters hang around because something bad might happen. The little girl left behind.

The kids in my class made me cards. It was a thoughtful gesture. I know the teacher and students meant well and wanted to make me feel better, but after flipping through them and seeing the words "Don't worry—Be happy" written repeatedly in vibrantly colored, hand-written letters across the page, I buckled. You could mark that down on the calendar as being the day I came to hate that phrase. It didn't even make any sense. "Don't worry—your family is dead." "Be happy—you're still here." The words did not soothe me in the slightest, they stung.

I would receive cards from other family members and friends in the mail following the tragedy. While their words were offered in kindness and empathy, they rang hollow. What I needed was a family. What I needed was love. What I was left with was uncertainty, tear-filled eyes, and a big stack of greeting cards. All the well-wishes in the world weren't going to fix this. Over time, the cards eventually stopped coming. The blank space in the mailbox matched the one left in my heart. "Don't worry, be happy, Jessica." I'm pretty sure that's no longer possible. I now worry every day. I am no longer happy. I don't even see how that's possible. I know anyone who ever lost a loved one can relate to the emotional aftermath in which I found myself following my loss. But what most people fail to realize is I didn't only lose my mom and my two little sisters that day, I lost everything. My home became the place "I used to live." My bedroom became a place where I would never sleep again. There would be no parting closure. I felt stripped bare. I lost everything associated with the life I had, all the things tied to my past, and every single thing that anchored me to my former existence. I was utterly alone. And utterly heartbroken.

Throughout my formative years:

Anger would become a balm.

Rebellion would become my medium of self-expression.

Resentment for being left behind would course through my veins.

Lost is what I would become.

And lost, I would remain.

STEPHANIE

Jessica's Best Friend

AGE 11

*A*bout a month after the funeral, Jessica and I found ourselves heading to Camp Mishindoh with my dad, who drove us there and dropped us off. It was somethin' that had been pre-planned by our parents before the murders happened. All the grown-ups seemed to think it would be a good idea for us to still go to camp together. I've been to this camp before, but Jessica hasn't. I know what to expect. It's basically a big camp where kids from Indiana, Michigan, and Ohio come to stay for a week of outdoor activities and camp life. It has a ton of cabins, surrounded by a large wooded area, with a lake. Each cabin has a bunch of bunk beds in it and holds about 10 to 12 campers, along with two counselors. It's a fun place. I'm pretty excited about it.

I admit I'm a bit nervous about how things will go. After all, Jessica just lost her entire family. I miss them. It's something you can't really forget about and find yourself thinkin' about many times throughout the day. I have no clue as to how she will be this week, whether she's okay or not, if she will be the same because of everything that has happened. It's not somethin' most 10- or 11-year-olds know how to deal with. Selfishly, I'm happy because I know I'll get to spend the entire week with her: just me, my best friend, Jessica, and a ton of other kids here to enjoy a week of camp.

This place has everything, and I mean *everything*: a large wooded area, a water slide, Bible study, puppet shows, water activities in the lake, kickball, other sports, hiking, scavenger hunts, bonfires: you name it. Surely, if there is anyplace on this earth where I can make Jessica feel better and get her to have fun, this is it. This is the place.

It doesn't take long for me to realize that the Jessica who showed up at this camp with me isn't the same Jessica I know. She is different now. It's in the way she carries herself. The way she sits in a room. She still looks the same. I can see that she's always payin' attention or watchin' what's going on around her, pretendin' to be with us, but somethin' is different about her. I sense it. It's somethin' I notice right away. She is now more of a silent spectator. She just sits, or stands there, watching. Always watchin', but not really engaging. Not really talking. Not really having fun with us. Not really. If somethin' happens that is funny, she does smile, but it's more of a smile of acknowledgment, not a true reaction. When she does smile, her smile doesn't reach her eyes. Her eyes seem flat. Far away. Distant. And when she laughs, it doesn't seem to come from a place of happiness, but more of a non-verbal nod to be somewhat present with the people around her. She's still here, with us, sitting with us, listenin' to us, joinin' the group, being a part of us, but not really.

I'm still so sad about what happened to her family. I've cried over it a lot. Part of me still wants to, but I want this week to be about her. I'll put my sadness deep inside me and try to just be normal around her. See if we can have fun and just be us. I'll hide my sadness from her, so things will be better for both of us. I'll see if I can help her.

Two days in to camp, Jessica twists her ankle while runnin' down a hill. I think one of her feet stepped into a hole or somethin', and that was it. Jessica went down. She ends up laid up in her bunk bed in our cabin after that. Just two days later, I twist my stupid ankle, when my foot steps off the edge of a sidewalk the wrong way, and yep, you guessed it, I end up laid up in bed, right alongside Jessica. I am honestly glad that it happened because it allows us to spend a lot more time together, just the two of us. It becomes the summer of twisted ankles. She and I both had bottom bunks right next to one another, so we would just lie there, in our beds, talking.

Still, any interaction that I or anyone else has with Jessica remains at surface level.

Me: "My ankle hurts."

Jessica: "Yep, mine does, too."

Me: "This sucks."

Jessica: "Yeah, it does."

Me: "It's a nice day."

Jessica: "Yeah, it is."

Me: "Well, that was fun!"

Jessica: "Yeah, it was."

That's exactly how all conversations with Jessica went.

It's like she's there, but she isn't here. She talks back or answers people when they speak with her, but *not really*. For days, I try really hard to get through *to the real her*, to Jessica, the friend I know, the one I love. It doesn't work.

It almost seems like Jessica is living her life in third person now. Like she isn't really Jessica anymore. The light is gone from her eyes. Every now and again, I see ever so tiny a flicker of the real Jessica come through to me, but then, as fast as it comes, it is gone.

As the days go on, I grow more concerned about her. Nothing I do to try to help draw her out of her shell or get her back to herself works. I feel like she needs help. I can tell she does. But I'm not sure what else to do. Since nothing I try is helping, I decide to approach one of the camp counselors, a kind, really pretty blond-haired girl we both like. I tell the counselor about what happened to Jessica's family, and how I think she needs help. That she isn't being herself anymore. The counselor and I both sit down and try to talk to Jessica about it. We try to help her. But that doesn't work, either. Nothing does. In that moment, I realize that while my best friend is still here with me, really, she is gone. She is a different person now. I'm not sure if I will ever get her back.

STEPHANIE

Present Day—2018

Looking back and remembering that summer we spent at camp, it's as though Jessica didn't have a voice. I don't remember it at all. I know she replied to me and others just enough to carry the surface level conversation along to avoid it being awkward, but I do not remember hearing her voice. I don't remember really connecting with my best friend, Jessica. It felt as though she was teetering on the brink. She had changed. She wasn't the same person anymore. It was palpable to me, even at 11-years-old. I saw it clearly, and couldn't do a damn thing about it. It was a feeling of extreme helplessness. I felt at a complete loss to help the friend I loved so much. I knew what Jessica was going through, but I couldn't fix it. I couldn't help her. Nor could the camp counselor. Nor could anyone else. She was too messed up over what had happened.

Jessica had changed.

She was different.

My best friend was no longer with us, although she still was.

She was existing from a distance, pulled deep inside herself, barely there, barely hanging on. Even when I was with her, sitting beside her, sleeping next to her, talking to her, or laughing with her as I was and did, I missed her, because my best friend, Jessica Pelley, was gone.

While I would always remain her friend in my heart and mind throughout all the years of my life that would follow, looking back I now realize that week we shared at summer camp in 1989 would mark the moment when I first came to the realization that I'd already lost her.

We all had.

JESSI

AGE 37
Present Day, 2018

*B*efore I tell you about my new home following this tragedy, I must admit these truths:

ONE: No one could have helped me. No one. That wasn't their fault, or mine.

TWO: My childhood ended when I was nine years old. The carefree, innocent days I had left to live were gone, right along with my loved ones.

THREE: It didn't take long for me to realize it was easier for me to be angry than sad.

FOUR: The anger is how I would survive this tragedy. My anger became an invisible armor, sparing me from sadness and emboldening my defiance in the face of contested authority.

Certain members of my family stepped forward to try to help me. But I was such a sad, angry, lost little girl, that their attempts to build a new normal for me would be unrequited in every way. They weren't to blame for the failure. Neither was I. I was attempting to learn how to live through an unlivable situation and the people around me tried to pretend I could assimilate back to some version of normal. Who the hell were they kidding? Not me. Normal was gone. Over. Lost. A thing for carefree little girls who still had families. I said goodbye to normal the same way I said goodbye to my mom, Janel, and Jolene for the very last time, unknowingly. Goodbye, family. And goodbye, normal. In one moment, it was all gone, as were they. I was left to face a lot of truths I had yet to discover, and to fight my way to normal, the new normal for lost little girls, like me. There wasn't anything normal about it. There never would be again. You could give me a home. You could feed me. You could mess up your own family structure to take me in. You could try to get me to talk.

You could even try to "fix" me, but people in certain situations are unfixable. It's a brutal truth and not one any of us would come to terms with until much, much later. If I had to declare one mode that would accompany me throughout the years that followed, it would be rebellion. Rebellion against people. Rebellion against what happened to my family. Rebellion against what happened to me. Rebellion against anyone's attempts at a new normal. Red hot rebellion, served up pretty much daily, by the hands of a lost, lonely, little girl named Jessica Pelley. Don't blame yourselves. And I won't blame me. We were all casualties of sadness, anger, and the dysfunction that flows from it. If anyone is to blame, it's the person who callously pointed a 20-gauge pump-action shotgun, loaded with deer slugs, at point blank range at the heads of my terrified loved ones, cocked the shotgun six separate times, then pulled the trigger on April 29, 1989.

INVESTIGATION
1989

Four months after the murders

In August of 1989, Jeff Pelley attended a keg party. Some peers approached Jeff and asked him if he had "really killed them." Witnesses heard Jeff state, "I'll kill you just like I did them" followed by, "I'll blow your eye out just like I did hers." (This was a reference made to little Janel whose eye was blown out by the shotgun blast that took her life.) "How could you do that to your sisters?" was the next question they posed to Jeff, who replied, "They weren't my sisters." Multiple witnesses were present for this verbal confrontation which turned physical and heard these statements.

Six months after the murders

Six months after the murders, Jeff Pelley, age 17, was charged on two counts of wire fraud for attempting to defraud his trust fund—the inheritance money from his father's estate—after he lied and attempted to manipulate the trust administrators into believing he had cancer and needed more than $20,000 to pay his medical bills, to try to gain early access to the funds. He would have received his first disbursement of the funds at age eighteen. Jeff was convicted and sentenced to six months of home detention for that crime.

JESSICA

AGE 10
Fifth Grade

O ne day, probably a month or a month and a half after I moved in with Ed 2, he and Lara pulled me into the sunroom to talk to me. It was a beautiful space filled with skylights and fancy white patio-style furniture. I was told that Ed 2 and the aunts decided I would be better off at Aunt B's house, because she had kids. She was my mom's youngest sister. She was only twelve years older than me, had a husband (we'll call him "What's His Name"), and also three young children under the age of six: one girl and two boys. They thought being around the kids would help me because there weren't any kids at Ed 2 and Lara's. They meant well. I'm sure it made sense to them at the time. But to me, no kids could ever replace the sisters I lost. It almost felt as though these kids were being forced on me, and me on them, and I was supposed to pretend to like it, even if I didn't. I think it made them all feel like there was hope. Like I could learn to be okay again. Like I could assimilate into their family and become one of them. They were wrong.

Aunt B's girl liked to play Barbies, and me, well, I liked to drive Match Box cars through big holes or to play in heaping mounds of dirt in the backyard. I was a total tomboy. They were girly girls. A dream playmate situation, it was not. And honestly, being around Aunt B's kids hurt me more than it helped. It reminded me I no longer had Janel or Jolene. These kids were not them. They never could be. I barely knew them, really. And at this point in my life, I didn't want to. It wasn't their fault. They were just innocent little kids stuck dealing with "bad Jessica" and all her baggage and problems. It was just a messed-up situation for all of us.

If you talked to my aunt and What's His Name, I'm positive they would tell you I was a handful. And they would *not* be lying. I was. Totally. That said, I was who I became because of circumstances. It never felt like a choice I made as an individual, but one that was thrust upon me by a murderer.

Not long after my family was killed, I remember Aunt B and What's His Name took me to church. It was on a Sunday, a beautiful, sunny day. A day when everyone else was drifting through a normal day of life. But not me. I was hurting, deeply. On the way into church, I threw myself facedown onto the grass and began screaming, "I JUST WANT TO DIE. I JUST WANT TO DIE. I DON'T WANT TO BE HERE ANYMORE. I DON'T . . ." I meant it. Every word of it. I'm sure it was quite a scene, a little girl in a church dress who appeared to be far too old for tantrums. But it's honestly how I felt at the time. Perhaps, it was my only way of physically dealing with the intense pain I felt inside. I know Aunt B and What's His Name had no earthly clue what to do with me. And I had no clue what to do with myself. I was in such a low place. I know I was an imposition. I know it was hell trying to live with me, let alone help me.

People got tired of dealing with my sadness. They were tired of seeing me cry. They were tired of me acting out or running my smart mouth. I can't blame them, really. What's His Name used to refer to me as a "shit head" on a regular basis. Let's be real, I was one. But I was also a little girl who was carrying more pain and emotional torment than she knew what to do with. I was a shit head. I don't deny that. But anything they did to try to remedy my behavior just made me feel even more isolated, misunderstood, or alone.

I always felt like other people having me around was a burden. Little Jessica was just so sad and so screwed up. Nobody could do anything to fix that. I learned to hate myself while I lived there. I also learned to loathe my existence. I would go to school and carry myself as a goody two-shoes, but I would come home and act like . . . yep, you guessed it . . . a little shit. The place never felt like home to me. I never felt like I was a part of a real family. I felt like the outsider. I also felt like a reminder of what they'd lost: Dawn, Janel, and Jolene. It was hard to be somewhere where you felt like you never fit it. Also, Aunt B was so young herself, she wasn't well-equipped to deal with this type of a situation. Hell, I'm not sure anyone would be. As I said, she was just twelve years older than me, so it was almost more like having an older sister. She was trying to raise her own family and get her own life in order. Dealing with me just further complicated her life. I know that now. And I certainly felt it back then.

It got to the point that What's His Name's words became verbal daggers that cut straight to the core of the angry girl I was. His words wounded me. In response, I acted out more. I talked back. I did things to piss them—and especially him—off. It was a dysfunctional cycle, and one which left me feeling worthless and spent.

Aunt B would come to tell me "It's time for dinner, Jessica." And I would respond, "I'm *not* hungry." A turf war would ensue, one that would hold no victors. We were constantly arguing. They were mad at me. I was mad at them, and it never got any of us anywhere. After a while, I remember thinking to myself, "I can't do this anymore." I really couldn't. I was sick of it. I'd had enough. No doubt, they had, too.

I was embroiled in a battle not only within my own home but one within my own flesh, too. I felt like I was being attacked from every angle. Internally, I battled the darkness. Externally, I battled those around me because of it. I couldn't be what everyone else wanted, needed, or expected me to be. I just couldn't.

JESSICA

AGE 10

*F*rom the age of 10, I began to play the world's most unfortunate hypothetical game: The one dealing with "The What Ifs." Questions for which I already knew most of the answers, but I didn't stop asking. It didn't help a thing. But still, the questions fired away in my brain. What if? Playing on an endless loop in my mind.

What if my dad never died?

What if my mom never met Bob?

What if my mom never married Bob?

What if we never moved to Indiana?

What if Bob never adopted my sisters and me?

What if Janel got to go to the slumber party at The Nameless Girl's house with me that night?

What if my sisters both got to spend the night at their friends' house, as requested?

What if Stephanie had spent the night with Jolene and Janel that night at the parsonage?

What if I had been home that day?

What if this never happened to my family?

What if this never happened to me?

What if I never find a way to get past this?

What if I never forget?

What if I never stop hurting?

What if Bob had never killed my mom and sisters and then turned the gun on himself?

What if I don't want to live anymore?

What if I just kill myself?

No, really. What if . . .

Behind each question a million emotions were buried, deeply entrenched beneath flesh and bone. While some of the What Ifs did fade a bit over time, they never disappeared completely. Even all these years later, I find myself wondering what my life would be like if Janel had been with me and had been spared.

And what if my mom never married Bob? That one hits me at my core. It's the one that ate at me a lot over the years. Well, if my mom hadn't married Bob, then ALL of them would be here with me now.

The What Ifs, for me, became a form of psychological warfare I waged against myself. It was a lot like playing that game Russian Roulette, but with torturous questions in place of the bullets in the spinning chamber, waiting to see if a person would fall. And knowing, way deep down inside, that the only person who could and would finally fall, was me.

JESSICA

AGE 10
(Present day)

The adults in charge of me thought it would be a good idea for me to visit The-Pissed-Off-Lost-Little-Girl-Whisperer. But I am being far too kind. I'm gonna call him Dr. Sunshine. I'm pretty sure you're thinking he was personable and friendly, given the pseudonym. But you would be dead wrong. And I am being facetious. Dr. Sunshine and I working together in therapy was a hopeless cause for all involved. It was like the psychologically clueless leading the lost. Let's be real, he was out of his depth with his sports psychology specialty when it came to me. In all fairness, the guy had probably read every psychological text ever written. Lots of books. Maybe even some pamphlets. He went to college, took classes, and landed a degree in psychology. That, I knew. But what he had in knowledge, he lacked in social skills, and I mean epically. To paint the full picture, he was an older man, partly bald with the most dry, dull, lackluster personality in the history of this planet, served with a side of condescension. Looking back, he kind of reminds me of the teacher on that movie *Ferris Bueller's Day Off*, but with less hair and no glasses. Anyone? Jessica Pelley? Anyone?

Helpful? Not so much.

In the beginning, I may have been angry—strike that—I was mad as hell. And now I found myself sitting in a room with some man who seemingly had no clue how to help me. A guy who lacked basic empathy, exuded no social skills, and had no couth. He was about as warm and fuzzy as a Styrofoam cup. A real dazzler, that one. If there was an award for awkward therapy sessions, he definitely won the title in my eyes.

Most of the time it seemed like he was reading off a template or some type of a formatted checklist or something. How do you feel about this? How do you feel about that? What do you remember about this? How does that make you feel? I'm pretty sure we all know how I felt about losing everyone in my family without me needing to articulate, but in the beginning, I tried to play along. I really did. I answered his questions truthfully and tried to express what I felt. He didn't seem to like a lot of my answers. Perhaps they didn't match up with the checklist he was reading from. It didn't take long to realize we were both entrenched in a fruitless mission—me, the lost little child in search of any type of actual help or guidance, and him—the clueless, socially inept leader of the world's most awkward therapy sessions, who didn't seem to be listening to what I was telling him.

What he lacked in proper social etiquette, he made up for with insulting remarks and a lack of constructive help. Just to give you one example:

DR. SUNSHINE: "What do you remember about your dad?"

ME: "Well, I remember that he was happy and fun. I loved him very much. We did a lot of things together. He spent time with me. We went to Frisch's Big Boy to eat; I always ordered these waffles covered in cherries and whipped cream. We went fishing together. My dad would go deer hunting and if he killed one, he would bring it home with him and I would see it in our garage. My dad made funny faces and laughed with me a lot. He was fun to be around. When I was with my dad, I always felt loved."

DR. SUNSHINE: "You were only five when he died. I don't think you can really remember your dad."

ME: (Um, yeah. Thanks for listening, doc.) My formal response was silence. Followed by folded arms across my chest and deciding we're all done here.

Yep, all done. What a waste of time.

He didn't want to hear what I had to say at all, unless it was what he wanted to hear. If this guy thinks he knows more about what I remember about my dad than I do, when I'm the one who actually knew him, that is insulting. You know why I remember the Big Boy trips, big guy? It's because they are the only times I ever remember going out to eat during my childhood. Ever. We didn't go out to eat, with the exception of trips to Big Boy with my dad. For me, it was like the Disneyland of dessert waffles. I remember every bite. As for the rest, I may not be left with a whole heck of a lot of memories regarding my dad, that I know, but what I do remember, I recall vividly. Why don't you tell me how you feel about someone in your life, Sunshine, so I can tell you it's total bullshit? Glad we cleared that right up. Thanks for basically calling me a liar. Is that on your checklist? Go ahead and check the box for "lost all chances of making any headway with the girl who desperately needs my help as much as the air she breathes." You passed that one with flying colors.

Other times, I would tell Dr. Sunshine I really wanted to see my gammy and paps—my dad's parents. He told me that wasn't a good idea and I shouldn't be around them anymore. Mind you, my grandparents had never committed a single negative action against me, not one. They were always nice to me. I didn't get to see them much, once my mom married Bob, but there wasn't a reason for it, other than my mom moving on with her life and taking us with her. I missed them. It became clear Dr. Sunshine was trying to keep me away from reminders of my past. But at this point, every person in my life after April 29, 1989, became a reminder of my past. Unbeknownst to me at that time, my grandparents missed me, wanted to see me, and were attempting to fight for grandparents' visitation rights. I just wanted a connection to the other side of my family. I wanted a connection to my dad. I wanted to be around both sides of my family. I wanted to be around people related to me, the more of them, the better. Anyone who could help me repair the links to my broken chain. But what stood between me and them was Dr. Sunshine.

My dad had nothing to do with this tragedy, but every bit to do with my happy days in advance of it. What did they need to protect me from in that regard? What did seeing his parents hurt? What did they ever do wrong? Keeping my dad's parents from me further fueled my frustration and loneliness. It had only been a matter of months and it already felt like I was building the foundation of a fortress I would dwell upon forever, one constructed of frustration, anger, hurt, betrayal, and loneliness.

Maybe the checklist told Dr. Sunshine that I needed to create a new life. In some situations, it would make sense. Maybe if I had just lost one person. But this was a situation where, more than anything in this world, what I needed was people I loved and trusted around me. I think he failed to realize the depth of my loss when my daddy died. Pretending he did not exist wasn't going to help any of us, especially not me.

I realize there probably aren't many people who can say they know how I feel or what I've been through, therapists included. But any halfway normal, caring person may have been able to help me. Unfortunately, I was chained to Dr. Sunshine. He was my lifeline to help. And by that point, the sun really did stop shining in my world. I needed help. I knew it. They knew it. Even Sunshine knew it, he just couldn't or didn't help. The darkness had already began to cloud over my soul.

To find yourself in a room, as a 10-year-old girl, truly wanting help and knowing you aren't going to get it—not here, not with him—well, that further fueled my frustration and hurt, and turned it to anger. By this point, we were leaving the slow burn stage and moving on to scorched earth. Is there a checklist for that? Is there a checklist for when a little girl loses every single person in her immediate family and gets told she doesn't remember her dad? Is there a checklist for how to *act normal* when your mom and little sisters are brutally murdered in their home? Is there a checklist for how to create a rapport with someone by calling them a liar? Well, I'm pretty sure there is a checklist for that last one. I saw Dr. Sunshine a handful of times.

I wish I could tell you I got a new therapist and got things sorted out. But that would be untrue. What I ended up with was a disdain for people I started out feeling I could respect and trust: the professionals, whom I desperately wanted to believe would help me.

Oh, before I close this chapter and forget to do so, I want to tell Dr. Sunshine, "thanks"—thanks *for nothing*.

Sincerely,

The little girl who remembers her dad.

(And needed *real* help desperately.)

STEPHANIE

AGE 12

Jessica's Best Friend
1989

After the Pelleys were buried, it was almost as though everyone forgot they ever existed. Church went on as usual, with a new minister leadin' it. He moved into the Pelleys' parsonage with his wife and children. You never really heard about the murders or the Pelleys again. I'm sure the town folk whispered, but it wasn't something anyone spoke of directly. It was almost as though their existence was wiped from the face of this earth. But in my mind, they were still there. They existed. I still missed them. I began to feel some animosity toward the whole situation. The minister lived in that house as though nothing bad had ever happened there. I have no idea how anyone could ever live there after what happened—but he did; church services continued every Sunday, and people didn't speak of the Pelleys anymore. I know it wasn't the new minister's fault, he was doing what he could to lead the congregation in his new role. He had to move forward, to help others to carry on. I guess it's not like I expected the church people to talk about them anymore, but there was just this huge void where they used to be. Did everyone else just forget about them altogether?

All I could think was "How dare you. How dare you live there and put a smile on your face and act like nothing happened." That's the thought that ran through my mind on a never-endin' loop. How dare they all forget about them and just move on. They were people. They mattered. I loved them.

It became a fight for my dad to get me to go to church every Sunday after the murders. I wasn't into it anymore. I just couldn't do it, I didn't want to. That place held a lot of positive memories from my past, but the space now, at least for me, was brimming with the bad memories, they overtook the good.

And when I was old enough to form my own decision, I quit all of it. I stopped goin' to church. It was too hard. It didn't feel right to me anymore. It no longer felt like the safe, sacred place it used to be for me. Now it was one that was no longer occupied by three little Pelley girls, my friends. It became the church Jessica no longer attended. She had moved to Grand Rapids, Michigan, to live with her grandpa—her mom's dad. The same room where we sat to hold that tragic funeral service was the same place I was supposed to now go to seek God. It was all too much for me. The podium, a place where Bob Pelley used to stand to preach his sermons every Sunday, was now occupied by someone else. I couldn't see the church the same way anymore. And frankly, I didn't want to. I didn't want to forget all about them and pretend like they never even existed. I couldn't. And I downright freakin' wouldn't.

Church services continued. People moved on with their lives. But I did not forget. I would not forget. Nothing in this world could make me forget. Not now, not ever.

And I couldn't help but wonder: How is Jessica doing?

JESSICA

AGE 12
1992

*N*ot long after I moved in with Aunt B and started to attend my new school in Michigan, I was told I had to participate in an extracurricular activity at school. I believe this was at the order of Dr. Sunshine with his sports therapy background. Aunt B didn't care which one I picked, but I had to choose something; I didn't really have a say in the matter. I wasn't mad about it, but I wasn't excited about it, either. I didn't really care. I decided the lucky winner was going to be cross-country running. Considering I was a kid who was afflicted with asthma, this may not have seemed like the most rational choice. But I figured running was easy enough, when compared with something far more involved, like learning how to play an instrument. If they were going to make me participate in an activity, I was going to pick something I knew I could do. I had two legs, and already knew how to run—just as we all do—so I chose cross-country running.

I joined the team, and I began to run. I ran, and I ran, and I ran. Surprisingly, I learned that I actually enjoyed it. It was just me, out there on the open road, feet pounding the pavement, no boundaries, no one trying to talk to me about anything, nothing to worry about, just the physical pain associated with running. I found comfort in the solitude. I found the physical act of running to be one of the only places where, while I was alone, I was able to be just me . . . and free. Free from all the emotional wreckage that created my new life. Free not to think about all the shattered splinters of my former life, the lingering what if's and unexpected heartache. Free to not think about the bullshit that led up to this point in my life. Free just to be, just to exist, just to run, and breathe, and endure, until I physically felt like I might collapse. After the tragedy, running, for me, became one of the only times I ever felt like I was not being pulled down by the invisible weight of the world's most emotionally exacting baggage. The one time I wasn't thinking about my life and how unalterably it had changed. I was just living in the moment. In between the footsteps. Focusing on each breath. Focusing on taking that next step.

With each step I took my legs burned with an intense pain searing through the muscles of my lower legs, as though they were ravaged by fire. My heart beat rapidly in my chest to the point it felt it might explode. My asthmatic lungs constricted, almost unable to fill with air each time I attempted to suck in a labored breath. But I continued to run. It was physical agony. Personal torture. Yet, it was a different kind of pain than what I was accustomed to, this one entirely physical. The choice to continue to run or give in to my body's physical pleas was mine alone to make. I was in control. It was my choice. I mentally willed myself not to quit. Not to give up on myself. I was the one and only person I knew I had. The one I could rely on. The one that wouldn't give up on me. I ran *through* the pain. I ran *for* the pain. I ran *in spite of* the pain. Over time, I ran for the release that pain gave me. I ran because it's the only time I ever felt free. And I, just as we all do, so desperately deserved to be free, even if only for a moment in time.

A blue sky.

A sunset.

Pebbles scattered on the roadway.

The beauty of nature.

The feel of wind on my face.

Warm rays of sunshine beaming down.

Happy.

Positive.

Alive.

FREE.

At least until I stopped running, anyway. My reality was one I could not outrun. All the steps in the world could never carry me past it. But I reveled in the minor respite the act of running provided to me. Running, for me, would become a close companion. An open channel of cost-free, lifelong therapy. I just didn't realize it at the time. Nor did I understand why I ran, what it took away, or what it gave me.

I ran to channel the inner rage I felt. To quiet the hypothetical questions calling to me from within: what if . . . what if they never . . . what if I had been home? I ran when I was really pissed off; when I was enveloped by frustration; when I felt I had nothing; when others didn't seem to understand me; when others didn't seem to care; when I was angry at the world; when I hated my life; when I hated everything, and at times, everyone; when I hated who I was, and what I was left with . . .

I ran.

MONA

Jessica's Mom's Best Friend
Early 1990

I waited a sufficient amount of time, in my own mind, to allow Jessica to get settled into her new home. I knew she was living with her Aunt B, Dawn's youngest sister. I hoped it would be a good arrangement for her, a place where she could find some new sense of normal and be able to move on with her life. I was so tortured, as an adult dealing with this tragedy, I had no idea how it would be possible for a 10-year-old to overcome it, but I certainly hoped and prayed she would. One day, I called Aunt B.

"Hi, this is Mona. I'm not sure if you remember me, but I was Dawn's best friend. I'm calling to check on Jessica and see how she's doing. Can I talk to her?"

"No, we don't think that's a good idea. The relationships of the past cause her too much pain. It would be too painful for her to have a relationship with anyone from her past."

"Well, can you tell me how she's doing?"

"She's fine. Don't ever call here again."

Click.

I certainly didn't like the answer, but I understood it. It seemed like a valid concern on their part. I wasn't sure whether they ever told Jessica I'd called to check on her. I also didn't know if she really didn't want to talk to me, or anyone from her past, or if that was something the adults in her life had decided on her behalf. Either way, I had no choice but to accept it. On some level, I guess I even had to respect it. But I certainly didn't like it.

I wanted to be able to check in on Jessica to see how she was. I wanted to take care of her, as Dawn's best friend, the way she had asked me to. But it was apparent I wasn't going to be allowed to be a part of her life anymore. From my talks with Gayle around that time, I wasn't alone in that. They wouldn't allow her or her aunts from her dad's side of the family to talk to Jessica, either. We were all cut off from her. They said it was for the best. But it sure didn't feel like it was for the best for any of us, including Jessica.

I know Gayle and her husband fought to try to get grandparents' rights. They wanted to see Jessica. It is a battle they did not win. There would be no rights. There would be no visitation. There wouldn't even be phone calls with Jessica. There would be nothing but questions.

How was she? Was she doing okay? Did she like her new school? How was it for her living with Aunt B? Did she like it there? Did she miss us? Did she ever think about us? Did she want to talk to us? Did she know we loved and missed her? Did she know there were these people wondering and thinking about her, hoping she's okay?

These were questions I know we all asked in our own minds and to which there would be no answers, at least not for a number of years, anyway. For some of us, the wait would be longer than others. But one thing we all held in common—those who knew and loved Jessica Huber Pelley—me, Gayle, and Jessica's paternal aunts is the fact that we were all cut off from Jessica. We were no longer allowed to be a part of her life at all. She was only nine years old. Then 10 years old. Then 11 years old. Then 12. And one day, she would finally be 13. She was a little girl who would grow up without us, those who loved her, for several years.

For Gayle—and Jessica's aunts—Jessica was all they had left of Ed, whom they'd lost just four years earlier. She was it. His only surviving daughter. And for all intents and purposes, she was just as gone to all of us, as the rest of them were. We'd already lost Ed, Dawn, Janel, and Jolene.

And now, we'd lost Jessica, too. Not to death, but to circumstance.

JESSICA

AGE 11
June 1990

For my eleventh birthday Aunt B wanted to throw me a sleepover, complete with a Slip 'N Slide set up in the yard for me and my friends and a camper for us to hang out in. I was supposed to be excited. It was supposed to be a day of fun. For any other 11-year-old girl, it probably would have been. But for me? Not so much. I tried to play along. I tried to act excited. I tried to pretend to feel the way Aunt B wanted me to feel and act the way my friends probably expected me to act. But let's face it, I wasn't a girlie girl. It all felt off.

I wasn't ready for all of that. The friends. The celebrating. The party. The pretending. I remember feeling as though they were drawing attention to me by attempting to throw this party, when I never even wanted it. Like, if they just tried hard enough, I would be normal. If we all just pretended the bad things had never happened, maybe we would forget them. But they didn't really *know me* at all. It was apparent. Forget girls in pink pajamas, I wanted to play in the ditch, dig for worms, and hunt fireflies. As a tomboy, a slumber party, like that one, was the *last* thing I'd ever want.

It all became too much. The pretending to be normal. Inside, I was falling apart. The essence of who I was breaking up and falling down in pieces around me . . . and here I was, at a party!

At one point, I ran out of the camper, crying hysterically. Aunt B, undoubtedly, thought I'd lost my 11-year-old mind. I'm sure she had no idea what was wrong with me at the time, didn't understand why I couldn't just enjoy myself and have a good time, and was completely clueless as to what had caused such a reaction.

While I know my Aunt B meant well and went to a lot of trouble to plan the whole event, it all felt forced upon me. My wounds may have been about a year old by that point in time, but they still felt like gaping wounds that *would not* heal. They ached. I longed for that which I could not have—my family. Their faces, words, hugs, smiles, and my real home. I missed them not just every day, but in every passing moment. Literally, every single moment. And no pajama party or Slip 'N Slide was going to change that.

Happy 11th Birthday, Jessica! "Let's open some presents and eat cake," said everyone, except me. They're still dead. I was still here. And I had no idea why. I didn't want to be here anymore. And it didn't matter at all. There wasn't a thing in the world I could do about it.

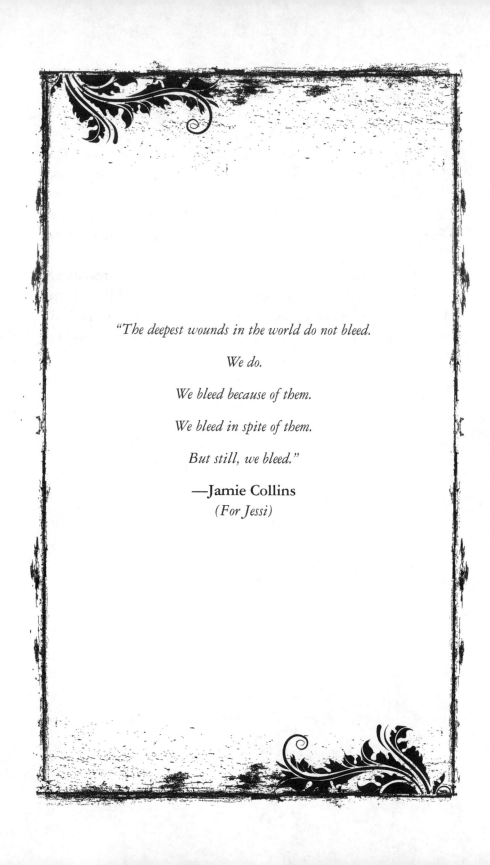

"*The deepest wounds in the world do not bleed.*

We do.

We bleed because of them.

We bleed in spite of them.

But still, we bleed."

—**Jamie Collins**
(*For Jessi*)

JESSICA

AGE 12

As told by Jessi, present day
1991

I remember the first time I put a thin, cold, sharp, steel razor to my flesh at the age of 12. I was in the seventh grade. It's not something everyone can understand, or ever will. Only those who have been pulled low enough to lurk beneath the depths of despair in life will truly ever get it.

Most people assume we want to do it; want to cut ourselves. We don't. They think we want to hurt ourselves. Not really. Some wonder if we do it for the attention. I think deep-down, we just need the not-so-subtle reminder that we are still alive. We need the outward physical pain to somehow displace even the smallest sliver of self-contained turmoil and pain we are carrying on the inside. A pain rooted so deeply inside of us, it sits in our bones. A sadness so boundless, it flows through every drop of our blood, every cell, every memory, and always will. No amount of cutting will ever accomplish that. Nothing can ever take its place. Not really. But it doesn't stop us from trying.

You hurt. Deeply. In a way that other people cannot understand.
A hurt that runs so deep it's fucking impossible to articulate.
You remember too much.
In some regards, too little.
You want to forget, but can't.
And here you are.
Pulled low.
Breathing.
Your lungs so heavy with sorrow, it feels impossible to breathe.
Impossible to think.

Impossible to carry on, pretending that it's all okay.

That you're okay.

It's not okay, not at all.

And you're far from fucking okay. Far, far from it.

The pain consumes you from the inside out.

You reach a point where you can't host that pain any longer. Not one more fucking second.

And that's exactly how you end up with a razor pressed against the soft flesh of your forearm, pressing down ever so slightly, then harder, and harder yet, until that first trickle of crimson spills from your veins and runs in a thin line, like a tiny, sorrow-laced river of red, across your bare flesh.

Trickling down.

Spilling out.

The blood runs freely.

Your heart continues to beat.

And it beats, and it beats.

Your lungs continue to shift in and out with each breath.

Nothing has changed.

But the pain you feel is now physical. It has shifted.

You aren't quite so deeply entrenched inside your internal suffering anymore.

You hurt. But this feels different. It's physical. Outward.

And in that moment, you realize you're still alive. You are still here. Who in the hell knows why? I don't. I didn't for a long damn time. And maybe that's what you really need to know in that moment—the one when you're embroiled in a war against yourself, as the blood begins to exit your veins—*that you are still alive*. You're still here. Do you care that you still are? That's the tricky part. The part the razor can't fix.

I'm not saying some people don't do this type of thing for attention. I'm sure some do. A cry for help, perhaps. But the individuals, like me, who cut as a means of emotional release don't do it for attention. It's quite the opposite, really. We hide it from those around us. We hide it from everyone. We almost feel shame for doing it, yet we can't stop. We don't want anyone to know.

We feel helpless. Like we're drowning in our own sorrow. Almost as though we're rotting from the inside out. We feel all alone. Maybe others care. Maybe they don't. Maybe they try to help us. Maybe they don't. In my case, I felt like I had nobody to talk to. Sure, family members took me in and attempted to care for me in their own way. But I felt like there wasn't anyone around me who actually gave a shit. Not one single person. That's how I felt. It doesn't necessarily make it others' reality. But that's the way I felt at the time.

Sometimes, the attention a person seeks to secure is actually their own. I know that now. I still wanted to live. I wanted to feel something, anything, that could dull the terrible pain I felt on the inside. While I wanted to die one thousand times throughout my childhood following April 29, 1989, damn-near-literally, that was never actually my intent each time I took the razor blade into my hands over the years. I just wanted my outward pain to help me to shift away from my inner pain. That was impossible. It truly was. Yet, simple lines of lacerations etched across my flesh hurt just enough that they could divert my attention away from the emotions bubbling below the surface within that threatened to crush me, to an outward manifestation of physical pain I felt.

And that, that was a wound I could tend to. It was one I could fix. An application of triple antibiotic ointment, a few bandages, and a handful of days later, I was on the mend. I was on my way to healing a wound. But the gaping wound that marked me from the inside, that would take much longer. It was the type that could never be healed, not fully. Never be fixed, not really. And now I know that it never will be.

Looking back, those years of lessons at the hand of a razor blade serve as a reminder that life, for me, is a choice. I sure as hell didn't choose to still be left here alone after my entire family was murdered. Not for a single fucking moment. But each day I remain here is a choice—one I consciously or unconsciously had to make each and every single empty, sad, lonely, happy, carefree or love-filled day, and still continue to today—my choice, the one I get to make for myself. It's something I had to learn over time. One of those lessons you don't realize you're learning in between the moments, until you find yourself there, holding the cold steel bar down upon your flesh and pressing down, yet stopping. A choice.

Will I do this, or won't I?

Will I stop right now, or won't I?

Do I want to die, or don't I?

More importantly, do I want to live?

Can I . . . really?

Cutting may seem like an extreme, and it is. It may also seem like a selfish choice, to some, but I had nothing left, and no one to hurt, not really. No one except for myself. I didn't really want to inflict harm upon myself. I definitely never wanted to hurt anyone else. I just didn't want to feel like I was hurting so deeply inside anymore. The pain was too much to bear. It was too much for me to carry.

Choosing to live is a choice. Most of us just don't realize we're making it every day.

We are.

And we do.

JESSICA

AGES 12 TO 13
As told by Jessi, present day
1992

We moved to a new house when I was 12. It was a one-story house with a basement. I had my own bedroom, which was exciting. I was still living with Aunt B and her family. It was not the best situation, but I was trying to stick it out. What choice did I have? I had nowhere else to go.

I loved to be outside. I felt freer when I was outdoors and not trapped inside a house, stuck within the walls of a building. I wanted sky and grass and birds and a cool breeze. I loved being around animals, especially dogs. Animals were there to love and accept me, unconditionally. Aunt B's dog was a calming presence in my life. A stable living thing I knew I could count on. It was a whole lot easier than trying to get along with people or make them happy. None of the emotional stuff mattered to a dog. He wasn't trying to get me to talk or attempting to fix me. He simply wanted me to pet or play with him. To just be. I guess you could say that animals allowed me to exist on my own terms; to hold the space I needed to hold in that moment, without judgment or expectation.

I was acting normal (well, normal enough) to get by. In junior high, I got good grades and everything. I hated math and history. In reality, I never really cared much about school at all, even before the murders. (I once started a food fight in the cafeteria, in Indiana, when I was in the third grade. At that point, my family was still alive. Why did I do this? Uh, I guess because it seemed like fun. I have no other answer.) All throughout my childhood, school sucked for me. My fifth through seventh grade years were no exception. I'd lost everything I had. Why in the hell would I care about grades?

I mean, really . . . it seemed like a joke. But I learned that if I acted okay enough at home and walked enough of a straight line at school, I could get Aunt B and What's His Name to back off, at least a little bit. By eighth grade, I was actually trying in school.

No part of me wanted to carry on, yet I had to. I could have won an Academy Award for the ridiculous amount of pretending I did from the ages of nine to eighteen. Those around me probably don't even realize how much I faked my way through existing. They may have thought I was bad or out of control, but even in those moments where they saw a glimmer of my pain or anger, I was hosting far more than they knew existed. I was three years past the tragedy, but it still nipped at my heels, so I did what I had to: I pretended. Heck, I think I may have even been trying to fool myself, at times. It looked better on the outside than it felt on the inside to live a lie, pretending to be a person I wasn't, and acting like I cared about life, when I didn't at all. I didn't care about anything anymore.

I ran my mouth like a rebel. I walked through life like a zombie. I felt like a shell of a person, an empty carcass, like what was left. However, I will say that deep, deep, deep within me, was a small ember of hope burning ever so slightly, of who I could be and what I could have in life. Barely there at all. Most days, I ignored it. I tried to forget about it or deny it. But still, that ember burned and flickered at my core, tucked away, rarely felt and barely acknowledged.

I found some salvation when I met a couple of kids who lived in our neighborhood. It gave me a few real friends to hang around. I remember playing in the ditch with Sarah. She lived in the woods and had a tree fort. I thought it was the coolest thing ever. Jake was my other friend. He lived pretty far down the street, maybe a mile and a half or so. I could ride my bike to his house, or he could ride his bike to mine, but it was too far to walk. The three of us bonded fairly quickly and spent quite a bit of time together. We were at that preteen age where it didn't really matter so much what you were doing, it was just always more fun to hang out with a friend.

We passed the time together: playing in the ditch, hanging out in the woods or in Sarah's epic tree fort, talking, watching television, listening to songs on the radio. Anything was more fun with them, than it would be alone.

While everyone at school knew my name was Jessica Pelley, none of them knew what that meant. My true identity remained my own secret to keep and burden to carry. I was hiding in plain sight among my peers. (Google wasn't born yet.) Honestly, I was tired of being Jessica Pelley. I never wanted to take that last name in the first place. It was Bob's last name and a bad memory in more ways than one. It was a name now associated with this horrible thing that happened in my past. My plan was to continue to perpetuate this new pseudo-normalish identity I now had going for me. Sure, it was strange I lived with my Aunt B, not my parents. But I could explain that away. I walked through elementary school and junior high on autopilot, pretending to exist, pretending to care, pretending to be normal. I intended to keep my own secret, until one day, I no longer felt I could. I no longer wanted to. I had a reason to out myself and my life's story, and I would do so, on a whim, without giving it a second thought.

When my friend Jake missed several days of school, it was enough of an extended absence that anyone who knew him couldn't help but notice. I didn't know why Jake was absent from school, but I wondered. I worried about him. Then, one day, I found out the reason for his absence. Jake's dad had died. He had committed suicide—hung himself. And in that moment, being there for my friend Jake and expressing to him how, and why, I knew *how he felt* in that terrible situation mattered *far more* to me than hiding *who I really was*. I wanted him to *know* that I knew his pain. I *knew* his suffering. I felt it all. I'd lived through it. I continued to live through it, just as he would learn to do. My concern for Jake's emotional wellbeing trumped any consequences born of me giving up my true identity. I trusted Jake and Sarah with that piece of highly personal information. I trusted that they wouldn't share it with anyone else. Whether they actually did, or not, I can't say.

All I know is that the day I found out about his dad's tragic death, Jake became another "Jessica" and I needed to and wanted to—I had to—help him through that hellish moment, as he took his first steps over the threshold of overwhelming sadness and life-altering darkness I lived in. It meant more to me than the preservation of my new life. Besides, it was all a sham and a lie. I was hiding. Always hiding. I was hollow, run down, torn up, and emotionally screwed up, to put it politely.

JESSICA

AGE 13
1992

One day, Aunt B took me to trade in my glasses for contact lenses. My moment in the cool kids' club had apparently arrived, thank God for that, and it was none too soon. Good God, I loathed the Coke-bottle glasses I'd worn throughout my childhood. I don't think they could have been any thicker or uglier. So, Aunt B and I paid a visit to the local optometrist. I got a pair of contacts to help my future attempts at preteen popularity, and we topped the day off with a stop for lunch at Pizza Sam's. I told Aunt B I needed to use the restroom. I was 12-years-old at the time, so she didn't think a thing about allowing me to go to a public bathroom by myself. Instead, I left the restaurant and took off running down a nearby alley. I ended up over at a friend's house. As I said, I simply "couldn't do it" anymore. I was done, one way or another. Running away felt like the only way I could escape what my life had become. The life I didn't want.

I didn't feel I had another place to go, but I knew I just didn't want to be there anymore. I didn't honestly care where I ended up. In that moment, I felt a bit lost, like a drifter. A person who had no ties, no real connections, and no real place to be. Anywhere had to be better than there. The cops showed up at my friend's house. I ended up in trouble with Aunt B and What's His Name.

Back at school, they assigned me to a counselor to help me deal with my problems, one of them being the fact that I seemed to be a living, breathing, talking, grief-stricken problem. I was placed with Mrs. H. I liked her a lot. I felt like I could trust her. I guess you could say I felt safe with her. It gave me someone else to talk to. Someone who was independent from my situation. I felt like maybe

I had a shot at getting Mrs. H to understand what it was like for me to live at Aunt B's and why I did *not* want to be there anymore. It was clear this situation wasn't working out for any of us. And I was fed up with this new life I was left to live with her, What's His Name, and their kids. Completely done.

JESSICA

AGE 13
1992

M y guidance counselor, Mrs. H, understands I don't like living at Aunt B's. I told her I won't go back there. I can't. If they try to make me go back, I'll just run away again. I told Mrs. H that, too.

Mrs. H said I can move in with her until they find me a foster home. She knows I need a place to stay. She knows I don't really have anywhere to go. So, I guess I have to wait until they find a foster home for me. I'm not sure how long that will take. I don't even know what it's going to be like.

I like Mrs. H. She is nice and really pretty. She's probably in her mid-twenties. She has dark hair and is thin. She has a husband and two little kids, both under the age of four. She seems to like me. That feels nice. I haven't felt liked by an adult in a *really* long time. Everyone I've lived with thinks I'm too hard to deal with. I'm too sad all the time. They don't like it when I cry. I'm too angry. I run my mouth when I'm upset. I try to be what everyone I've tried to live with seems to want me to be on some level. Normal. Happy. Moving on. Those are things I no longer am. And as for the moving on part, I have no idea how I'm supposed to do that.

For the first time since this happened, I feel like someone— my guidance counselor, Mrs. H—is on my side, and I finally have someone in my life that I can trust. With Mrs. H, I'll have a safe place to live, until they find me a real place. She's a counselor, so she must understand what I'm going through and why I feel the way I do. Why I act the way I do. Maybe her house will be like having a real home again, at least for a little while. I've already forgotten what that's like, because mine is gone.

Mrs. H said I'm going to sleep in the loft upstairs. It's kind of like an attic. There are stairs leading up to it, no windows at all, and there's a door at the bottom of the stairs. I don't really have much of my stuff to bring with me, but I'm just so happy to be here, with Mrs. H, in a place that feels safe, until things work out for me. I lay my head down on the pillow and for the first time in a long time, I feel like I might have a chance at having a kind of normal life. I think about the potential my new home has and how grateful I am to have it as I drift off to sleep.

In the morning, I wake up, I realize I have to pee something fierce. I mean bad. I walk down the stairs to make my way to the main part of the house, where the bathroom is located downstairs. I turn the knob on the door, and it is locked. I am locked in. She actually locked me in here. I keep trying to jiggle and turn the handle to get the door to open, to make sure it isn't just stuck or something. It is truly locked. I am so upset and so sad right now. Does she think I'm some freak that would actually try to hurt her or her kids or something? I'm a lot of things. Bad. Angry. Sad. But I would never hurt another person. She doesn't know me at all. While stewing in the realization that the door is locked, I stand in the loft, teetering my weight back and forth on my feet, because I have to pee so bad by this point, I'm about to pee my pants. Finally, about twenty minutes later, I go jiggle the door handle again, and lo and behold, it is unlocked. It opens with the first turn of the knob.

I go and find Mrs. H and ask, "Why did you lock me in?" She denies it. But the door was freaking locked. Trust me, I had to pee so bad, I twisted that knob a million ways to Sunday. It was to lock me in. To keep me away from them.

So much for a safe place. With me here, she clearly doesn't think this is one.

So much for trust. There is none.

So much for a place that might actually feel like a home again for a little while.

I'm so hurt she thinks that way about me. It cuts me to the core. It hurts in a different way than all the other things that hurt me. While I may not like myself, or like my life very much anymore, I would never hurt another person. Never. And the fact she's worried that I could makes me hate myself, my life, and the fact that I have no one and nowhere to go, even more.

Why am I still alive?

Would anyone even notice if I was gone?

No one wants me. Not even a guidance counselor can understand me or help me.

What am I going to do? Will this foster home they are finding me be any better?

At age twelve, instead of worrying about what movie to watch with my friends or what color to paint my nails, I have to worry about where I am going to live. What will it be like? Will I ever again find a place where I fit into this world?

I have no one. I have nothing. I feel sad, unwanted, unloved, and alone.

I wasn't sure where to go from here. But I sure hoped it was better than where I'd been.

Next stop: foster care.

JESSICA

AGE 13
1992

I think I only ended up staying at Mrs. H's house for two days before they let us know they'd found a foster home for me. I can't even begin to tell you all the thoughts that ran through my mind, when it came to that. Me living in foster care. In a foster home with people I didn't even know.

Will they be nice to me?

What will it be like?

Will they have other kids?

Will it be a good or bad place to live?

What will their house be like?

Will it be awkward living with complete strangers?

What if they are weirdos or bad people, what then?

How long do I get to live there?

Will these people help me have a normal life?

The fact is, these people would never be my parents, not really, no matter how good it went. They were just strangers to me, who were taking me in and giving me a place to live. It was going to be so weird no matter what.

When I first met them, they seemed okay. They were an older couple. I remember arriving at their house. Holy smokes! I couldn't even believe it. It was a huge house on a lake. A beautiful house, like the kind you see in magazines. I'd never been in a house like that before. I felt excited about it. Still a bit nervous, of course. But at least I was going to get to live in a big house on a lake! It had the most amazing backyard and the back of the house had big picture windows that overlooked it! How bad could it be? (Please tell Cinderella to lace up her shoes and grab a broom. We'll get to that in a minute.)

Upon arriving, I learned they had other kids. I believe they were foster kids. It was a bit awkward trying to get to know not only your new fake parents, but also some kids, too. Not long after I moved into The Lake House, I realized I would, in fact, need to lace up those shoes and grab that broom. Cleaning that big house was our job. Literally.

Looking back at the time I spent in that house, I don't remember how nice it was, or how much fun I had playing with those other kids in that big, beautiful backyard. What I remember is cleaning. It was all normal household chores, but those chores seemed to be neverending. Sweep the floor. Wash the dishes. Dust the house. Vacuum the carpet. Clean this. Clean that. Do it all again. This was not the house of hopes and dreams, it was the house of dust and mop, from top to bottom, over and over again. I really did feel like a makeshift, foster child's version of Cinderella. The only reason they kept all these kids around was to clean their mansion. I'm not sure if they were truly trying to grow a family, or working to enlist a cleaning crew.

I never felt like The Lake House was home. I never felt like it was a place where I belonged or mattered to anyone. They didn't really even know me. I didn't know them. I didn't want to be here anymore than I wanted to be at Ed 2's, or Aunt B's, or locked in Mrs. H's attic.

Perhaps this is where my future fixation for proper cleaning was born. (We'll get to that later.) But for now, I have to figure out where in the heck I go from here. The truth is I have nowhere to go.

I still have no one.

I have no real place in this world.

I don't fit in anywhere.

I am lost. And broken. And alone.

I'm not sure if that will ever change.

But I will pick myself up, dust myself off (right along with the many pieces of wooden furniture in this house) and figure it out.

JESSICA

AGE 13
1992

I was so freaking tired of not having a real home. I didn't belong anywhere or feel like I belonged with anyone.

I had a friend in choir who knew my living arrangements had fallen apart. Ed 2 was still my legal guardian on paper, but I had no desire to move back in with Ed 2 or Aunt B and I'm pretty sure they wouldn't have been any more thrilled with that prospect than me. One day, I was talking to my friend, Choir Girl, venting about how I had no idea what I was going to do or where I was going to go to stay. I felt like I was out of options.

That's when Choir Girl turned to me and said something along the lines, "Hey, my mom takes in foster kids, you know. You should come live with us! Do you want me to talk to my mom about it?" Did. I. Ever. I desperately needed a home. Somewhere to stay. A place where I could try, by some immaculate miracle, to have some semblance of a normal life. You bet I was interested! At least I would be living with a friend. That would be fun. Surely, it had to be better than all the other places I had tried.

Choir Girl's mom agreed to take me in. I was grateful. I felt like maybe I finally found my fresh start. I was excited. I wasn't sure what to expect, but it felt like the best option I had.

Living at Choir Girl's house was pretty darn good. It was the most normal living arrangement I'd had. Choir Girl's Mom treated me like I was normal, like I was just another friend of her daughter's from school. She didn't tiptoe around me, like I was broken. She didn't try to get me to talk. She didn't pry. And for the first time in my life since my daddy died, I felt like I was around an adult who wasn't either judging me or attempting to fix me. I liked being left alone to deal with my own problems. I liked not having someone looking at me as though I was broken or messed up. I liked feeling like I could be normal. I could talk if I wanted to, or I didn't have to. It would be okay either way.

There were rules at Choir Girl's house. I'm not saying Choir Girl and me never broke any of those rules, because we totally did, but we were pretty good for the most part. We had curfews. We did chores. I listened to what her mom told me to do and did what she asked. I didn't want to mess this up. For me, this was the closest thing to a normal home I'd had. So long as I followed the rules and didn't cause any trouble, I had a place where I felt comfortable and safe. A place where I felt like I fit in okay enough and wasn't a burden or a bother. A place where I could take care of myself and just be me. And it was fun living with a friend. I had someone to talk to. Someone in whom I could confide. And for the first time in a really long time, a place and people that felt comfortable and right. I lived with Choir Girl for three years.

After that, I stayed with my boyfriend at either his dad's or his mom's house. I also stayed with friends. I continued to be a nomad. By this point, it was my new normal.

JESSI

2016

*I*t wasn't until I was telling this part of my story to my cousin, Jamie, that I realized why I was able to probably assimilate so well under the supervision and tutelage of Choir Girl's mom. She, herself, had grown up in foster homes. In fact, she had lived in numerous foster homes, numbering into double digits. I never realized it at the time I lived there, but she knew the way to approach me because she knew what it was like to be the foster child. To be the one who did not belong or fit in. She knew what it felt like to not have a home or a real family. And something tells me, the reason she knew how to communicate with me and deal with me and my emotional baggage is because at one point in her past, she was me. She would not pry. She would not judge me. She would not try to fix me. On some level, when she looked at me, she probably saw her younger self. And for that, I am truly grateful.

JESSICA

AGE 13
1992

*W*hen I was in eighth grade I dyed my hair a vibrant shade of mahogany red. I wanted something different. The truth is, when I looked at a mirror, what I saw staring back at me was a girl I did not like. Nothing was ever going right in my life. Things were so messed up. I was so sad. I was pissed off all the time. Even when things were going okay, I still didn't have a family. Not liking the essence of who you are as a person is a difficult thing for a person to reconcile. The girl with the mousy brown hair lived inside a shell. She was a person who was afraid of the world. At least, that's how I felt when I saw her.

When I emerged as the girl with the fiery red, shoulder-length hair, I felt different. I looked different. People around me in school acknowledged me and seemed to talk to me more. I liked what I saw when I looked in the mirror. I didn't look like me. I looked like someone else. And I liked that *a lot*. I had always felt different than everyone else around me. This new color hair was a way to show the reality of what I felt on the inside to the world in an external way. The contact lenses helped me to look like a new person, too. At one point, I even had some bangs cut to accentuate my new colorful style. I was digging this new look. It was fierce. Bolder. It sure beat the hell out of being the sad, plain, boring Jessica.

I'll never forget the first picture I saw of myself after I embraced the new look. I was wearing these cool shorts with brown embroidered embellishments and a long-sleeved green shirt. When I looked down at that school photograph, it was like I was peering upon the face of another girl. This girl looked happy. She didn't look like someone who had all the problems I had in life. I liked her. I liked the look she had. It felt like I was staring down at the photograph of a girl I wished I could be. One who didn't have a bunch of problems. One who wasn't missing her parents. One who had a real home. What I saw was just a pretty, vibrant, happy girl. And that girl was me, yet at the same time she wasn't.

I was goodie two-shoes at school. I never swore. I'd managed to pull myself together on the outside. All the ugly, unhealthy ends dangled loosely on the inside. Internally, I was rotting from sadness. I was drowning in anger. But outside, it didn't show. I could rein it in. I could act like someone I didn't feel like being. I didn't get into trouble at school. I began to care about my grades for the first time ever, and was actually pulling straight A's. I wasn't interested in joining any extracurricular activities or hanging out with other people, but I was getting by.

That mahogany red dye would be the first color of many. Throughout my junior high years, I dyed my hair every color of the rainbow. Initially, I used Kool-Aid to dye it. I could easily get my hands on that and it was cheap and easy to do. I had blue hair. Then red. After that, I began to use real hair dye. I went from red, to orange, to yellow, to green, to purple, to blue. It was as though I was searching for the color that felt the most like "me." My nickname in school became "Rainbow Brite," for obvious reasons.

I looked like the girl I wanted to be. One who was happy and carefree. The only problem was, that girl was never going to be real to me.

JESSICA

AGE 13
1992

When I was 13, I began to take notice of a certain boy. My friends and I hung around the same circles as this guy did. I was now in junior high and he became my first infatuation. My friend and I used to follow him home. Not in a creepy, stalker sort of way, but more of a "Hey, you're really cute and I'd like to get to know you better, so I'll just follow you around, so I'm near you, type of way." Thankfully, he liked me, too. It wasn't long before he asked me out.

He was tall, really good looking, had long hair, and wore baggy clothes. He had a bit of edge to him. He also liked to smoke pot. At that point, not a lot of kids our age did drugs, so it made him a bit of a bad boy. While I didn't do drugs, I always felt like I didn't fit in, so we were perceived alike by others in that way. He treated me well. I was friends with his sister. His mom adored me. We spent a lot of time hanging out at his house. Obviously, with me still living at Choir Girl's house, family life where I lived wasn't exactly typical. He didn't seem to pay it any mind.

First Love and I dated for about a year. We were each other's first romantic relationship. We were each other's firsts in other things, too. He eventually dumped me for another girl. Talk about devastating. Here I was, all alone, and he was moving on with another stupid girl. That type of thing wasn't easy to survive in junior high. It's something everyone around you notices or asks you about constantly, so it takes a long time before you feel like you're over it. It was even harder for me, as a broken person.

It's incredibly difficult to accurately convey how hard it was for me to lose the one and only person I felt loved me in life—that boy with edge who treated me well—my first love and the first boy I ever gave myself to. It crushed me. In a way, it felt like losing my family all over again. Once First Love was gone, I was alone again. Completely alone. And I didn't do well with being alone at all. For me, alone was a trigger to past emotions, the ones I buried deep inside myself, so I wouldn't have to think about them or feel them.

When I was alone, those terrible feelings would resurface and eat away at me, bit by bit. They would strip away at the happiness I had claimed and what little of me remained. I felt so sad, lost, and totally scared that I would always feel this way. Afraid I would never have anyone in my life who mattered again.

It was difficult having no true connection to anyone. I decided to reach out to my gammy and paps, whom I loved dearly (and bear absolutely no ill will towards) because there was no longer anyone around to stop me, like Aunt B and Ed 2 had. That connection helped a bit. They were excited to reunite with me and we talked on the phone every now and then, but I truly felt alone in this world. Completely and totally alone.

When something bad or significant happened in my life, it would signal the start of that vicious mental cycle in my head: Why did my family have to die? Why am I here all alone? What if this had never happened; what would my life be like? Will I ever feel like I have a normal life? Will I ever feel loved again? Will I always be alone? It would be followed by thoughts of what all that meant: You are alone. You have no one. You never will. It's just you. You may never have anyone who really loves you again.

Then the emotions would begin to overwhelm me. They would present as a gentle wave, at first, but before I knew it, I was drowning in sorrow and floating in pain. No matter how hard I tried, it always felt like the large pieces of the life I'd managed to gather together was being pulled out from beneath me, just like in 1989. I was falling. I was sinking. I was struggling to breathe. It was a hellish pattern; one which I had no freaking clue how to break free from. I could make my way a few steps ahead, then BAM, out from under me it went and in came the pain.

I wanted to give up one million times, maybe even before high school. I'm pretty sure that's an accurate number. But something inside me wouldn't give up. I fought to exist, even when I didn't know why. I fought to become better, even when I had no idea what the point was of trying. Maybe, one day, I would figure out the reason I was still here. And maybe, one day, I wouldn't feel so alone.

JESSI

AGE 13

1992

$\mathcal{W}$ hen I was 13, I sat down one day to write a poem to get my feelings out on paper. It was at the end of my eighth grade year. I was still in deep mourning over my break up with First Love. The loss hit me hard. So, let's just say it was a dark poem. And I mean *really* dark. The kind that makes any person reading it think the person who wrote it is really screwed up and must be on the verge of doing something stupid. I'm gonna have to paraphrase a bit, but it went something like this:

> You have to do this.
> No, you can't do this.
> Yes, you can.
> You're going to do this.
> I take an expensive bottle of sherry from my
> foster mom's liquor cabinet.
> I put the pills in my mouth.
> Pain.
> So much pain.
> I can't bear it any longer.
> Swallowing.
> Fading into darkness.

It was far more eloquent than that and a lot longer—it took me a long time to write—but that's the gist of it. A person in the throes of sadness, making the decision to kill herself. While I know I wrote some dark stuff, it was just to get it off my chest. I had no intention of actually doing it, killing myself. But somehow, writing about it made me feel better, like a form of release. After I wrote, I felt lighter, at least a little bit, anyway. Hey, there are a lot worse things a girl could be doing, given my circumstances, than writing dark poems. I'm just saying.

I was still living at Choir Girl's house at this point. One day, Choir Girl's younger sister, who was in high school at the time (years after I wrote the darkness poem), apparently had to write a poem for a class of hers, and unbeknownst to me, she stole my darkness poem, and turned it in as her own. My poem. My thoughts and feelings. Her project and grade. Not only does the theft of intellectual property amount to plagiarism, but if one steals the darkest of dark poems of another, it also leads said poem thief to be approached by one of the school's guidance counselors, lectured, and told she needs to undergo a psychological evaluation. That's what she gets for stealing my darkness, and my words. Trust me, no part of me is making light of suicide. It's no joking matter. I'm really glad the school took swift action. They should. But you gotta admit that it's kinda funny Choir Girl's sister thought she was getting away with stealing my work and passing it off as her own, without my knowledge, and ended up getting herself into some major trouble over it. I didn't find out about this until *way* after it happened.

It was my darkness to carry. And my darkness, alone. No, I didn't have any desire to kill myself. But yes, I was feeling that dark, alone, sad, and low on the inside. I just wasn't going to do anything stupid, like that, because of it. At least I hoped not . . .

JESSI

AGE 15
1994

*W*hen I was 15-years-old, still living at Choir Girl's house, my former stepbrother, Jeff Pelley, reached out to ask if I wanted to come and visit him in Florida, where he lived with his wife. I was honestly shocked to hear from him, since I hadn't heard from Jeff or Jacque since the murders. I asked Choir Girl's mom if I could go. She knew Jeff was my former stepbrother—and was clearly oblivious to any suspicions cast upon Jeff back in the day, as was I—so she didn't have a problem with it. I told him I could come. Jeff booked me a flight.

I found myself seated on my first flight, alone, and like most first-time fliers, prepared to die at any given moment when the plane shook with the slightest bout of turbulence. My fear of heights certainly didn't help things. Jeff and his wife had registered me for that "supervision" option where the flight attendants would help me, as a minor child, onto the plane, escort me off the plane, and keep an eye on me during the actual flight. I was also unsure how my visit with Jeff was going to go. After all, I hadn't seen him since I was nine years old at our family's funeral, back when our lives were intermingled at the parsonage. My memories of Jeff were not fond, to say the least. In a way, I felt stupid for going to visit him. I had no idea how things would unfold. I think my own curiosity is what led me there. Was he still a mean person? Would he treat me the way he used to? I wanted to see if he'd changed and, perhaps, if we could have a better relationship. After all, we were both older now. I was interested to see what he was now like, as a grown man all these years later. (I am guessing he was around 22 or 23 years old at the time.)

As fate would have it, the plane did not, in fact, break into a million pieces at an altitude of 30,000 feet and we did, eventually, land on the concrete runway unscathed. I was relieved to set my feet upon the ground, but still harboring a stomach full of nerves as I pondered how the reunion with my former stepbrother and his wife would go. It would be okay. That's what I kept telling myself. The flight attendant walked me off the airplane and into the waiting area of the airport, where I saw Jeff and his wife waiting for me. I recognized him immediately. He looked older, but his dark eyes and dark hair made him easily identifiable. I could see the similarities in his appearance to his dad, Bob. They seemed happy to see me. We hugged it out and exchanged a few words. The warm introduction helped to ease some of my nervousness. Jeff seemed nice, not how I remembered him at all. That was good. That glimmer of a seemingly decent person standing before me helped to alleviate some of my apprehension and worry and made me feel a bit better about how this visit would go.

We exited the airport, walked out to their car together, and then Jeff drove us to their house, which was small, but nice. I was excited to learn they not only had a hot tub, but were also the owners of a pet squirrel, which was slightly weird, but totally cool, all at the same time.

Once we arrived at their home, his wife showed me to the spare bedroom where I would be staying. She left me there to get my stuff settled. I heaved my suitcase onto the bed and began to unpack my things. Not long after, Jeff walked into the bedroom where I was unpacking and stood there—almost as though he was lingering— for a moment. I felt his presence. He then asked me, "Hey, *who* do you think did it?" I obviously knew he was referring to the murders. (It bears mentioning I'd never been told anything beyond what I was told in that driveway in front of the parsonage back in 1989: that they were gone. I think I later found out they had been shot. But, I didn't know anything beyond that.) I immediately responded with, "Your dad. I think your dad did it." Jeff said, "Oh, okay . . ." He then changed topics.

It seemed like a bizarre question for him to ask me right out the gate after all these years. After all, I was only now 15, and also coming from an uneducated place of understanding about the murders. As a nine-year-old kid, I held the belief that the murders had actually been a murder-suicide. I had believed that Jeff's dad was the one who killed my family before turning the gun on himself. And now, here Jeff was, all these years later, asking me this question. It was even more odd that he would ask me this question within a few minutes of me being in their home. It wasn't in the middle of a casual conversation. It was the basis of a conversation almost the moment I arrived there.

I knew our family had been shot in our house. That's it. No stories. No details. Nothing about what the detectives thought or had collected as evidence, much less whom they suspected to be my family's killer. I categorized this interaction with Jeff under the category of weird, most definitely weird, but moved past it. After all, I was going to be there for several days. There was no going back. He seemed nice now. Everything would be fine. At least, I hoped it would.

Over the next few days Jeff and his wife took me to the mall to go shopping and bought me several outfits, consisting of some adorable cut-off shorts that had ruffles affixed to the bottom of them and some cute crop tops. They also took me out to dinner at Red Lobster. As a kid with no parents, I didn't really get to go out to dinner or shopping much, so to me, it was a special thing.

We also spent a lot of time at the beach and rode jet skis in the ocean. There was one point when Jeff knocked me off the jet ski on purpose. I fell into the ocean and came up gasping for air. In that moment, I had a flashback of the way things used to be between Jeff and me. He laughed after the fact and seemed to be playing around, so I just played it off like it wasn't a big deal and didn't bother me. That one moment with the jet ski *didn't* bother me. The feelings that bubbled up because of it, that past emotional baggage between us, well, that *did* bother me. But it was a fleeting moment. I tried to stay in the present and not to allow those negative feelings to creep in. Nothing good could come from it.

When we parted ways at the airport terminal, Jeff said, "Maybe you could come back again." All in all, it was a fun weekend, notwithstanding the weird question that would punctuate the beginning of my stay. I flew home and resumed my life. I didn't give much more thought to the question, but I didn't forget about it, either.

Jeff emailed me a few times after that. At one point, I learned that his wife had given birth to a son. His exchanges with me were few and far between, and more informational in nature. I wouldn't see Jeff again for another twelve years.

JESSI

AGE 17

1996—1997

*D*uring my senior year of high school my school hosted a talent show. I have always loved to sing. It's something I always did with my sisters, back before my life went to hell. It seems like a lifetime ago. I guess music and singing is something that always allows me to feel closer to them, after I lost them. This talent show seems like the perfect place for me to showcase my vocal skills. I'm in choir now and have sang in the choir since the seventh grade, but I don't think a lot of people realize the passion I have for singing. It allows me to set a small piece of my soul free. All I have to do is sign up, pick a song or two, practice like crazy, then get on that stage and sing my ass off. I decide to go with "Hero" by Mariah Carey and "One Sweet Day," by Mariah Carey and Boyz II Men, in that order. I even talked a guy friend of mine into singing the guy's part of "One Sweet Day" with me. I practice the songs endlessly. I have to get it right. It has to be perfect.

The big day finally arrives. I am excited, a little bit giddy, and slightly nervous, too. But I feel ready. This is my moment, the one I'd eagerly practiced for, probably a thousand times from the moment the talent show was announced until now. I walk up the stairs, make my way onto the stage, take the microphone in my hand, and dedicate the songs I'm about to sing to my family: My mom, dad, Janel, and Jolene. The whole room gives way to silence. I'm not sure how many people actually knew what had happened to my family, but it was apparent from what I'd said that they were no longer with me. All my teachers knew what had happened to me. It was as though everyone in the room sensed how big a deal this was for me, to get up on this stage to do this. I dedicate the first song to my dad. And I begin to sing the lyrics to Mariah Carey's "Hero."

I sang with everything I had: every memory, every scar, every hope, every dream, every tear, every moment of love, loss, and longing, everything I had in me. I sang the song to my daddy, for him, to my family, in honor of them, and the only way I had them in my life, in memoriam to them. I pour my whole heart into every note, every word, every chorus, every-single-soul-seizing-moment of it. When I finish the first song, everyone applauds. I'm happy they liked it and feel proud, but I'm trying to keep it together, because I know I'm about to sing the next song and this one, it takes all of me to get it right. I'm going to sing it from my soul. I say an appreciative, "Thank you," and go right in to the next song, which I sang as a duet with my guy friend. I dedicate it to my family.

Tears well up in my eyes and threaten to fall as I finish the last chorus of the song, but do not drop. I'm right on the brink, emotionally and as authentic as humanly possible, pieces of my soul stripped away and lain bare for all to see. As for the tears, it seems I wasn't alone in holding them back. In that moment, through my voice, I had allowed people to catch a glimpse of my pain, my sorrow, my life's story, and my true self. They could hear it in the timbre of my voice. They could sense it in the emotions I poured through the words. Teachers were crying. Some parents had tears streaming down their faces. Even some students were crying. After letting go of the last note I just stood proudly on that stage, full of emotion, but feeling like I did what I came here to do. I sang because of them. I sang for them. I honored them, in a way that meant a lot to me, because I missed them with every cell of my soul.

In an interesting turn of events, there happened to be a guy in the auditorium that day, one student's grandfather, who happened to work for a local record label. He approached me, handed me his card, and offered me a recording contract. This is the part of the story where I'd love to tell you I hit the big time and became a famous singer. That said, you've never heard of me as a singer, so it's clear that didn't happen. I decided that going to college sounded like a more solid plan. I passed up the deal.

I know, I know, be young and throw caution to the wind, live your life out loud, no regrets, and all that. I'd done my fair share of it. But for once in my crazy ass life, as a crazy ass girl, I was trying to do what seemed to be more practical and made sense from a logical standpoint. I wanted to be successful in life. I wanted to be able to provide for and take care of myself. I didn't want to be forced to depend on other people for anything anymore, not after graduating high school. I was done feeling like a second-class citizen or an accessory to those who actually belonged. I wanted to have a real job—a career—and a reliable income. A real place to live. I wanted to make my own way in the world. To me, college, it seemed, would give me the best shot at all of that. A real chance to stand on my own and a way to exist on my own terms.

Just me.

Before closing this chapter, I should probably mention that during high school, after living at Choir Girl's house for a few years, I ended up moving in with Aunt M from my dad's side of the family for a while, maybe four weeks. One day I hung posters on the wall of my bedroom at her house and she ordered me to take them all down. It was my room. But it was her house. She tried. I tried. But it didn't really work out.

I would live with my new boyfriend's mom, while he lived at his dad's house. I would later move in with him at his dad's house for a while.

And there were times when I was pretty much living with friends and crashing on their couches throughout high school. I did end up back over at Choir Girl's house from time to time because it's a place where I always felt like I could return. For me, the wandering did not end.

MONA

Jessica's Mom's Best Friend
1997

I always wondered what happened to Jessica after my last call to Jessica's Aunt B, the one where she told me never to call again. I complied with her wishes. I hoped it was truly what was in Jessica's best interests, but it certainly didn't feel like it, at least not to me. I felt like she needed to be able to talk to people that knew her. To see or ask questions of people who knew her parents. It gnawed away at me that I had no idea where she lived, or whether she was doing all right. I hoped she had found some way to live a semi-normal life and maybe even managed to find a way to be happy. She was so young when the tragedy happened, that I had to hope it was possible she had a normal childhood.

I never left Midland, Michigan, the place where Dawn Hayes and I had grown up and spent our teenage years together. I still drove by our high school on occasion. Some of the places in Midland would spring up a memory of Dawn and the time we'd spent together before everything unraveled and she was ripped from my life. In some ways, it helped to be there. In other ways, it hurt. But either way, it was my hometown and the place where my husband and I decided to raise our two children.

One day, I was sitting in my kitchen drinking a cup of coffee and reading the Midland paper as I always did. I always liked to stay abreast as to what was going on in our city. Usually, not a whole lot, but it was still interesting to know about, nonetheless. I finished the news clip I was reading and turned to the next page. On it, I saw the most vibrant, happy looking blond-haired girl smiling in a picture. At first, it was just her vibrant smile that caught my attention. But then, I thought to myself, "Wow, she looks just like Cher" (one of Ed's sisters that I'd known, growing up). As it turns out, the reason she looked so much like Cher is because she was *related to Cher*. It was her niece. Smiling in this photograph was Ed Huber's daughter—my best friend, Dawn's daughter—looking right back at me. It was Jessica Pelley. I couldn't even believe my eyes. It was Jessica! I immediately got up and ran to show my husband. It made me so happy to see her and how she'd grown into a young woman. She was so beautiful. She looked so happy. The caption below the picture confirmed what I already knew to be true, it *was* Jessica Pelley. She was a member of a local church choir and that was the reason for the photograph appearing in the paper.

I did what any person in my situation would do. After I calmed myself down a bit, I picked up the telephone, and dialed the number to the church. "Hi, my name is Mona and I'm calling about an article and picture I saw in the paper that featured some members of your choir. I used to know Jessica Pelley. I was best friends with her mom, Dawn. I lost touch with Jessica over the years and I would *love* to be able to talk to her now. It would mean a lot. I think she'd be happy to hear from me. Is there any way you could give me her number?" Of course, the answer to that question was a hard and fast "no," due to privacy concerns, which I completely understood. So I went with what seemed to be the next logical question, "Well, I completely understand that. How about this, would it be possible for me to give you my number and you could just give it to her in case she wants to call me?" The answer to that question was a softer "no," but still a no, nonetheless. I understood the church's position, but that didn't make it any easier. I was so close to Jessica, in my own hometown.

I did strongly consider the possibility of just showing up at the church for a service, so I could try to see her and maybe talk to her there. But I really didn't know if she would want to see me or would even remember me. The last thing I would ever want to do is bring her more pain. Maybe she was moving on with her life and to be reminded of the past would be painful. I definitely didn't want to do anything to harm her wellbeing. The internal conflict drove me crazy. But at least I got to see her. I knew she was still alive. So beautiful. I did find some solace in that. I cut out that newspaper clipping, placed it into a picture frame, and put it on a shelf in my living room. It gave me some small sense of connection to her.

It was my hope that the photograph conveyed her reality and that she really was living a normal life and was as happy as she looked in that black and white photograph staring back at me. Whether or not that was true, I had no way to know. I was so close to her, yet so far away. Midland isn't that big of a place. I wasn't sure if we would ever meet again. It's possible we could even run into one another somewhere along the way. And when, and if, we did, she might not even remember who I was. Whether that would be a good thing or a bad thing, I couldn't say. I just hoped above all else that she was happy and had a chance to lead a successful life.

JESSICA

AGES 9–17
Present Day, 2018

*I*t's the little things that dismantle your attempts at normalcy in the early years following a tragedy like the one I lived through. Things other people never even notice send an emotional tsunami crashing through your carefully constructed walls, breaking you. Things like making crafts for Mother's Day or Father's Day. It's normal for all the other kids. But not for me. Heck, even the kids missing one parent can manage to make the token craft for the other parent, but not me. Not anymore. For me, this became one of the perpetual reminders of my brokenness. My emptiness. A cold, hard look at what remained. Yet another one of the times I could no longer deny I was different from the others. While other kids were creating vibrantly colored ornaments or making hand-painted gifts with glue sticks and glitter, my mind was flashing back to a hellish day in 1989. To say I felt sorry for myself would be inaccurate. I was angry. So angry. And so *not normal*. Really, how could I be? How could *anyone* be after what I'd been through at age nine? Let's be real. I was damaged.

Any time I went to a friend's house I was given a glimpse at what normal looked and felt like, what other kids had, and all I lacked. Even the divorced families were normal. They may have had two homes, but they still had parents who cared for and loved them. Parents who cooked them meals, bandaged scraped knees, washed their clothes, yelled at them about cleaning their dirty rooms, picked them up from school, and loved them unconditionally. People who told them goodbye every time they left the house and good night each time their head hit the pillow. That made it painful for me to be around other people, normal people, and even more difficult to be around their families. But it sure beat being alone.

Speaking of alone, that's another thing I hated. I felt utterly alone, even in a crowded room. I felt like there were now two distinct factions: me and the rest of the world. Another thing I would come to loathe was holidays—all of them. The holidays killed me. They would never again be the same. For me, they felt more like this:

Another Christmas without my family.

Another birthday with no family.

Yet another Easter without my family.

The birthday of each family member I lost, a perpetual reminder.

Other kids looked forward to holidays; they were enamored by them, just like I once was. I had memories of wearing the Wonder Woman costume at Halloween with my sisters beside me. I also had memories of me beneath the Christmas tree shaking presents. I still knew that holidays were supposed to be about time spent with family, home-cooked meals, decadent desserts, and special memories made. But after the tragedy I began to dread them.

Even when people made an effort to include me in their family holidays, I always felt like a second-string attendee. The plus one that didn't belong. Sure, as a kid I wanted a trimmed tree with presents beneath it, beautifully decorated birthday cakes, cute costumes, and themed parties, but more than anything, what I wanted was love. What I longed for was acceptance; a place where I mattered and belonged. I wanted special memories to replace some of my sorrow. Something to dull the ache. Someone to fill the emptiness.

The anger ate away at me, like a crow picking at bones, it stripped me to my core. I swung between trying to forget about my past, to wishing people would remember it, or realize what I'd been through and acknowledge it—acknowledge me—broken pieces and all. At that point in my life, had I still been a Girl Scout, I undoubtedly would have earned a merit badge for "walking through hell and back," canvas sneakers, empty smile, and all. It's not easy to straddle the edge between denial and reality. But it's a place where I would dwell for a long time. I lived between the extremes. The normal girl. The messed-up girl. The girl who wishes she had died at least 100 times each day. The girl who forgot what it feels like to stand in the sun. Even on my worst days, there was the quiet whisper of a warrior within me, something that told me to stand and hold strong. If only I could learn to hold my head a little higher. If only I could find a way to live, and a reason why.

While the other kids were trying to decide what color dress to wear and what sports to play, I alternated between giving up and fighting back. One day, years and years away from ornament handprints and hollow smiles that never touched my eyes, I would see the value in it—the value in me. I could really live again. But first, I would have to live through some of the darkest days I would ever know.

JESSI

AGE 38
Present Day—2018

*Y*ou want to know one of the things I came to loathe in life? The looks I get from other people. The ones I've come to know all too well over the past 29 years. The reaction is almost scripted, really. At this point, I think it's fair to say I tend to present myself to people in one of the three distinct ways:

ONE: I am Jessica Pelley, the survivor of the horrific murder of my family (rather insultingly referred to as the "Prom Night Murders"), a tragedy, and the only one left of my immediate family of five. (We're all fucked with this approach. Trust me.)

TWO: I am Jessi Toronjo. I'm normal. (Well, aside from the hot pink hair, anyway.) You will never know something tragic happened to me. I'm just like you. Yep, normal. This is my default setting. This version of me is easier for both you and me. It can be hard to dodge some questions occasionally, but deflect, deflect, deflect, act normal, and we're there.

THREE: You actually know me: the real me. You know that I am Jessi (the resilient one still standing in the light), but also know that I am also Jessica (the broken little girl who spent years shrouded in darkness). Not too many people get to know this version of me—the real me. It's an elite club by personal invitation only. At least it was, until I decided to tell my story publicly in the pages of this book.

And that brings us back to the looks of pity. Any time I show up in life as Jessica Pelley, the girl who tragically lost her entire family to a gruesome murder in 1989—cue the look of crestfallen pity from any person standing within an earshot of the story. When I tell people about my past, the transformation takes place in 20 seconds flat. In that moment, I go from being normal, as Jessi . . .

to poor little Jessica in a person's eyes. And there is no going back, for either of us.

I refuse to accept pity, even when bestowed by a well-intended offeror. I accept that I have a past that is unlike most others. I accept that I am human and flawed. But most of all, I accept that I am here and no different than most people in many ways. I don't want what happened to me to become a chasm that separates me from everyone else around me.

I fought my way through the darkness. I fought my way back to the light. I stand stronger because of yesterday. I remain hopeful for tomorrow.

I lost so much to the past. I refuse to lose anymore.

I am Jessica, and I am here for a reason.

JESSI

AGE 18

1997–1998

*W*hen I turned 18, I approached Ed 2 and begged him to let me borrow the money to buy a house. Jeff, Jacque, and I were each to receive inheritance money from a life insurance policy Bob held. We would receive these funds in two separate increments when we reached certain ages. I told Ed 2 that if he would let me borrow the money I would pay him back with the initial inheritance allotment I received.

Ed 2 said I was too young to buy a house, but he was willing to lend me the money to buy a mobile home. While it wasn't exactly what I had in mind, it was a fresh start. The one that, in my own mind, I desperately needed.

Even though Ed 2 and I *didn't* get along well over the years, understood one another's viewpoints on pretty much *nothing*, and I never really thought of him as "grandpa," I am grateful he loaned me the money to buy that trailer, until I could pay him back with those guaranteed funds. Yes, I did pay Ed 2 back, once I received the first installment of my inheritance money. It put me on a path to building a new life for myself. It really was a step up. I felt it.

I bought a three-bedroom mobile home. When you hear the term "mobile home," you may not think much of it. But it was nice. The master bedroom was so large, it was actually bigger than the living room. There was a set of French doors off the master bedroom that led to the master bath that had "his" and "hers" sinks and a huge garden tub. It was really nice. It was new and beautiful. I loved it.

It was my first real home—a place that actually *felt like home* to me—in nearly a decade. I liked finally living in a place that was mine. There was power in having something all your own, not being forced to rely on other people or feeling like a burden. It was a place where I could live on my own terms, in my own way, exactly like I wanted to. I guess you could say I felt free. Free from trying to fit into places where I didn't belong. Free from trying to be what everyone else around me wanted or expected me to be. Free from having to rely on the generosity of those around me in order to survive. I was free to just be me. And that felt good. Hell, it felt better than good. It felt fucking fantastic!

I decorated the living room in cheetah print and hung Elvis memorabilia all over the walls of the master bedroom. I had a healthy appreciation for good music, and Elvis songs were definitely that, plus my daddy was also a fan. It reminded me of him. I also placed exotic potted plants all throughout the trailer, sixteen of them, to be exact. My home was exactly what I wanted it to be.

My then boyfriend (we'll refer to him as "the Boyfriend") moved in with me. We had dated each other for about three years. He and I had already lived together for several years at either his mom's or dad's house during our high school years, so us cohabitating as a couple wasn't anything new. It was nice having this place, with him, to call home. It was also great not having to live by anyone else's rules.

This trailer was my first gateway to normal. My chance at living life on my own terms. If I had to work hard to make that happen, by working a bunch of bullshit jobs I'd rather not work, so be it. I was totally down for some adulting. I would learn what it was like to be responsible by going to work to pay my own bills. I would learn what it was like to buy my own groceries. For me, it was exhilarating to finally be in a position to make my own way. I didn't need to rely on anyone else now, I just needed me. And I was the one person I knew I could always count on. The one and only person I always had.

The Boyfriend and I ended up breaking things off not long after we moved into the trailer together. He wanted kids. I did not. I was only 18-years-old. I had goals in life. Since we both wanted different things, we reach an impasse. There was no point in us staying together. We parted ways, amicably. (I broke up with him.) He meant a lot to me, but we each ultimately went our separate ways because our paths diverged and we were smart enough to realize it.

I wanted to move forward with my own life. I can tell you that new life of mine involved working at a uniform laundering company to pay the bills, and a whole heck of a lot of partying. I liked going camping with friends, too. When I wasn't at work, that's where you could find me: partying my ass off or camping.

I liked my new life. It suited me well, for a while.

JESSI

AGE 18

1997-1998

$\mathcal{W}$hen I was 18, I decided I wanted to reconnect with my cousins—Aunt B's three children—the ones I'd lived with for several years of my life. So, I called Aunt B to see how everyone was doing and, also, asked to see my cousins. She said before I could see them I would have to go for a psychiatric evaluation. A psych eval. What the *actual* fuck. Are you kidding me? Really??? I was at a total loss. I had no words. It stung. I felt just as misunderstood in that moment as I felt running away from that stupid, pink slumber party all those years ago.

I'm sure Aunt B was just looking to protect her own children, but that didn't do a thing to assuage the intensity of the jab. The sad thing is, I wanted to see my cousins so badly, I actually played along. I did it. I went for the damn psych eval. It appears I passed, as Aunt B did allow me to see her children afterward. I guess little girls who have their entire lives upended and derailed don't grow up to be psychopaths, after all. Who knew? I did, that's who. I was a lot of things, but a psychopath was not one of them.

It's a hard thing to explain what it does to you when people think you're more screwed up than you actually are—when it's all trauma-induced issues, mainly—and screwed up in ways that in reality, you are not. Was I a bit of a rebel with a smart mouth? Abso-freaking-lutely. Did I grandstand and turn bantering sessions into full on verbal wars, escalating otherwise normal human interactions the entire time I lived with What's His Name and Aunt B? You bet. Did I push their buttons? Yes, I did. Regularly. But was I a fucking psychopath? That would be a big, huge, bold, hell NO. And it hurt so bad to think she, my aunt—my mom's younger sister—actually thought that about me to the point that she made a psychiatric evaluation a precursor to me being able to reconnect with my long-lost cousins. The ones I wanted to see and missed because they held some small connection to a piece of my childhood.

I felt so blindsided by Aunt B, so incredibly misunderstood. Let me be clear: I was NOT a psychopath. I could probably be lumped into quite an array of adjectives on a long list of other things, but *that* wasn't one of them. Not even on my worst day.

I was a little girl with a dark past.

A little girl carrying sadness, rebellion, and rage like accessories borne of darkness.

What I was NOT was someone who would ever want to harm another person. Ever. Period.

I continued to be a lost little girl in a grown woman's body and mind, who was incapable of understanding how I could have been any different than I was. I did the best I could with the tragic cards I was dealt in life. I played that messed up hand the only way I knew how, one sad or angry card at a time. I guess I did all right, because it allowed me to survive.

I was a woman who began to feel like a discarded remnant from everyone else's past. And apparently, I was now someone who could or should have turned out to be a psychopath, but wasn't one. Proving someone wrong never felt more disheartening. It was just one more heap of hurt on the trauma pile that I was carrying. But really, what's one more piece on the pile?

TYSON

(AGE 21)

Meeting Jessi (Age 16)

May 1996

My name is Tyson, but a lot of people call me "Ty" for short. I guess I should probably tell you a bit about myself. I was born in Midland, Michigan, but we moved around a whole lot when I was growing up. It's not that we lived in a long list of states—the number was four—it's just that we moved into and out of those four states on a rotational basis. It got to the point I didn't even try to make friends anymore because I figured we wouldn't be there long. By the time I hit junior high, I knew how to pack the back of a U-Haul truck with the best of 'em. It's always been me, my mom, younger brother, little sister, and my stepdad. My real dad's never been in the picture. I don't know him. The messed-up part is that I spent all the years of my childhood believing that my mom's husband—my brother's dad—was my father, too. I guess they thought it would be easier. It sure as hell wasn't easier, at least not for me, once I found out. I'm not sure how I was supposed to feel after learning I'd never even met one of my parents. They said that my real dad worked for the fair. From that moment on, every time the fair came to Midland, I went on the prowl in search of him. My brother would join me in my quest of looking for my long-lost dad. It was constantly in the back of my mind. Did I look like him? Did we have anything in common? Would he even want to get to know me? I never found him. I never had answers to any of those questions. It's something I learned to deal with as time went on. But it still sucked, all the same.

I'm a people person. I have a lot of friends. People seem to like hanging out with me at parties. I have a quick wit and a good sense of humor. I take pride in the way I look. I take the time to style my hair and wear nice clothes. I have no trouble landin' a girl, and if I wanted a relationship, I'd have no trouble findin' one. But I'm not that type of guy. I'm known as a guy who likes to drink and have a good time. I love doing stuff outdoors, like camping, hiking boating, riding a jet ski, you name it. Anything active. I'm into all that, always have been. I served a two year stint in the Army right after high school. My dream at the time I enlisted was to become a pilot, but, uh, that didn't quite work out as I'd hoped. They gave me a vision test that showed I was color blind. There wasn't a path to piloting with a seeing impairment. Once my plans of a future flying career were derailed, my thought process was, "Well, if I can't fly the plane, then let me jump out of it!" No part of me was kidding. I have a bit of an adventurous streak. Sign me up for anything fun; I'm down. I became a paratrooper in the 82nd Airborne, 35th Signal Brigade, S1 Headquarters. I made 23 jumps in the year and a half that I spent jumping out of airplanes for a living. It was fun while it lasted.

I'm not above taking risks. And I love to have a good time. If there's a party, I'm there. If there's a pretty girl around, I'm probably interested, likely hitting on her, and could get her interested in me, if I wanted her to be. It's actually hard to avoid them falling for me though. I may not be into relationships, but at least I'm honest about it. I'm just looking for a good time. If my buddies are camping, that's probably where you'll find me, if I'm not out on the lake on my boat. And partying is at the top of my list. Throwing back beers or drinking Jim Beam mixed with Coke—the soda, not the shit you snort up your nose—and having a damn good time doing it. That's the way I choose to live. In the middle of the party. Being around cool people who like to have fun and living it up; that's my number one priority. Nothing more. Just a good time.

I met my buddy's girlfriend today when I stopped by to hang out with some friends. She was smokin' hot. And I mean smokin'. Like, she could be a model type of hot. The type of chick that makes you do a doubletake. She had long, straight, platinum blond hair, a beautiful face, and a killer body. I mean, I am a 21-year-old guy; what can I say? It's something I couldn't help but notice. She's my buddy's girl, so it's not like I'd make a move on her or anything. She seems nice, likes to party, and is easy to talk to. He's one lucky son of a bitch. And you better believe I gave him a hard time about it.

After she left I leaned over to my buddy and in an animated voice said, "Maaaan, I'd *marry* that girl! I don't wanna get married, but I would marry *her*!" She was the total package. He laughed in response. It was playful banter among guys, nothing more. Me giving my buddy shit for "dating up."

The day after I met Jessi my buddy told me that some messed up stuff had happened to her in the past. He told me her entire family was killed when she was just a kid. Murdered. That she was real young when it happened and no longer had any parents. Her whole family died. That is so fucked up. I can't believe that happened to her. Honestly, I can't believe that something as messed up as that could happen to anyone. How terrible. I feel bad for her. That is such a terrible thing to be forced to deal with as a kid. I don't know how a person gets past something like that, but she seems to be doing okay. I mean, I never would have known that had happened to her, if he hadn't told me. She's bubbly, talkative, friendly. She doesn't seem affected by it, and if she is, it doesn't show.

JESSI

AGE 17

May 1998

I'm hanging out with one of my guy friends today. We're looking for something to do later tonight and he asked me, "Do you want to go to this party?" "Sure," was my reply. I'm always down to party. I assume the guy is likely pretty cool because my friend usually hung around fun people, but didn't know if I'd know anyone else there besides him. I mean, really, who cares? I'll get to drink and have a good time, regardless. It is the weekend, after all.

We climb into his car. He drives us to an apartment complex where, presumably, his friend lives. We step out of the car, shut the car doors, and began to walk toward a nearby apartment building. I'm pretty much just following along beside my friend right now. I don't have a clue where we're headed. It's then that I look up and on the landing beneath the apartment building we're approaching, I see Tyson, my ex-boyfriend's friend, whom I met a few years ago.

Holy-Mary-Mother-of-Hot-Men. I'm not even kidding. Upon seeing his striking, six-foot-eight-inch stature and incredibly attractive face with his mouth turned up in a sexy smile, I immediately call out, "Tyson!" And he replies, "Jessi!" We hadn't seen one another in probably three years by this point and had met only the one time, but the recognition was instant and the connection, at least for me, was undeniable. There was a pull I had no desire to struggle against. Upon realizing this was his apartment building, and he was actually the one throwing the party, my breath caught in my throat and I felt the immediate onset of butterflies in my stomach. Let me tell you about Tyson. He's super tall, which is a major turn-on for me. He has the body of a god—he's stunning—with striking blue eyes, and sandy brownish hair which is longer on the top than on the back and sides that he spikes up in the front with gel. Tyson wasn't a boy. He was a man. If I had to compare him to an actor, he was a young Brad Pitt, but taller and more built, with the charisma and swagger of Matthew McConaughey. Not only did Mother Nature bless the man, but he's dressed like a freaking fashion model off the pages of a magazine. He's so freaking hot. I have no idea what's going to happen tonight, but you bet your ass I'm looking forward to it!

I desperately attempt to rein in my nerves and smother my internal giddiness so it doesn't show, as Tyson and I hug and banter about how long it's been since we've seen each other. We then step inside Tyson's apartment—you know, the one I'll be hanging out at tonight—for the party.

I drink a few bottles of Zima—you know, that clear, sweet, "girl" beer from the 90's—and throw back several shots of vodka along the way. Granted, I'm always down for getting drunk and having fun, but at this point the liquor is serving a dual purpose. I'm trying to settle my nerves, just as much as I'm seeking the thrill of a buzz.

We hang out for several hours. We talk, drink, and shoot the shit. Everyone is pretty wasted and I am certainly no exception. I admit I am totally and completely shit-faced, which is why I decide I have to dance. I ask Tyson if he can play some music. He, I, and a few others move into his bedroom, where he has a speaker, so we can listen to music. I'm standing in the middle of the floor as I begin to move my body to the beat of a hip-hop song. I'll admit, I am making every effort to look sexy. And then, I decide to peel off my top and toss it away. Yep, me standing there, in the middle of the bedroom floor, in front of Tyson and a few others, dancing my ass off. You bet I was putting on a show. I wasn't shy when it came to my body or being naked in front of other people—remember, lots of Zima and vodka—and lord knows, I have it *bad* for Tyson. When I see his eyes on me—and only me—it only serves to fuel me further. After a few moments of dancing, I continue to peel off layers of clothing, until I'm standing in the middle of the room wearing only my panties. I stop, look at everyone else, and yell, "ALL RIGHT, it's time for everyone TO GO!!!" I then begin to usher everyone else out of the room, closing the door behind them. That left Tyson and me, two drunk people who were magnetically drawn to one another.

Perhaps you think this sounds like the story of a crazy, drunken girl who was out of control, seeking attention at a party in all the wrong ways. And maybe you're right. Perhaps you believe it to be the makings of a proverbial one-night stand. But you would be wrong. Tyson and I drank together the entire night and had a lot of fun. I did spend the night with him that night. That's as much as I'll tell you about that.

We both loved to party. We were both free spirits. In fact, so much so that me stripping my clothes off that night didn't make him think any less of me, it allowed him to see me for the free-spirited, crazy girl I was; the fun girl whom he admired. Our personalities clicked completely. Our physical chemistry was off the freaking chart. We were like fire on fire. Together, we sizzled. It was hot. We craved one another. If I'm being entirely honest, we were always intertwined. It didn't take long for me to fall for Tyson. Not long at all. Heck, I'm pretty certain it happened on night one. The moment I saw him standing on that patio, I knew. The moment he said my name, I knew. The moment he hugged me, I knew. The moment I stepped into his apartment that night, I was a goner. And the moment I decided to strip my clothes off, without a care in the world, drunk off my ass, forcibly removing all bystanders from his space, so we could be together, you better believe I knew. Without a doubt, I knew.

But I had no way to know that one night and our chance encounter with each other all those years after our initial introduction would shape the rest of my life.

TYSON

AGE 23
May 1998

I'm standing at the top of the stairs outside my apartment building, waiting on my buddy to get here. I'm throwing a party tonight. Should be a good time. I see him pull up, park his car, and open the door to get out. The passenger door opens, too. And that's when I see her—beautiful fucking Jessi—walking up to my building beside him. Oh man. Holy shit. I can't even believe it. She is so fucking hot. It's been a few years since I saw her, but, man, one thing is for certain, she's only gotten better looking. As far as I'm concerned, this party just got a *whole* lot more exciting. Hell yeah.

She calls out, "Tyson!" And I reply, "Jessi!" and she runs up and gives me a big ol' hug. This girl has no idea the effect she has on me. I'm tryin' to act cool about it, but if there is *any* chance I can get with this girl tonight, you better believe I'm gonna attempt it. Once she lets me go, we walk up the stairs, and into my apartment.

I've already got people over, probably 15 or 20 of 'em. Jessi brought a six-pack of Zima with her. Why anyone drinks that shit, I'll never know. I guess it's a girl thing. She starts drinking. I walk into my kitchen and make another Beam and Coke. This ain't my first. I've been drinking *long* before now. There are people sitting and standing everywhere. It's not like my apartment's that big, so it's pretty packed. We're all just sitting here drinking, shooting the shit, having a good time, and a few people begin to pass a joint around the room. What can I say? It's a party.

I can't even believe Jessi is standing in my living room right now. Can't even believe it. What are the odds? She is off the charts hot. I'm looking forward to seeing where things go tonight. I'm down for whatever. My buddy definitely fucked up when he let *her* go. They broke up years ago, so as far as I'm concerned, she's no longer off limits. Bro code only extends so long. And looking at her, oh man, you can forget about it. I'm down for whatever.

Jessi just said, "I want to dance." So I decide to move a speaker into my bedroom so she can dance. Hey, I'm here to please. If the girl wants to dance, that means I get to watch her shake her ass. I'll gladly comply.

She turns on a station playing a hip-hop song and begins to sway to the beat. Oh man, this girl. She's hot enough standing still, but when she's moving her tight little body to the music like that, she's sexy as hell. There's no shame in staring. Any man with two eyes would be. I'm just gonna sit back and enjoy the show. She sees me watching her and I don't give a damn. I want her to know I see her. I'm watching her. That I want her. With our eyes locked, it's then that she grabs the bottom of her shirt and pulls it up over her head and throws it across the room. What. The. Fuck. (And I mean that in the best way possible.) A moment ago, this was my bedroom, but now, it's a place of nirvana. I can't take my eyes off her. Surely, she's not gonna take anything else off. No way. That was it, just the shirt.

Then, I see her unbutton and begin to shimmy out of the pants she's wearing. Holy. Fucking. Shit. This girl is crazy. Not crazy in a bad way; crazy in the coolest and most intriguing way possible. She's like a female version of me. Wild. Fun. Free. Doing whatever in the hell it is she wants to do, when the feeling strikes her. Her confidence is a big turn on. The sensual way she's moving her body to the music is mesmerizing. She's got my attention. She knows it, too.

Jessi stops dancing and begins telling everyone to get out of the room, well, everyone except me. She shuts the bedroom door behind 'em. Now it's just the two of us in this room. Jessi and me. In that moment, I think to myself, "I'm so lucky she chose me." Not because she's clearly looking to have a good time tonight, but because I've got it bad for this girl. Who wouldn't after watching that show she just put on? This will go down in history as being one of the best house parties I've ever thrown. No doubt about it.

As for the rest, I think I'll keep that to myself.

JESSI

AGES 18 TO 22

1998–2001

*F*ollowing the night of the party and spontaneous sleepover at Ty's place, he and I became inseparable. Either I packed a bag and stayed at his house, or he threw some stuff in a bag and stayed at mine, but we were together pretty much every single day and every single night after that. The two of us, the "party people," had quickly merged into a unit, an unexpected couple, a legitimate thing. It was the overnight stay that transformed into something more than either of us expected.

Tyson and I watched movies. We talked. We laughed. We drank a lot. We attended parties together. We did a lot of stuff outdoors. We went camping. We went out on his boat on the water. We hung out with mutual friends. We went hiking. We rode jet skis. We laid out in the sun by the lake and drank beer. We went canoeing. Wherever he was, I was, too. It happened organically. We were consumed by one another in the best way possible.

For our first official date, he took me to Ruby Tuesday's. That restaurant was the place where I discovered his first flaw. Ty had just taken a bite of his fajita and I hear what sounds like a gagging noise. I think to myself, *"What the hell? Is he choking or something?"* I say, "What's that sound?" He admits, "I just took a bite that had too much cheese in it and it made me gag." We both laughed. Flaw number one: gagging while eating fajitas. (Check the box on that.)

Any time I was around Ty I had butterflies in my stomach and felt like I was floating on a cloud. Like the air I breathed was lighter in his presence. It felt good to like someone that much. Who am I kidding? I was completely and totally infatuated with the man. Game over. Done deal. Sign me up for whatever this was turning into between us, because I was lost, and found, all at the same time. I was falling fast and loving every minute of our time together. It felt so good to love someone, to finally, really, truly, love someone. That's something I hadn't had in such a long time, I forgot what it felt like. It scared me a bit. Loving a person made me feel vulnerable. Emotionally fragile. Susceptible to heartache and loss because it opened me up to the potential of losing someone else in my life again. But the magnetism between us dissipated my fears. It transcended every doubt I had. I couldn't deny myself the love I felt for him, not even if I'd tried. I was all in.

Tyson became my rock. My lover. My best friend. My constant companion. The man who made me happy, rocked my world, and made me feel more whole. I, Jessi Pelley, am irreparably and unequivocally in love with Tyson Toronjo. No doubt about it.

JESSI

AGE 18

1997–1998

*T*hree months after reuniting with Tyson, he moved into my mobile home. I started a job at a place called Educational Training Center, a childcare center where we watched children for people who were studying to earn their General Equivalency Diploma (G.E.D). I loved working with the kids. It was refreshing to be around them. They were so innocent and said some of the funniest things. I loved that about them and enjoyed interacting with them and teaching them new things. It was a fairly small center and there were typically three or four of us working in the classroom at any given time. The center was sectioned off by age, with the babies kept in a separate area that was gated off from the rest of the excited children who were mobile, curious, and looking to play with anything that piqued their interest.

One day, about three months into the job, something occurred that changed the way I felt about the place. It was lunchtime for the kids—their parents always packed and sent lunches for the children—and the kids had just sat down to eat. A little boy about six or seven years old, who had special needs of some type, had a meltdown. I don't remember if he didn't like his food or what the issue was, but he began to throw a tantrum. This particular child was known for sometimes having physical outbursts. We all knew this. My coworker, a lady, grabbed the little boy, knocked him down onto the ground, pinned his hands down, and sat on him in an effort to gain control over him. I said, "You need to get off of him." She said, "He's freaking out." I replied, "Well, you can't be sitting on him like that. There's a way to restrain a child and that's not it." I was pissed. This was no way to treat a child. I immediately went to our boss and told her what had transpired. I said, "You can either fire her or I'm leaving. I will not work in this type of an environment." She didn't fire her. I never went back. I couldn't, not after that.

I could not stand to see a child, much less one with special needs, treated that way. It's not like he was trying to be malicious. He just had his own personal issues. He had some violent tendencies, but it wasn't his fault he was that way. At his age, that's the only way he knew how to deal with life's challenges. I can tell you one thing, that lady who improperly restrained him is lucky I didn't punch her in the face that day.

I would find my way back to caring for, teaching, and loving children at another time and place, one that didn't allow stuff like that to go down. I simply could not and would not tolerate the mistreatment of what others perceived to be "bad" kids. They were children, and only that. Innocent. Still learning. Not bad. Just children.

JESSI

AGE 18

1998

*T*y and I, by some miracle of fate, managed to stay together as a couple. We grew past those days of slamming back beers, Jim Beam, and vodka and grew into more mature people we would eventually become. As cliché as it was, two free-spirited, crazy, fun, party people had somehow ended up together, in a committed relationship that would seemingly stand the test of time. Who said one night stands never work out? Not me and Ty, that's for sure. We continued to live together as a couple in my mobile home, the place we would live for the next three to four years.

We continued to work, drink, party, camp, go boating, watch movies, go on dates, and hang out like couples do. But, uh, it's probably fair to say we had more fun than your average people, because we did. That initial attraction was the bond that sealed our souls and bound us, one to the other, from that moment on. Ty worked construction. He installed windows and doors, hung siding, did roofing, pretty much anything that wasn't plumbing or electrical work. He was a hard worker who often worked long days and would party into the nights.

AGE 20

On August 11, 1999, we welcomed our newborn daughter, Dakota (we often refer to her as "Kota"), into the world. I was 20 years old. Tyson was 25. No, we weren't married at the time. (If you're thinking about that stupid ass saying about putting the cart before the horse, save it. I've heard it enough.) We were two people, madly in love. We were still figuring things out. It's not like we planned it. But we welcomed it, just the same. And we loved our baby daughter to the moon and back. We were in love with one another and now had a family to call our own.

Our relationship continued as it always had. As a new mother, I had more tasks than time. Our hands and hearts were full.

AGE 21

On December 22, 2000—a little over a year after our daughter was born—we celebrated the birth of our son, Austin (his nickname is "Austi"). We now had a toddler and a newborn baby at the same time. That's not easy for anyone to manage, but especially not a young couple who was used to partying our asses off, now assimilating into the world of full-on adulting and working, as well as the parenting of two little kids. Thankfully, motherhood came naturally to me. I loved my children. Dearly. Ty was a good dad, too. He loved me and the kids. He was still working construction, which wasn't an easy job, to provide for our family. We were finally making our own way in the world. I had the family I always hoped to one day have.

All of that said, shaking Ty from the partying lifestyle proved to be difficult, if not altogether impossible, as time went on. I was at home with two young children and, by that point, wanted to live our lives together as a formal family unit. Ty wanted that too, but that didn't mean he wanted to give up doing what he wanted to do: drinking with friends, staying out too late, tipping back beers, and having fun. I'm not saying I never went out, drank, or had fun. I did. I just did it a whole lot less than he did at that time in our lives. We fought a lot. Our early years together could be summarized as incredibly passionate and equally as intense. It was filled with a lot of memorable times and happiness, but oftentimes, it was also filled with a lot of fighting. He would verbally lash out at me. I would verbally lash out at him. It was a perpetual cycle.

Most people assume I likely had a hard time going through the pregnancies and births of my own children with my family being deceased and gone. But the truth is, my babies kept me busy.

Making the adjustment to taking care of someone full-time didn't leave me time to think of much else. The emptiness that was my former family continued to be what it always was, a gaping hole I did my best to move past. I will say that the older they got or when the holidays rolled around, I thought about it—my family, that hole, their absence. I knew I had no family to introduce to my children and no home filled with my family to visit. It sucked that my kids would grow up without that part of me. That they would never know their grandma—my mom—or their two aunts—my sisters who would have adored them. My hole would become their hole.

I took it in stride as best as I could. After all, we still had Tyson's family. We went to his mom's or his sister's house for holidays. I felt welcomed there. I knew they liked me and over the years, loved me. But no matter how many years passed or how many people were there for me, they would never be the family I had lost. It was an unspoken part of the past that would always linger above me. That loss, that void, that reality, is now my husband's and children's loss, as well.

AGE 24

By the time early 2004 rolled around I'd decided enough was enough when it came to our lack of a formal relationship. We had sold the mobile home after living there three to four years and bought a house together, but we still weren't married. In my mind, either we were going to get married or we were going to break up (at least, that's what I said—whether or not I'd actually make good on that threat, we'll never know). I was 25-years-old by this point in time. Tyson was 30. I mean, the reality was we already were a *real* family. And I wanted a *real* relationship to go along with it in the form of marriage. It was either that or a hard goodbye. Thankfully, Tyson didn't want to walk away from me any more than I wanted to walk away from him. On June 12, 2004—six years from our first official date at Ruby Tuesday's—we got married. It was a small wedding with mostly just Tyson's family and our close friends. Dakota was four and Austin was three.

I wore my mother's wedding dress, the one she wore on the day that she married my daddy. It was made of white lace and had a long train. Tyson wore a black tux with a white shirt and white bow tie. We were a couple with no real budget to speak of, so it was a small affair, but one filled with love. The colors for our wedding were red and white, with a yellow accent in our wedding flowers. I was truly happy. Tyson was everything I ever wanted in a man. He was my everything. And now he was my husband. We were a real married couple with a beautiful family.

About three years later, in 2007, Ty decided to start trade classes to become a journeyman doing electrical work. He had to attend four years of classes and work 8,000 hours in the field to earn that designation. In 2011, he became a Journeyman. The pay raise associated with that position working for the union definitely helped to provide a better living for our family. And that's exactly what we were: a family. I *finally* ended up attending college at Delta College to obtain my early education accreditation in 2013. It was a long time coming, but I did it!

Before we close this chapter, I should probably take a minute to tell you that while Tyson obviously knew about what had happened in my past, he didn't know much beyond the fact that my family was murdered in our home when I was just a kid, at nine-years-old. It's something I never talked about with anyone. Tyson would not know the details of my past until he would one day read the pages of this book.

For better or for worse. In sickness and in health. Until death do us part . . .

JESSI

AGE 38

Present Day–2018

I'm not sure when the numbers first became important to me, but they did, and it happened fairly early on. The dates began to serve as formal reminders of what I'd lost. Most people only have one set of numbers to contend with for a lost loved one: the date the person was born and the date on which the person died. But for me, the dates have become intertwined in a twisted new form of normalcy.

Let's look at it this way:

There are 365 days in a year.

My dad died on January 2nd. (Mark that date down on the calendar.)

He was born on February 3rd. (Mark that date down on the calendar.)

It's been 29 years, since my mom and little sisters died on April 29th. (Mark that date on the calendar.)

Their funeral was on May 3rd. (Mark that date down on the calendar.)

My mom's birthday is July 1st. (Mark that date down on the calendar.)

Janel's birthday is August 22nd. (Mark that date down on the calendar.)

Jolene's birthday is July 11th. (Mark that date down on the calendar.)

I was born on June 20th. (Mark that date down with the other holidays.)

Then there were the "special" markers:

New Year's Eve of every year. (One more year without them.)

Valentine's Day of every year. (One more year without them.)

Easter of every year. (One more year without them.)

July 4th of every year. (One more year without them.)

Halloween of every year. (One more year without them.)

Thanksgiving of every year. (One more year without them.)

Christmas of every year. (One more year without them.)

See where I'm going with this? The reminders were never-ending. The numbers are relentless, and they find me, wherever I am. Over and over again. Year after year.

I've lived through 29 Easters, 29 Thanksgivings, and 29 Christmases without the family members I loved most, and lost. For me, all of the dates became perpetual reminders that cast me into a place of internal suffering, even when I was strong. It's hard to explain to other people. You have to mark at least 15 dates of darkness down on the calendar to even step into the arena.

I also lived through not only all these dates 29 times, but a total of 10,585 days. That's 254,040 hours without my dad, mom, and sisters. More than 15 million minutes without my family. I won't even tell you the number of seconds. It may seem ridiculous to count time in this way, but when you lose a dear loved one, especially as a young child, you no longer count in weeks, months, and years. You begin to count in hours, minutes, and seconds. Each hour without him. Each minute you'll never talk to her again. Each second you feel so alone.

Normal people don't count seconds. But what if your loved one was clinging to life in the ICU and you heard a "Code Blue" ring out over the intercom, and the medical personnel goes flying by—how long is a second then? When a baby is born and there is no cry that fills the air, how long does that second last? There are times when the only thing appropriate to count are the seconds.

The days I was actually counting the seconds were my darkest. It's so much time. It takes so long. It's overwhelming to realize how long your life will be when you find yourself counting seconds. All the seconds, minutes, and hours I've cried my eyes to a freakish shade of red, or that I've been so damn mad because Janel should be here with me, or that I've wondered why I had to be here alone.

My family members will each live on in my heart every day. But they will also each continue to visit me in the form of these numeric reminders throughout the year. On the bad days, they will remind me in the form of seconds, minutes, and hours spent without them. With 60 seconds to a minute, an hour can feel more like a year.

The numbers don't lie.

And they don't stop coming either.

JESSI

AGE 23

The Cold Case Team

2002

O ne day in 2002, I received a knock on the door to my mobile home. When I pulled it open, I was greeted by two detectives who showed me their badges and told me that they were part of a cold case team that worked to solve old cases. My first thought was, "Holy crap, it's been a long time. What could they possibly be here to tell me?" In a way, I was obviously happy to see them, but still kind of in shock because so much time had passed. It had been nearly 13 years since the murders by that point. It dredged up some old feelings. Feelings I'd spent years of my life avoiding or attempting to bury deep inside myself. The detectives standing on my front porch knocking on my front door brought it all back.

I had lived the 13 years before that believing Bob had killed my family and then turned the gun on himself. It's what I had pieced together in my own child's mind. As a minor, I was pretty much off-limits to the police and detectives at the time the murders occurred. They did interview me at the park once at a picnic table with Ed 2. I remember that. But what could I really tell them at age nine? They had to soft-pedal anything they spoke about or asked me. And the family members I'd lived with refused to even speak the names of my dead relatives, much less talk about the horror that transpired in our house that day. I don't think they just spared me from it, they wanted to spare themselves from it. I think they were hiding and pretending as much as I was. So, the only version of events I had was the one I had created in my nine-year-old mind. But here I stood, a 23-year-old woman, with a cold case team on her front porch talking to me about the things I'd never been told. It was shocking, to say the least. I wanted to know the details. Yet part of me was scared to hear them. It was kind of like driving by a catastrophic car accident on the highway. You don't want to look at it or hear about what happened, yet you can't turn away from the mangled metal and lives ripped apart or lost. That's the way it was for me. I straddled the line between those emotions like a thin balance beam, worried that a fall was inevitable.

The two detectives and I took a seat in my living room. One of the first questions one of them asked was, "Let me ask you one question: Who do you think killed your family?" My immediate reply was, "I think Bob did it. That he killed them and then offed himself." The detective followed that with, "Well, what if I told you I could prove to you that it wasn't Bob that did it; that it's not physically possible. I could prove it to you by showing you these pictures I have with me. If I can prove to you that Bob couldn't possibly be the one who did this—that he couldn't be the one who committed this crime—*then* who do you think did it?"

With no hesitation, his name left my lips: "Jeff. If it wasn't Bob, then it had to be Jeff." I said it with confidence. I said it with conviction. Hell, based on my past personal history with Jeff, it wasn't a stretch at all. It was logical. He terrorized me on a regular basis. He made verbal threats against my sisters to get me to comply with his sadistically twisted games. The detective nodded his head. "That's exactly right," he said. He went on to say that the original detectives had believed it was him all along, but they weren't certain there was enough evidence to bring it to trial without the murder weapon. They still hadn't found the rifle all these years later, but here they were in my living room to tell me they were arresting my former stepbrother for the murders of my family.

They were here to finally bring him to justice. That's a big word: JUSTICE. It had been 13 years—13 long, damn years—but in my mind, my family's killer still deserved to be held accountable for the atrocities committed on April 29, 1989. For killing people who didn't deserve to die the horrible way that they did. You bet I was interested in obtaining that small semblance of justice. And after they proved to me, through pictures and evidence, that my internally forged assumptions from childhood couldn't have possibly played out, I knew it was Jeff. Bob couldn't have shot himself the way he did. And Bob was believed to be the first person shot that day. In the chest and again in the throat and face. Bob wasn't the killer. His son was.

They left a business card and said they would be in touch. There aren't enough years in a lifetime to keep a victim from wanting to obtain justice for those who were murdered. Thirteen years, 40 years, 100 years, no matter how many years could have passed, a killer had not yet been held accountable for this horrific crime, the one that annihilated my childhood and stripped me of the life I was supposed to have. Justice wouldn't bring them back. It wouldn't fix anything, not really. But it sure as hell would make the person who pulled that trigger pay the price for the execution of his own family. Jeff didn't deserve to just carry the atrocities in his mind. He deserved to carry them behind prison bars.

Whether they would be able to convict my former stepbrother, Jeff Pelley, after 13 long years on a heap of circumstantial evidence and no murder weapon, was yet to be determined. I was happy they were working to obtain justice for my family, no matter what came of it . . . or didn't.

JESSI

AGE 23

2001–2002

*W*hen I was 23, I landed a job working at the Holiday Inn. That's where I worked at the time the cold case detectives knocked on my door. It was my job to clean the common areas of the hotel: the lobby, convention center, bar, and other places. It was a bullshit job, but I didn't mind it, and it helped to pay the bills. I liked the cleaning. It allowed me to indulge my semi-neurotic tendencies for doing things a certain way—the only way it would be done properly—my way.

At this point in my life, I was pretty much in my "I don't give a shit" stage. Although we'd been together for years, Tyson and I fought all the time. Let's just say the transition from two partiers to a family unit did not go smoothly in the early years. To say I was busy, as the mother of a three-year-old and a two-year-old, was missing my reality by twelve football fields and twenty miles. I kind of sunk into home life, but Ty had a harder time making the adjustment from Mr. Life-of-the-Party to nights on the couch, at home, sans drinks and friends. We fought a lot back then. And by a lot, I mean pretty much every single day. We were engaged in those damn circular arguments couples have. It sucked, for both of us.

In those days, Ty chose his friends over me. Repeatedly. It was an ongoing battle for me to try to get him to stay home or leave a friend's house or yet another party to come home. My God I loved that man, but at the same time, his partying ways drove me freaking crazy and made me miserable.

Tyson was the only person I felt I always had. When our relationship seemed to be teetering on the brink of implosion, I didn't deal well with it at all emotionally. Losing Ty would mean losing everything. The one person who knew me. The one person who loved me. The one person to whom I felt like I belonged. But we were two young people, two young parents, and two former hard-core party people trying to find our way toward some sense of a stable home life and domesticated normalcy. I felt emotionally off-kilter. Ty would agitate and piss me off. Yet, I was drawn to him. I felt keyed up, like I had no control over the way things were going in our relationship and life. I felt like my whole world could shift out from under me in one second, flat.

Ty picked his friends and parties over me time and time again. I would get pissed and refuse to talk to or acknowledge him for hours or days on end. At one point, I told him there was a guy at work who I thought "was really nice and I might like . . ." I was a pretty open person, as far as sharing my true feelings went. Why bother hiding the truth? Let's just say that didn't sit well with Ty. At all. He seemed to realize he could lose me if he didn't change his ways. Oh, he'd still go out, but then he'd try to make it up to me by cooking dinner and bringing it to me at work. I would simply scoff at him and say, "I don't know why you brought that, I don't even want it." I was just hurt. Angry. I wasn't looking for a plate of chicken Alfredo, what I really wanted was more of his time and attention. For him to get his shit together and stay home with me and the kids, instead of living it up with other people.

During the same time, I was going through those dramatic fights with Ty, the cold case team had knocked on my door. So, now I knew Jeff had killed my family. I knew they were going to arrest him when they left my house. What I didn't know was how things would turn out and whether he would actually be convicted. It's like the past crept back up on me and was, again, a part of my conscious reality.

I began to lose significant gaps of time. But I wasn't throwing back Bacardi wine coolers or taking recreational drugs at the times this was happening. And it wasn't sleep deprivation either, despite the fact that I was a young mom running on a lack of sleep—persistent insomnia my constant companion, even when I was exhausted—with two little people clinging to my legs, downing cans of Dr Pepper as jet fuel to make it through the work day. After losing a period of time, I would come to and realize I was at work, at the Holiday Inn, but I had absolutely no idea how in the hell I got there. It was like I was still awake, but on autopilot. I was still functioning physically and acting normally, by the accounts of those around me, but I wasn't checked in, mentally. It was truly bizarre.

These memory gaps occurred on a regular basis while I worked at the hotel, so much so, that it became a running joke amongst me and my coworkers. "Well, it looks like Jessi spaced out again!" "She musta did that thing again where she checks out!" I would approach them with what *had* to seem like *entirely ridiculous questions*, such as, "Hey, do you know how I got here today?" or "Did I just get here?" or "Do you know how long I've been here?" You can triple the awkwardness when the person to whom you are directing these types of questions actually happens to be the individual who *drove you* to work that day or you are informed that you've only been at the place where you now are for an hour. How could you forget that? Really? You rode with her. You worked for an hour already. Weird. I felt like a time-jumping freak who was losing her grip on reality. My coworkers found this type of thing amusing and simply chalked it up as me being ditzy. This occurred on at least ten separate occasions during my stint of employment at the hotel.

My blackouts also crept into my home life. I would wake up and realize I was at home. I guess you could say in these moments, I became aware of my surroundings and thought to myself, "How in the hell did I get here?" I had no memory of what had transpired prior to my moment of mental awakening. This definitely made my days and weeks interesting. I had no idea what had transpired or what I had discussed, done, participated in, or accomplished, much less with whom or when, or how long I'd been in the place in which I found myself standing. It's the only time this had ever happened to me. Perhaps I am just ditzy. Maybe I am losing my mind. But perhaps I'm just one messed up person, with a messed up past, who does weird stuff for which there is no reasonable explanation.

JESSI

AGE 24

2003

$\mathcal{A}$fter quitting my cleaning gig at the hotel, I worked at several different jobs. Hell, at one point, I even worked at McDonald's for a few months. That job totally sucked. I then cleaned offices and banks in the evenings for a cleaning company for a while. And in 2003, I landed a job working at another KinderCare taking care of children ranging in age from birth to twelve. I was 24-years old-at the time. Based upon my past experience at that last childcare center, I was slightly apprehensive, given what I had witnessed with that little boy. I had realized since then that the owner of a daycare facility's attitude was likely a determining factor for what would be tolerated and allowed to occur.

I immediately clicked with the lady who was to be my new boss. We'll refer to her as "Boss Lady." Little did I know that over time, Boss Lady would become one of my close friends.

At the new center, I once again found that I loved working with the children. I thrived in the structured environment. I could clean the way I wanted to. I could plan the day and run it as I deemed fit, so long as I complied with the safety guidelines, facility standards, and all the rules. If my quirky soul insisted a child's piece of artwork needed to have five pieces of tape on the back, placed precisely so, that's how it was done. (Yes, I would actually pull the pieces of artwork back from the wall which were hung by other teachers to check the tape situation and would neurotically redo them, if they failed to meet Jessi's five-pieces-of-tape-rule. Crazy, I know. But it's true. I fixed them every single time.)

Working with young children filled me up. It gave me something my soul desperately craved. I could love kids and they would love me back. They needed me as much as I needed their constant presence in my life. I loved their innocence. The way they viewed the world. How they hadn't yet learned everything they one day would and weren't encumbered with all of the issues, difficulties, and decisions in life they one day would face. They were vibrant, full of energy, playful, engaging, and happy—well, at least for the most part—and so precious, curious, fun, honest, and kind. They were little beings of laughter, love, and light. Nothing seemed to diminish that light. I absolutely loved it. My time spent at work wore me out some days, but it never felt like work. I had the type of job most people never find: one I loved.

Over time, the children I became closest to were the difficult children. The ones with special needs, emotional issues, developmental delays, behavioral issues, or other problems. The kids most grown-ups would likely view as being out of control or bad. To me, they were not bad. And they weren't out of control, although it certainly seemed that way to any adults around them. They were simply children who were doing the best they could. In so many ways, I felt as though I *was* them. I had made bad choices. I had meltdowns. I had done things I shouldn't have done. (Remember that time I threw myself down on the grass, in a dress, on the church lawn proclaiming I wanted to die? Yep. Stuff like that.) I could identify and relate on a level that most people couldn't.

These challenging children were little people to whom I could relate on a deep psychological and emotional level. I saw their difficulties. Their deficits and strife. I saw their personal burdens, their struggles, their frustrations. I felt their pain. I knew, regardless of a particular child's issues, they were issues beyond that child's control. And all that anger, rage, throwing of items, crying and screaming, and flailing fits of arms and legs were an indication that in that moment, the child was feeling incredibly frustrated, sad, misunderstood, or angry.

"Miss Jessi" became the one you called to the room for the assist, when a child was out of control, no matter who the child, what the issue, or where the classroom was in the building. I was the first string. The one you called in to be the fixer. I was there any and every time I was ever asked. I always will be. It's precisely where I want to be, in that moment, with that child. Trying to help him or her to get back with the rest of us, back in the moment, into a calmer reality, out of the fit of rage or item-throwing tantrum, back to a calm and happy space. When other teachers may have been somewhat intimidated by those troubled kids, I was bold and fearless. When other teachers, quite credibly, feared getting punched in the face or kicked in the stomach by a child throwing an epic tantrum, I was the one who would make my way beyond that invisible wall or rage to greet the child, as he or she really was, to give him or her—that hurting little human being—the hug I realized he or she so desperately wanted and needed, even if they didn't realize they did.

I knew exactly what that felt like. To rage. To be frustrated. To feel like no one understood you. To feel like no one cared enough to find a way *to* you: the real you, not the raging you. I would *never* allow any child in my presence to ever feel the way I had, or allow them to be responded to without the compassion, understanding, kindness, and love they so desperately needed and deserved. It wasn't just my job, it became my calling and a bit of a personal mission. One day, in a fit of rage, a little boy stomped on one of my feet (that already had a hairline fracture) so hard, I had to wear one of those stupid, cumbersome leg boots. Over time, that same foot would be stomped on and reinjured by two other children in the throes of anger and pent up frustration in the years that would follow.

I know now why I had to get *to them*—to those children—*why* I had to hug them, why I had to get in there, past that invisible wall of rage, into the depths of the child's emotional pain to help him to trudge back out the other side of it. I wasn't just saving that child. I was saving myself, my past self. What I was saving was another future Jessica.

Once I got the child somewhat calmed down, I would always hug him or her and hold them for as long as they needed me to. That's what they needed in that moment. And I would say all the things I knew he or she needed to hear: those things that I never did hear, at least not in a way that mattered to me. "Calm down. It's okay. You aren't bad. You just made a not-so-good choice. It's okay. You get to make new choices from now on. You can be better. It's okay. It's going to be okay. I'm here for you. I'm right here with you. You are a good person. I'm not going anywhere. I love you and everything is going to be okay." Beneath those words laid my unspoken promise: "You'll never have to feel the way I felt, because I'll say what you need to hear." Every single time. Always.

I've now worked with Boss Lady at one of the two KinderCare centers she owns for the past 14 years. I still love it as much now as I did when I first started. I was promoted to Assistant Director. I continue to gravitate toward the lost, broken, or challenging children. I still thrive on the routine of the place. I am still routinely called in as the fixer. And yes, I still put five pieces of tape on every piece of art, placed precisely so, every single freaking time.

THE ARREST

August 10, 2002

On August 10, 2002, when I was 23-years-old, Jeff Pelley was arrested at the airport, after stepping off a plane in Los Angeles on his way home from a business trip to Australia. He was 31-years-old and working for IBM at the time. I have no idea what he did there, but it appeared he had created a successful life for himself. He was living in Florida with his wife—whom he'd married, got divorced from, and remarried again—and their son. That little boy's world was going to implode. I took absolutely no solace in that. It broke my heart. I knew what it would be like for him to lose someone as I did. But a person can't just execute an entire family and get away with it.

Two days later, on August 12, 2002, a headline on the front page of the *South Bend Tribune* read, "PELLEY ARRESTED; SON HELD IN 1989 SLAYING OF FAMILY." The slaying of my family. The slaying of *his own* family. It's hard to put into words what it's like to put those two sentences next to each other, whether it's in my mind or on the page of a book. Jeff killed his own father. He killed my mom and my two precious little sisters. And here he was, 13 years later, finally being arrested. He was charged with four counts of murder and extradited to Indiana to face the charges.

They had never found the murder weapon, a 20-gauge Mossburg 500 pump-action shotgun. (Remember that gun of Bob's that was missing from the gun rack that held a bow above our parents' bed?) The prosecutor planned to bring this case to a jury based on strictly circumstantial evidence. There were no fingerprints. (After all, Jeff lived at the crime scene, the parsonage was his home.) There was no DNA evidence. (The last outfit Jeff was seen wearing was found inside the washing machine, so it was inconclusive to luminol testing, indicating either the presence of laundry detergent or blood. No one could say which it was.) There were no eye witnesses to the crime. What the prosecution had was a timeline for when the murders had occurred. It was a 45-minute window. One that ended with every curtain being drawn shut, every window closed, and every door locked. No sign of forced entry. Four people soaked in blood after being brutally executed in their own home.

In my eyes, Jeff had gotten away with what amounted to a horrific execution for too long. The fact that he'd gotten married and worked at a job in corporate America meant *nothing* to me. It simply meant that a killer had managed to pull his life somewhat together after destroying my life.

It was time for Jeff Pelley to face a jury of his peers for the crimes he committed all those years ago. I hoped they would find him guilty. You bet I did. I hoped they would take his freedom away from him, the same way he took everyone in my life away from me. Swiftly. And without regret.

THE TRIAL

July 12, 2006–July 21, 2006
17 years after the murders

My family's case finally made it to trial in the summer of 2006. I was now 27-years-old. By this point, 17 years had passed since my family was murdered. Seventeen arduously long years. Six thousand two hundred and five days without them. That was the tally. Not that anyone else was counting the days as I felt them. Although Jeff probably was counting the number of days he'd spent in jail by the time his trial rolled around—four years— but I digress.

The detectives drove all the way from Indiana, where the trial was to take place, to where I lived in Michigan, to pick me up the morning I was scheduled to testify. It was a little over a five-hour drive. Plenty of time to think, wonder, and worry about what was going to take place later that day. I was nervous, but ready for closure. Questions floated through my mind: "How will I feel when I see him again?" "Will I cry?" "Will I freak out?" "What's this going to be like?" I wasn't sure what to expect at a trial. The detectives said what they could to try to put my mind at ease, but it was something I'd never done before. And it was a big deal. It made me nervous knowing I'd have to walk up there to the stand, in front of what would likely be a room full of people, several attorneys, a jury, and a judge, to testify in front of all of them about the worst part of my life. But the time for justice had come. I was prepared to take the stand, answer the questions honestly and to the best of my ability, and to tell the jury everything I remembered from 1989, nervous or not.

Once we arrived at the courthouse, they took me to an office to wait in a more private area. The anticipation of this monumental event hit me full-force. My stomach was flip-flopping, my heart beating fast, my mind racing, and I broke out in a cold sweat.

A little while later, I was moved to wait in a hallway of the courthouse until it was my turn. There, I felt completely out of place. Others, random strangers, made me feel as though I didn't belong there. Here I was, the sole survivor of the Huber clan, and I didn't feel like I fucking belonged at my own family's trial. How messed up is that? You may find yourself wondering why that is. For starters, it probably had a lot to do with the fact that no one even knew who I was, even by name, or identity. A man approached and asked, "Did you know them?" Meaning, did I know my own fucking family. The answer to that question is, unequivocally, yes. I loved them. I missed them every single day.

People I didn't know would approach to ask questions like, "Who are you?" A question to which I would reply, "I'm a sister, to the ones who died." This was met with the response, "What . . . you're a sister? I didn't know anyone had survived. I thought they were all dead." Well, there I stood, a grown woman with hot pink hair. I was Jessica Pelley, in the courthouse, at my family's trial, feeling like I didn't belong. Realizing people didn't even know I existed. They didn't know I had even survived, that I was the only Huber girl left. It's not that I expected anyone to recognize me by sight, but even after they heard my name or was told I was "a sister" to that family, it still seemed to be completely new information to them.

As nerve-wracking as it was to be there and feel like people never even knew you existed, there was no place on this earth I would rather have been in that moment. It was time for Jeff to finally face his fate.

I was ready to walk my ass into that courtroom to look Jeff straight in the eyes. To answer every question asked of me and finally get some sense of closure. Some may think I had it out for Jeff, but I don't think that's accurate. I simply wanted him to face up to what he had done, for him to look me in the eyes, and to *see me*. To acknowledge what he did to my family and what he had done to my life. What I wanted was that moment of acknowledgment.

I know what you did, and so do you. We're both here today and you're sitting exactly where you need to be in this courtroom, as am I. More than anything, I wanted me and Jeff to share that unspoken moment of acknowledgment for all that had transpired in our lives.

You will see me. You will all see me now. You will know I exist. You will know that I lived through this horrific event because I was away at a sleepover. But I still exist. I'm still here. I've been here all along. I've lived every single day without them. Suffering their loss. Longing for the life I could have had, but not for what happened. I'm here today to testify. For the first time in seventeen years: You. Will. See. Me.

I nervously approached the stand. I agreed to tell the truth, the whole truth, and nothing but the truth, so help me God. I meant it. I took a seat. And the questions began.

DIRECT EXAMINATION OF JESSICA BY THE PROSECUTOR, MR. SCHAFFER:

Q. Ma'am, would you state your name for the record and please spell your last name for the court reporter, please.

A. Jessica Toronjo.

Q. Would you spell that?

A. T-o-r-o-n-j-o.

Q. You go by Jessie (sic)? *{This spelling error appears in the court's actual transcript.}*

A. Yes.

Q. Jessie (sic), do you live here in St. Joseph County?

A. No.

Q. Jessica, in 1989, did you live here in St. Joseph County?

A. Yes.

Q. (sic) Was your last name back then?

A. Pelley.

Q. Jessica Pelley?

A.   Uh-huh.

Q.   And Robert and Dawn was your stepfather and mother, correct?

A.   Yes.

Q.   Jessie (sic), were you home the weekend of April 29th and 30th?

A.   No.

Q.   When was the last time you were in the home?

A.   I was home that Friday.

Q.   April 28th?

A.   Yes.

Q.   Do you recall what time you left the home?

A.   I didn't really see what time it was. It was before dark but after dinner.

Q.   Where did you go for the weekend?

A.   I went to a friend's house.

Q.   How far away from your home?

A.   It took about ten minutes to get there.

Q.   Do you remember who it was?

A.   I think her name was ▇▇▇▇▇▇ I don't remember her last name.

Q.   What time during the day did you decide to go to her house?

A.   It was earlier, probably early afternoon.

Q.   Were you staying there—were you the only family member going over there?

A.   Actually (sic) it was supposed to be my sister Janel and I.

Q.   Did Janel go with you?

A.   No.

Q.   And did you make an inquiry before you left that Janel could go again?

A.   Yeah. I asked my mother if she could still go and she told me that she couldn't.

Q. When you made the inquiry with your mother, where were you at?

A. In her bedroom.

Q. Is there anything on the walls in your mother's bedroom that you remember?

A. Yeah, they had a gun rack. It was made of wood. And he would keep his gun and his bow and arrow up there.

Q. Did Bob use guns and hunt?

A. Yes.

Q. Did Jeff use guns and hunt?

A. Yes.

Q. Did they have a lot of guns?

A. I just remember the one, and then Jeff had a BB gun. I don't remember a lot of other guns.

Q. That day, April 28th, when you were in your mother's bedroom, was there a gun in the gun rack?

A. Yes.

Q. Jessie (sic), I will show you what has already been entered as State's Exhibit 33, do you recognize that?

A. Yeah.

Q. Is that the way it looked when you saw it?

A. Yes.

Q. Did it have a gun, or was it empty like that?

A. No, there was a gun.

Q. There was a gun in it when you left on Friday?

A. (Witness nods head).

Q. When was the next time you were in the home?

A. I wasn't.

Q. Never went back to the home?

MR. SCHAFFER: No other questions, Your Honor.
THE COURT: Counsel.

CROSS-EXAMINATION BY THE DEFENSE ATTORNEY,
MR. BAUM:

Q. May I call you Jessie (sic) also?

A. Yes.

Q. Jessie (sic), you know Jacque Pelley?

A. Yes.

Q. And what is her relationship to you?

A. Stepsister.

Q. She's Jeff's full sister?

A. Yes.

Q. From his father—his father's first marriage, from Bob's first marriage?

A. Yes.

Q. And you know Jeff and Jacque's mother passed away and thereafter Bob, Reverend Bob married your mother?

A. Yes.

Q. And you were all living as a family at the parsonage adjacent to the church?

A. Yes.

Q. How old were you in 1989?

A. I would have been ten in June.

Q. So at the time of this incident you were nine, almost ten?

A. Yes.

Q. Do you recall a time sometime before April of '89—let me withdraw that if I may.

Q. Do you know Thomas Keb?

A. The name sounds familiar. I couldn't tell you who it was.

Q. Do you remember a time before April of '89 when someone, perhaps Thomas Keb, came over and took some guns that Bob—Reverend Bob gave him out of the house?

A. No, I do not remember that.

Q. How old was Jacque at the time when you were nine, almost ten, how much older was Jacque?

A. I think she was fourteen.

Q. Shortly after this incident were you—did you talk to an investigator? I know you were young. Do you remember a Detective Botich?

A. I remember being at a park, but I don't remember faces.

Q. Or names?

A. No.

Q. At some time very soon after the incident do you remember being asked if you knew where Jacque was, where the police could find Jacque to tell her about what had happened?

A. I don't remember.

Q. You don't remember telling some officers who were trying to locate Jacque that she was at Huntington College at a seminar?

A. I don't remember.

Q. Do you remember telling any officers that Jeff was at Great America?

A. Yes, I do remember that.

Q. And was that on Sunday morning?

A. I didn't get there until I think Sunday afternoon. My friend's mom had dropped me. We were actually going there to be dropped off.

Q. This was before Jeff had been brought back to South Bend?

A. Yes.

Q. And some police officers wanted to know if you knew where Jeff was, right?

A. Yeah.

Q. And you did, you knew Jeff was at Great America?

A. That's what I had been told, yes.

Q. When have (sic) you been told that Jeff was at Great America?

A.   Before I left.

Q.   On?

A.   Friday.

Q.   That he was going to be going to Great America?

A.   Yeah, that he was going to be there.

Q.   Who told you that?

A.   I think it was my mother.

      MR. BAUM: Thank you, Jessie (sic). I have nothing further.

      MR. SCHAFFER: Nothing else.

I stepped down and made my way back into the hallway of the courthouse. I was glad it was over. My time in the courtroom went more quickly than I thought it would.

AUTHOR'S NOTE

The trial spanned ten days and over 40 witnesses were called. There is no way we could share everything that transpired in the courtroom. Jeff Pelley did not testify at his own trial. In an effort to share sufficient evidence, as well as the defense's theories, we are including summaries of the attorneys' closing statements during the trial, along with some direct quotes to summarize the evidence presented to the jury at trial.

As a witness in the case, Jessi was called to the stand, but she was not aware of any of the testimony presented at trial, aside from her own.

From an authenticity standpoint, I felt it important to share that while it is clear from Jessi's trial testimony that she apparently knew The Nameless Girl's first name when she took the stand at Jeff's trial in 2006, she *cannot* recall it now. While I am no psychologist, it is my belief that she has re-repressed this memory in the years that followed her testimony, in much the same way she has blocked so many pieces of her painful past. To maintain the integrity of her story, I am not going to reveal to Jessi what

The Nameless Girl's name actually is, until we publish her story. We wrote this book true to Jessi's life, as she lived it. And for one million dollars today, she could not, for the life of her, recall the name or any other details about her former friend.

PROSECUTOR SCHAEFFER: "This case comes down to one thing; that 20 minutes from 5 o'clock to 5:20. Because the most important thing from this stand what you didn't hear the last ten days, you didn't hear one person who saw the Pelleys alive after 5:15. And there was only one person that was in the house before 5:15, he sits right there. Only he knows."

" . . . When you go back in that jury room think about this case hard, look at the pictures. It's not a quick decision but it's got to be a thorough decision. Examine those pictures very, very closely and remember what happened to those little girls in the basement. Imagine what those little girls went through and what the family endured and they scream to you for justice . . ."

For three days the jury deliberated. With each vote taken over the course of the first two days, they came closer to reaching a consensus.

Robert "Jeffrey" Pelley was found GUILTY on four counts of murder.

The Sentencing

October 17, 2006

On October 17, 2006, approximately three months after the jury's guilty verdict, a judge sentenced Jeff Pelley to serve 160 years in prison for murdering my family—40 years for each life he took—to be served consecutively.

Justice had been served a little over seventeen years later. It certainly beat the alternative. He'd experienced enough of that—freedom, happiness, a life working at IBM and business trips, a family, a home, all the normal things people have. But over the years he carried inside him one significant thing most other people do not ever have to carry, the guilt associated with murdering his own family, and mine. I can only hope the weight of it was as heavy, oppressive, and agonizing as my loss.

He'd lived thirteen years of his life a free man, prior to his arrest in 2002. That's thirteen years of freedom I never had. I was consumed by people and places that no longer existed on earth, but only within the confines of my mind. I remained shackled to my tragic past. Hell, I didn't need bars. I had memories and gaping holes to remind me every day of what I'd lost.

One hundred and sixty years behind bars sounded just fine to me. I would be here to live another 40 years of my life without each of them—God willing, of course—my mom, Janel, and little Jolene.

Let's be real. *My* sentence wasn't 160 years, *it was life*.

THE APPEAL

The Indiana Court of Appeals, 2008
19 years after the murders

Jeff's lawyers had raised six appealable issues, which could potentially overturn his convictions at the trial court level, and on April 8, 2008, an opinion was *finally* handed down by the appellate court, nearly two years after Jeff's conviction. The appellate court's opinion read:

"Robert Jeffrey Pelley appeals his convictions for the four counts of murder. Pelley raises three issues, which we revise and restate as:

I. Whether the trial court abused its discretion by denying Pelley's motion to dismiss, which requested discharge based upon Ind. Criminal Rule 4(C);

II. Whether the trial court erred by denying Pelley's petition to appoint a special prosecutor;

III. Whether the trial court committed fundamental error by admitting hearsay statements of a victim;

IV. Whether the trial court abused its discretion by excluding Pelley's evidence that someone else may have committed the offenses;

V. Whether the trial court abused its discretion by excluding evidence regarding the delay in bringing charges against Pelley; and

VI. Whether the evidence is sufficient to sustain Pelley's convictions.

Because we find the first issue dispositive [relating to or bringing about the settlement of an issue], we need not address the remaining issues. We reverse and remand."

"Reverse and remand." Two monumentally significant words for all involved. In other words, the appellate court agreed that Jeff's convictions should be overturned, based upon the first issue set forth above—"whether the trial court abused its discretion by denying Pelley's motion to dismiss" based upon the time clock issue and right to a speedy trial issue he raised.

Jeff's arrest had occurred in 2002 and he did not face trial until 2006: he spent a period of four years behind bars. The State and defense attorneys had spent a significant amount of time fighting over the Pelleys' counseling records, including Jeff's individual counseling records, from their counseling sessions prior to the murders. The State fought to obtain them. Jeff's attorneys fought to block the family's records as a whole based upon privilege (with Bob and Dawn being deceased) as well as Jeff's individual records. It was a lengthy battle. And after the State finally did obtain them, the parties fought about whether they should be introduced at trial. Ultimately, the trial court did not allow the counseling records in at trial. The legal battles over the records drew on for years, resulting in the State filing an interlocutory appeal (an appeal based on an evidentiary ruling, which meant the case was stayed, or frozen, until the final ruling on that interlocutory appeal). And all the while, Jeff sat in jail. That was his argument regarding the time clock and speedy trial. The delay caused by obtaining and arguing about counseling records and their admissibility at trial. Granted, Jeff could have sped up the process by agreeing to waive the privilege to his own records, but did not do so. That was his right. And so the legal battle had continued.

The opinion went on to state:

"The relevant facts follow. In April 1989, seventeen-year-old Pelley lived in Lakeville, Indiana, with his father, Robert Pelley ("Bob"), his stepmother, Dawn, his fourteen-year-old sister, Jacque, and his three stepsisters, nine-year-old Jessica, eight-year-old Janel, and six-year-old Jolene. Bob was the minister of the Olive Branch Church, and the family lived in the parsonage next door to the church.

"On Sunday, April 30, 1989, the Pelley family did not appear for church services, and parishioners noticed that the Pelleys' vehicles were in the driveway, the doors to the house were locked, and the blinds and curtains were drawn. Parishioners obtained a key to the house and found Bob, Dawn, Janel, and Jolene dead from shotgun wounds. Officers located Jessica and Jacque, who had spent the night with friends, and Pelley, who had attended his senior prom on Saturday night, had spent Saturday night with friends, and had gone to Great America amusement park in Illinois with friends on Sunday.

"Although Pelley was questioned regarding the murders, the State did not charge him until August 7, 2002. At that time, the State charged Pelley with four counts of murder. Pelley was arrested on August 10, 2002 . . .

"We conclude that Pelley was not responsible for the delay caused by the interlocutory appeal. In so concluding, we find the Indiana Supreme Court's comments Huffman fitting here,

This case confronts this Court with an extremely unpleasant but compelling responsibility. We realized that the defendant was ultimately convicted following an arduous jury trial. Such cases extract an enormous personal toll from the witnesses, jurors, and others participating. Resulting costs are significant and burden our taxpayers, and the time devoted to such trials and subsequent proceedings operate to delay the resolution of other pending controversies. It is with extreme reluctance that we must consider setting aside the defendant's conviction, thus rendering futile the results of the jury trial which found the defendant guilty beyond a reasonable doubt.

502 N.E.2d at 908. The one-year period under Rule 4(C) had already expired when Pelley agreed to the July 2006 trial date during the October 2005 pretrial conference. Pelley had no duty to object at that time, and his January 2006 motion to dismiss was timely. The trial court abused its discretion by denying Pelley's motion to dismiss . . .

"For the foregoing reasons, we reverse the trial court's denial of Pelley's motion to dismiss, which requested discharge under Ind. Criminal Rule 4(C), and remand to the trial court with instructions to grant Pelley's motion to dismiss.

"Reversed and remanded."

The Honorable Judge J. Friedlander dissented, meaning he disagreed with the Majority's conclusion that the trial court should have granted Pelley's motion to dismiss, stating in his dissenting opinion in pertinent part:

"First, the facts of this case are unique and not likely to recur with any frequency. Second, there is no suggestion here that the State could have done anything to speed up the process of determining the legality of its request to discover the FCC {counseling records} records, short of abandoning it. Third, and most significantly, the delay here is attributable to the judicial process itself, i.e., the movement of cases through the appellate courts, which is entirely beyond the litigants' control in precisely the same way that a congested trial court calendar is beyond their control. Thus, I believe the time necessary to pursue an interlocutory appeal to its conclusion may be characterized as an 'emergency' or caused by court 'congestion' within the meaning of Crim. R. 4(C) so as to justify a continuance of the trial date for a reasonable time beyond the one-year limit. In view of the time it takes an appeal to wend

{the word used} its way through the appellate process, to hold otherwise could and in many cases would effectively deny the State the option of pursuing an interlocutory appeal of an unfavorable evidentiary ruling.

"I would affirm the trial court's ruling on this motion."

This is a lot of legal words to say that the Indiana Court of Appeals sided with Jeff Pelley's legal arguments and agreed that his convictions should be overturned, based upon that decision.

Reversed.

Remanded.

Two "r" words and a lot of legal lingo that meant nothing to me, on paper, but, in reality, meant that my family's killer could be set free. I was fucking terrified. If Jeff got out, life as I knew it would be over. It was an unfathomable nightmare, reincarnated into reality. By this point, I'd spent the past four years of my life knowing that Jeff was actually the one who killed my family. And this court had just done something that would potentially set that bastard free. The person who killed my entire family could walk the streets again, a free man. Free to live his own life. Free to make his own decisions. Free to not pay the price for the people he killed. How was that even possible? I couldn't even begin to grasp it.

I was told that Jeff had won his initial appeal, but that didn't necessarily mean he would be released from prison. The State would appeal the decision to the Indiana Supreme Court. I hoped and prayed that the supreme court would allow the convictions to stand. I had to believe that *could not* and *would not* happen. Not to me. Not to my family. Not to those beautiful people left lying on the parsonage floor on April 29, 1989.

It felt like my whole world was crumbling. Nothing made sense anymore. The pendulum of justice has swung the other way, totally unexpectedly, and opened a trap door for Jeff to potentially crawl or fall through.

The statements Jacque and I gave to the media following the appellate court's ruling ran opposite ends of the gamut. Jeff and Jacque were thrilled as hell. Excited. Jubilant. Celebratory. It was apparent from the interviews Jacque gave to reporters. It was a living dream come true scenario for Jeff and his family. Jacque was likely popping champagne bottles that evening and throwing confetti in the air, as I was mentally setting out an elaborate plan on how to leave my own family out of fear.

For me, the lone survivor of my family who was slain—and whose killer was potentially about to be set free—it was hell on earth. It was my darkest day, besides the one that put me in this reality in the first place. I rarely spoke to reporters, but following that appellate court decision, I did give a brief statement to one who asked me for a comment. The gist was that I was scared to death my family's killer would potentially be set free.

The prosecutor's office advised me they would appeal the decision all the way up to the Indiana Supreme Court. They tried to put my mind at ease by telling me that Jeff couldn't be set free until after the supreme court's ruling, and then, *only* if the supreme court actually agreed with the appellate court's decision to overturn the jury's verdict.

I would live the days, weeks, and months of my life after the appellate court's decision with my fate skittering in the balance, walking on emotionally treacherous terrain, gripped in a state of absolute panic. I couldn't even imagine the possibility of my family's murderer going free, but it was a potential reality.

He could walk.

And if he did, I would have to run.

APPEAL

The Indiana Supreme Court
Three years after the conviction
One year after the original appellate opinion

O n February 19, 2009, at 9:24 A.M., the Indiana Supreme Court *finally* handed down its decision. The one we had all been desperately waiting to receive for a grueling year—actually, three years since Jeff's initial convictions. Me. My family. Jeff. Jacque. Every single person in both respective sets of families. Our friends. The people who lived in Lakeville, Indiana, collectively. And every person who knew us or knew about the tragedy and realized this decision possessed the power to drastically impact all our lives, regardless of which side of the divided situation a person found himself or herself on. This decision was everything. For all of us.

"On Petition to Transfer from the Indiana Court of Appeals, No. 71A05-0612-CR-726

Robert Jeffrey Pelley appeals his convictions for the murders of his father, stepmother, and two stepsisters. We affirm Pelly's convictions. We hold that the Criminal Rule 4(C) period does not include the time for the State's interlocutory appeal when trial court proceedings have been stayed. We also hold that the evidence was sufficient to support the convictions, and the trial court did not err in its challenged evidentiary rulings or in denying Pelley's motion for a special prosecutor.

"The State presented sufficient evidence from which the jury could conclude beyond a reasonable doubt that Jeff committed the four murders: evidence of motive, access to a weapon of the type used, and presence at the site were all established. Alternate explanations seemed implausible. The home was locked, suggesting a person with a key had been at the scene, and Pelley's account of his activities

at the time was inconsistent, and on the videotape, sometimes flustered. Pelley argues that his convictions cannot stand because the State's theory of the crimes is 'inconsistent with the laws of nature and human experience.' Pelley contends that a teenager, within twenty minutes, could not kill four of his family members, put his clothes in the washing machine, pick up the shotgun shells, take a shower, get dressed, draw the blinds, lock the doors, fix his car, and dispose of the gun and shells. Although the time window is narrow, we do not believe it is inconsistent with Pelley's guilt. Pelley was described at trial as a 'very intelligent, young man,' and his statements throughout the week that he would not be able to attend all prom activities suggest that the murders were premeditated and planned. The jury could reasonably conclude that Pelley performed the necessary actions within the available time. Pelley also points to inconsistencies in the accounts given by police of the length and content of the second police interview and who was present. He also cites inconsistencies between Jessica and Jacque regarding the presence of the shotgun in the master bedroom on Friday evening. Pelley also points out that despite extensive police effort, no murder weapon has been located, and he had no visible bruising from a shotgun in the days following the murder. However, none of these is conclusive of innocence. It is the jury's role to weigh these factors, and the jury found Pelley guilty beyond a reasonable doubt."

Never in all my life had I been so relieved to hear a piece of news. Jeff would *not* be set free. He would remain behind bars, where he belonged, for taking the lives of my family members. I cried. I was happy, but it was a somber type of happiness that felt somewhat hollow. It would not change anything that had happened in my life. It would not bring back my mom, Janel, and Jolene. But it did help me to know Jeff wouldn't be set free after being found guilty. I didn't have to live my life gripped in a state of perpetual fear. I didn't have to leave my family behind to go into hiding. A tremendous burden was lifted. It didn't change the reality of my life's situation, but what it did give me some small sliver of peace. While I would never have my family back, at least I knew the person who murdered them, as he looked down upon them in their final moments, would serve his time. Justice for the family I no longer had, for the broken girl he created, and the broken woman still here to know his fate.

Jeff Pelley would live behind bars for a total of 160 years.

And I would live my life as best as I could behind the invisible ones that forever marked my life.

JESSI

AGE 30
2009

On the drive home from work tonight, I decided to listen to a new CD I bought by Bruno Mars. There was one song on it I loved. Yep, one of those old-school moments when you buy the whole CD for one song. (For what it's worth, this was before the iTunes uprising. Paying $13.99 for one song. Yep, those were the days.) I already listened to my favorite song a few times in a row, so I decided to just let the whole CD continue to play, so I can see if I like any of the rest of the songs. Not long after, a melody began to play, accompanied by Bruno's soulful voice. He had me at the first chorus. About 30 seconds in, my heart dropped, and I was in the throes of emotional pain, my heart heavy, my breathing labored, and I began to bawl. The words to that song hit me deeply. It was as though they came straight into my body and struck the little girl I used to be, making their way directly to Jessica. While the song caused me to experience a flood of emotions, what it also made me feel was a connection. It was as though it was written for me. I guess that's what good music does for you, it hits you at your core and makes you feel something you didn't feel before you heard it. It reminds us of things. It stirs us emotionally, at least the good songs do.

I'd grown up singing songs with my sisters. We loved music. We sang together at church. We sang at home. We sang in the car. We sang all the dang time. After they were gone, over the years, music became one of the things that allowed me to express in an outward way the stuff I felt on the inside. There was a lot of darkness and sorrow. But music was an outlet. I couldn't deny the emotions I felt when the right song played. They flooded through me, and allowed me to feel again, even if just for a moment. A flicker of what it felt like to sing, to feel, to live, to love, to remember.

Truth is, people do think I'm crazy for still talking to my family, even though they are gone. But I don't just *believe* they are still out there somewhere, still here with me, I *know* they are. And for me, that particular Bruno Mars song embodied everything I felt.

Each night, when I lay my head down on my pillow, I pray to God first, then I talk to my family to tell them that I love them and say goodnight to them. Every. Single. Night. And in that song, the way I felt was put into words perfectly. It almost felt like I could connect to my sisters just by hearing it, that they would be listening to it at the same time I was. I knew this was the song I'd been waiting to hear. From that moment, I knew I was going to add it to a tattoo I'd started to forever memorialize my sisters on my left wrist. There was already a music note to symbolize each one of the three of us on my flesh. But I had been waiting . . . always waiting . . . to add the perfect score and words to that tattoo. This was it. From the moment I heard it, I knew: this was the song.

Me and tattoos? Yeah, I have a lot of them. Over the years, it became my way of giving myself visual reminders of the most significant people in my life, my family. Each one of my tattoos means something special to me. I have names, dates of birth, symbols, and more. It's a tangible way to see them every day— to honor them, remember them—with black ink on my skin. It's not like I could ever forget them, but tattoos are my way of making them an extension of who I am and carrying them with me everywhere I go, every day, always.

"Talking to the moon," just like Bruno Mars said in the song. You bet I am. I'm not gonna stop, either. I'll be talking to the moon until the day I die. It's one small part of "the after."

STEPHANIE

Jessica's Childhood Best Friend

AGE 32

I'd written a letter to Jessica dozens of times, both in my head and on paper. I'd spent all the years of my life since 1989 thinking about Jessica, missing her, wanting to find her, and hoping that I one day would. I'd searched for "Jessica Pelley" on Google many, many times. The same articles always popped up about the murders. Nothing new or notable, and they always led nowhere. From what I found, Jessica didn't seem to speak to the press much. Jacque did. I assumed Jessica was married, but I didn't know her new last name, until one glorious day when a new article popped up after Jeff's appeal. I found myself staring at her new name: Jessica Toronjo. A quick search on Facebook took me to the beautiful girl I'd known all my life as Jessica Pelley. It was her! I couldn't even believe it. I finally got to send that letter I'd written to her over and over and over again, throughout the years. I didn't know how she would react or if she would even respond. But I was just so damn happy to finally have found her! The rest didn't matter. I was so fucking happy. I just needed to reach out. It didn't matter how she reacted. It's just something I HAD to do for myself. And whatever would come of it, I'd live with it.

I typed that letter one last time, and this time, I actually hit "send."

From: Stephanie
Date: Some day in 2009
To: Jessica
Subject: Stephanie Sue

I think I have wrote this letter a hundred times, each time it was much like writing something to yourself and tucking it away, just to get it off your chest. As I sit here right now, I cannot believe I am looking at your beautiful face. Jess, I have been looking for you for almost 12 years. I don't know if you remember me or not. My name is Stephanie, we were close when we were younger. I have carried a picture of you & I at camp for many years. Each time I look at it, I say, "Someday I'm gonna find her, and tell her I miss her . . ." For 12 years I have said this to a piece of paper, so you can only imagine how I feel right now!!! I have been torn about you for a long time. I have gone thru my life, grown up, had children and have never lost sight of trying to find you. I have huge tears in my eyes right now just knowing that you are actually gonna get my letter this time! It seems all the letters I have wrote in the past have been 2 or 3 pagers, but tonight I am at a loss for words . . . Just seeing you, the little I can see of you is a huge sigh of relief for me. I don't know how you feel about reconnecting with me, I would LOVE nothing more than to be able to talk to you!!! I have so many questions for you! But, if not, I do understand. I honestly do. I never in a million years thought I'd ever see you again, I'm just happy to have found you, just this lil bit. To know you are somewhere is good enough for me. Attached is the picture I have talked to for so many years . . . yes I'm a dork! I hope if nothing else you find humor in it— I hope this letter finds you well and striving for everything you deserve in your life. I will leave it to you to write me back, I will prolly be biting my nails until u do! Jess, a part of me is at peace now that I have been able to write this to you!!! I hope you remember me, if not, I have pics of me too at that age!! LOL! Please know that you have been in my heart for a long time, and tho you never knew it, I have missed you for many years . . .

I hope to hear from you soon!

Much love, Stephanie

P.S.

I kept saying 12 years, no, no, it's been 20. It was since I was about 12 that I started lookin!

JESSI

AGE 30
The E-mail from Stephanie

The e-mail from Stephanie leveled me. I read it wide-eyed, with my jaw dropped. It was a pivotal moment. This was someone who *knew* me. Honestly, I didn't remember Stephanie, as I had unintentionally blocked a lot from that time in my life from memory. Her name and face didn't immediately register. But it was clear that she knew me. The real me. The "me" I was way back when. The "me" before the murders. The "me" who ran through the cornfield with my sisters, crawled deep and dirty into nearby ditches, rode my bike like I was paid per the pedal, ate a big breakfast every Sunday morning before church, and sang songs. Jessica. Jessica Pelley. That's who she knew. Me.

My second thought was "Holy shit, that's a long time to look for one person and for that person to be me!" Everyone else in my life had pretty much given up. But here was Stephanie, the girl I grew up with, who had searched for me for 20 years. The one who kept photographs and old newspaper clippings. The one who followed every television show each time a station aired my story. And unbeknownst to me at that time, the girl who had not only visited, but also cleaned and cared for the graves of my family throughout the years. She was the one who placed memorial flowers on their tombstones. She was the one who brought her young son, complete with a sponge and bucket, to help her scrub the dirt and debris away. She still lived in that little town where we grew up. The one where I used to live. She still loved my family. She still loved me.

My reaction was one of surprise, mixed with elation. Of course, I wanted to call her! It didn't take long for me to remember her, once I saw the picture she sent of us together as kids. The one of us standing in front of the parsonage. We were best friends. She knew my sisters. She knew my mom. She knew me.

I thank God every day that she looked for me, finally found me, and that she reached out to me. Having that connection to my past means so much to me. Nowadays, I consider her my sister. That's what I call her. While she is neither of the sisters I lost, she knew Janel and Jolene. She loved them. I still have her. And she has me. We are sisters in spirit in this journey called life. I'm so grateful to have her along for the journey.

We would not only stay in touch with regular e-mails and calls, but over time, would become close.

P.S.

Stephanie—Um, I'm sorry for that one time when I visited the cemetery to see my family a few years ago. The time when I took those pretty pots of flowers someone {you} had so kindly purchased and placed on their graves. The ones I took home with me that day, when I said goodbye to them. I was just passing through town and felt deeply compelled to take a small piece of them with me that day. The flowers. It wasn't until you visited my house quite a bit later that I learned that you were the one who put them there. Remember, you found them sitting on my fireplace mantel and started cracking up? After you explained to me why, I did, too. Sorry, but not really.

Sincerely,
The Flower Thief

MONA

Jessica's Mom's Best Friend
November 15, 2010

As I told you earlier, I went to high school with Jessi's mom, as well as her aunts (Ed's sisters). I had connected with a few of Ed's sisters on Facebook over the years. On November 15, 2010, 21 years after the tragedy, I was sitting in the computer room of my house. I was on Facebook. All of a sudden, on the Facebook feed of one of Jessica's aunts, up popped a photograph depicting the face of a beautiful, bright pink–haired woman. She looked just like one of Ed's sisters. It was Jessica! Tears immediately began to stream down my face. After all these years, I was looking right at the face of the beautiful young woman Jessica had grown up to become. I couldn't even believe it. Through my tears, I yelled out to my husband, who was in the living room, "I found her! I found her!" He had absolutely no idea what I was talking about and walked down the hall into the doorway of the office.

"You found who? What are you carrying on about?"

I replied, "Jessica! I found Jessica! Dawn's Jessica!"

It had eaten away at me over the years, ever since that day I saw her platinum blond-haired, smiling face in that newspaper photograph 13 years earlier, to know she was so close to me, living in the same city, but I had no idea where. To be so close to this person I wanted to know and to have no way to contact her gnawed at my conscience, much like a puppy nibbling away at a bone, and it tore at me emotionally bit by bit. I had always hoped I would bump into her at some point. After all, we lived in a small town. And here she was, finally, staring right back at me—big green eyes and a radiant smile—beaming at me from the screen of my computer. The girl who was my best friend Dawn's long-lost daughter. The girl who was little Janel and Jolene's surviving sister. The little girl I'd looked for since 1989 and thought about on countless occasions, and here she was, within a social media arm's reach, just one message away.

Now, if I'm being entirely honest as Dawn's best friend, the pink hair and all those tattoos Jessi had, clearly depicted in the pictures, did take me aback a bit. Don't get me wrong, she looked beautiful—so radiant and happy—but all I could think to myself was, "Your mother would have a conniption!" Because Dawn would have. But inside, it also made me laugh, remembering back to all the times I had conversations with Dawn about Jessica during the early years of her childhood. I remember Dawn telling me, "This child does not take after me at all." She didn't say it like it was a bad thing. It was just a statement based on reality. She was totally Ed's daughter, as far as her personality went. Dawn and Jessica went head-to-head a lot. Jessica was a boisterous little girl with a free spirit, who was strong willed, adventurous, and didn't follow the rules. Well, I guess in hindsight, maybe that bright pink hair and those tattoos aren't so surprising after all. Maybe that's exactly how I would expect her to look, if I really stop to think about it. I was just so happy to see her and to know she appeared to have moved on with her life. She was a wife. She was a mother. She had a home and family now. I could tell that from looking at the pictures on her profile.

I was excited, but I wasn't sure what to say or if she would even remember me because she was so little at the time everything transpired. I had no idea how she would feel about me approaching her after all this time had passed. I knew it would be important for me to verify my identity for her, so she wouldn't think I was a person stalking her or something, so she would know what I said to be true. I honestly didn't think she would remember me. There was no basis for her to really know me. Her mom always lived in another state with Jessica, Janel, and Jolene (dubbed "the girls" during Jessica's childhood). Then, once my youngest son was born severely handicapped, we had pretty much lived at University of

Michigan Hospital for the first three years of his life. No matter what, I knew that I had to reach out, regardless of any of those considerations or how she would perceive it, so I cobbled together a simple, honest, and heartfelt private message and sent it her way, along with a request to connect.

Mona: Jessica, I am your momma's friend from high school. I have known you since you were born and have been trying to find you. I am also best friends with your Aunt [name intentionally omitted] Huber and knew your dad Ed Huber as well as your Huber kin. I'm not sure if you remember me, but I remember you and know your family. I would love to connect with you.

Mona: Jessi, this is the profile pic, a recent one. I just saw it tonight and wow it took my breath away how much you resemble your mom in this picture. Brought tears to my eyes, sweetie. I know that she must be so proud of the amazing young woman you have turned out to be and the fantastic mom you are. Love you sweetie.

Anytime you are free, I would love to get together. I haven't spent time with you since you were a little girl; really little, I would say about 6. So glad I found you on Facebook because I always wondered what happened to u and lost contact with your mom's sisters over the years. Seeing you all grown up and the wonderful woman you are just makes my heart so happy. It's like we still have a piece of your mom, dad (Ed) and your sisters living on through you and your children. I see a lot of your mom in Dakota [Jessi's daughter] also. My fondest school memories are of hanging out with your Aunt, your dad, Eddie, and your mom. We had lots of fun and your mom always had the same beautiful smile as you do. I don't think I can ever remember a memory I have of her where she wasn't smiling or laughing. Love you hun.

Jessi: Awwwww, I am so glad you found me too! When I figure out a day I will let you know! Yes, this pic was from December. We really need to get together and chat!

The more we messaged back and forth, Jessica—who now went by "Jessi"—made it clear she didn't have an active memory of me, but she did have vague memories of her mom talking about me, mentioning me by name, or knowing that her mom was "talking to Mona" on the phone. We talked about our lives now, the type of day we had, general stuff like that. It was pretty much all surface level. I was just happy she knew that I was who I said I was and had held a place in her mother's life. We kept in touch via private messages on Facebook. I was yearning to see her, but I didn't want to pressure her in any way. I was excited to now be in contact with her, but afraid. It's not like I really knew her. I knew the little girl she used to be. Based on what her Aunt B had told me the last time I called not long after the tragedy, I didn't know if being in contact with someone from her past truly might damage her or dredge up bad feelings. Hurting her is the last thing I would ever want to do. But I had sworn to myself that if I ever found her, I wasn't going to be absent anymore. That absence between us was something I did not choose. It is something none of her family from her daddy's side chose, at least not in the early years of her living with Dawn's family, anyway.

Then one day, fate intervened. I was at the chiropractor for a back adjustment. I was seated in the waiting room, flipping through a magazine, when the front door to the office swung open, and in walked Jessi with her daughter. She was here, in the same room as me! As soon as I saw the pink hair and that smile, I knew. I exclaimed, "Jessi!" She replied, "Mona!" I ran over to her, wrapped both of my arms around her, and for the first time in 21 years, I held her. I was overcome by emotions that came rolling over me in deep waves, dragging my breath away, and infusing my spirit with a newfound hope. I was so grateful and elated at being able to see Jessica in person, meet her daughter, hear her voice, and to hold this dear, sweet girl. It was everything I thought that moment would be. More. It was more. It was a silent dream. It was everything.

I cried the entire way home.

JESSI

AGE 33
August 2012

One day Boss Lady, my close friend at the childcare center where I worked, told me about a psychic/medium she sometimes visited to seek spiritual guidance. She swore this lady was spot on with her information and advice. She wasn't a psychic who advertised, but one who gleaned customers simply by word-of-mouth referrals. Boss Lady knew about my past and what had happened to my family. She thought it might be interesting for me to go see this lady who I dubbed "The Spirit Whisperer." The lady's name was Sherry Shaffnitt. Boss Lady said, "Just go with me one time and see what happens."

I consider myself a spiritual person, but I had never visited a psychic. I had no clue what to expect. I didn't know how she would go about her business and wasn't sure what the visit would entail. I hoped to get answers. I wanted to hear something from my mom and sisters. Was this even real? I had no idea. I was kind of excited about the prospect of communicating with my family members who passed, but nervous at the same time. I was naturally skeptical and tried to rein in my expectations, so I wouldn't feel disappointed if nothing happened.

I know seeing a psychic medium for guidance may seem completely crazy to some people, but I thought to myself, "I can't see or talk to my family anyway, so what do I have to lose?" The answer to that question was nothing, aside from the $60 I paid to talk to her.

We walked into the psychic's house—that's where she does the readings—and it was a small, nice, normal house. Boss Lady and I split the session. Boss Lady went first. I sat in a chair in the corner and listened to her session. Then, it was my turn. The only thing

Boss Lady had told the Spirit Whisperer was, "I'm going to bring a friend along with me; her name is Jessi." Not only did Boss Lady intentionally *not* give the lady my last name—which would be my married name, not Pelley, even if she had given it—but she gave her no information about me whatsoever. This lady had no way of knowing who I was, much less my background or the pertinent parts of my personal story.

I sat down across from her in a recliner chair that rocked, near a window. She was a pretty lady with shoulder-length strawberry blond hair that appeared to be naturally curly, with those big, round roller-style curls. She was pretty. She seemed kind. Once the session began, she appeared to breathe deeply, looked like she was meditating, and kept her eyes closed the entire time. The first things she said was, "Oh, you have a lot of people with you. There's a little loud girl right out front. She's yelling at me, trying to get my attention. There are so many of them talking to me at once, I'm having a hard time making sense of it all." As I said, the psychic's eyes remained closed. But Boss Lady and I were both wide-eyed and glancing at one another in a look of collective bewilderment.

The psychic knew something had happened to them, that they had died, but not how or why. She had a hard time making sense of it. She knew they had passed when they were young. She knew they had all gone together under unusual circumstances, but nothing beyond that. My response to any questions the psychic asked me were simply "yes," "no," "I think so," or "I don't think so." I was intentionally being vague. More than anything, I think I responded that way so I would know what she was saying to me was legitimate. While seated in that room, I showed no emotion, but in my mind, I was elated.

She told me, "I've *never* had this happen before. I've *never* had so many people come through to talk to a person before. If you'd like to come back for another reading, I'd be willing to do a free one, so we can try to sort all this out." She seemed not only perplexed, but incredibly curious. I wasn't sure what it meant when you puzzled the heck out of a Spirit Whisperer, who made her living talking to dead people, but I was sure excited to attempt to figure it out.

I knew it was my family. That's who was coming through to talk to her. It was probably little loud-mouthed Janel, right out front, trying to get her attention. I didn't know if it was my entire family, but it was clear at least some of them came through to talk to her, or rather, to talk to me. You bet your ass I was going to come back for that free reading! I would be counting the minutes until our next session.

JESSI

The Psychic Medium:

The Third Reading
August 2012

{This is a transcript of the audio recording of this session. It bears mentioning that Jessi lost the second tape, so that's why we skipped from the first one to the third one.}

PSYCHIC: The date is August {inaudible} 2012 and this is a reading with Sherry Shaffnitt. So, yeah, your mom was here first and um, you know, it was kind of curious. I asked you if you know they are always around you and you do feel them. It's almost like you carry them with you wherever you go. And, you know, I was talking with your mom, more of like a mom to mom, and . . . what do you think? She's all grown up now. And, you know, obviously, the tattoos, the different color hair, you know, and I'm like, "Mom, what do ya think?" And she said, "You know, even if I would have lived, she would still be that way because that is who she is." And, it's all love and support. Really that you march to a different drum and you dance to a different beat, and it's who you are in your soul. And had your mom lived nor had anything been different, you would still be the person that you are today. Do you understand?

JESSI: Yeah.

PSYCHIC: So, definitely. Anyway, so I just wanted to share that with you because we were talking about you, and I wanted to let you know what she said. So, I look at her and ask her what she wants to share. She has said this before, but she will always say this to you, that she is very proud of you. And that all of the painfulness that you have had in your life, not only losing your family, but other, after that, she calls them "child tragedies," you know, the different changes in your life, changes in your job, changes in your relationships, and friendships, and all of that and how that's been for you, and so she just really, in her word "admires" you and that you continue to go on and are so strong of an individual, that she's just really proud of you. She wanted you to know that.

She encourages you to continue thinking that, that that is going to happen. I asked her what else she wanted to share. Um, it's interesting because she's saying, in her words, "your sisters have grown up." That, you know, sometimes it's difficult for you to imagine because you think of them as how little they were at that age, right?

JESSI: Mmm hmm.

PSYCHIC: But they can, and again, it's not so much a physical body but they have grown and matured and are also walking with you, or helping you. And that you think of them often and it's almost as if, in your mind, you still have a family. Like, you know, you believe they're still there for you. And anyway, your mom is very pleased about that. And that you continue to be family, even though they're over in this other dimension. And she also says that, "Of the survivors, if you will, that you are a survivor, that the other girls wouldn't have done so well. That um, if you will, it's like you were chosen to stay. And um, continue on that path, and they are very supportive.

Not that it would be brand new, but did you get a new car?

JESSI & BOSS LADY: [laughing loudly—because Jessi just got a new truck]

PSYCHIC: Does that make sense to you?

BOSS LADY: Yes. Yes. [laughing with Jessi]

JESSI: Oh, that was funny!

PSYCHIC: All right, well, that would be a "yes"?

JESSI & BOSS LADY: Yes!

PSYCHIC: The only reason is, she brings this up is that they are helping you. Yeah.

JESSI: [laughing] Sorry, that was just kind of freaky.

PSYCHIC: Yeah. I'm like, well, since your mom is so good at this, I'm gonna say, "Mom, I'd like to win the lottery." All right, well good, so you already know that and I'm just affirming or confirming that she is being part of your life and helping, even though she's on the other side, she's still helping you.

JESSI: Yep.

PSYCHIC: Very good. And then one more change is going to occur or has already occurred, to live someplace different. Have you been thinking about that?

JESSI: Not right now. Maybe much, much later down the road, but . . .

PSYCHIC: Well, are you living in an apartment?

JESSI: Uh-uh. No.

PSYCHIC: Well, I'm gonna leave it with you and we'll see what happens!

PSYCHIC: Do you live on your own?

JESSI: Yeah.

PSYCHIC: And by yourself?

JESSI: Well, not technically by myself, but . . . [I was alone a lot because Ty worked out of town.]

PSYCHIC: Yeah. Okay. I don't know, for some reason, a feeling that that can change and it's changing for the better, so that it puts you in an environment where, I don't know, for lack of a better word in describing it that kicks it up a notch, you know, that you have a better environment. Um, and so I'm not really sure what all of that means, but I'm gonna leave it with you and we'll see what happens, and how, or if, that changes. But it seems not that you are a luxury person, that you don't have to have grand things and you're just fine with the regular stuff, if you will, but I really see that's there's opportunity for you to live in an upgraded kind of an environment. And that it's important to you, and it will feel better. It's not necessarily important to you now, but when you get there, you'll be like "Whoa, this is *really* nice." And so, I'll leave that with you and we'll see how it unfolds.

JESSI: Okay.

PSYCHIC: But those are the things she wanted to mention that she had seen, and knows, and is a part of going on in your life. That was the big thing for her when she left here, leaving as she says, "One of her babies" was that it was just of upmost importance to make sure that you were taken care of, and so she continues to do that. Yeah.

Do you have any questions for her, before I move on?

JESSI: I don't know. I don't know how to word it, like questions for her. I mean I have some . . .

BOSS LADY: I have one.

PSYCHIC: Okay, go ahead.

BOSS LADY: Well, I'm curious to know and I'm sure you would be, too, about when Jessi went back home [to Lakeville, Indiana] for the first time this year and what her mom would think of that. What does she think of that?

PSYCHIC: So back home, meaning back in the house?

BOSS LADY: No, not back in the house. But where it happened.

PSYCHIC: But back in that, yeah. Well, you know, when you were asking the question, the answer came back, and it was her holding your hand, and walking with you. And um, you know, so I went a step further and I'm like, "What was that like for you?" for your mom to be there. And she said, "Well, it doesn't have the emotional connection that it would for you." Um, it's uh, she calls it "her place of departure." That's interesting. That, you know, crossing over.

JESSI: Right.

PSYCHIC: And we all look at that in a very different way. Not only that particular situation, but many eyes, so they all look at it in a different way. But then also on a more philosophical level, similar to what we had talked about before, where when your eyes are closed, you know, where ever you pass, you pass. And so, she just calls that her point of departure. Where she left this earth plane and went to heaven. So, it wasn't quite as emotional for her, but she's very . . . I asked her "how does she feel?" And she said that you needed to do that to come full circle and to really close it. And that it was very, it was brave of you, it was healthy for you, and it was, for lack of a better way of saying it, it was "successful" for you. Does that all make sense?

JESSI: Yes.

PSYCHIC: Yeah, and so it's like, close that book and uh, yeah, it defines me, it's who I am, it's what happened to me, but it's not going to, you know, like *run* my life. And just going back there and doing that, it's sort of like facing the lowest point of your life. And it was, like she said, "very brave of you." And it was very helpful for you. It really like, it freed you, in some sense. And so, uh, yeah. So those are all of her thoughts on that. And very supportive, obviously, because she was right there with you. Yeah, yeah, yeah.

And for you, it was lots of emotion, but also, release. Yeah. Just a very, it was a good experience. I mean, for what it needed to do, right? Yeah. And for closure. Yeah.

I asked her if she had anything else that she wanted to say and, it's almost as if, um, it's like she's with you all the time. You know, it's not like she has to talk a whole lot. Like she talks to you every day, just like you talk to her every day. You know, even if it's not, it's still like you walk together, and so it's not like, "I can see you!" it's like, "Yeah, I saw her yesterday." You know, and so there's not a ton of things to be revealed because, she says, "you spend a lot of time" and not that you remember this all the time, "but you spend a lot of time together in dream time with her. With them." Yeah. And are always like, know the latest of what's going on. Yeah. Very good. I thank her for coming in and uh, giving so much love to you, and she goes, "You know, I would never leave you." And so, she hasn't. At all. And very much is a part of your life.

I let her energy go and your sisters, as well, they send much love. But mostly, mom's the spokesperson for them. And um, lots of love and support to you, and they'll continue to be with you.

But she steps aside because she wanted your spirit guide to have an opportunity to come through and to give you some encouragement.

And the whole thing of the sensitivity, that's really important, too. Really protecting yourself from negative energies, and, have we talked about that before?

JESSI: Yeah.

PSYCHIC: All right, okay.

JESSI: The negative energy, yes.

PSYCHIC: And so, protecting yourself from that negative energy because, you're just like a walking sponge. You soak that up, yeah. It's interesting because he [Jessi's spirit guide] was, to get around other like-minded people and he was, like showing me people that I know that you should meet because you guys would click, and you know, some different friendships that . . . not, like, whacked out on a spiritual path kind of a thing, but are like, open to, and aware of, and really, I don't know, that there could be some opportunities for some new friendships that get you away from some of the people that are energy zapping you. And that, that would be important. He calls it "meeting your people." So, it would be people that loved you, people that supported you, not people that came to you and said, "what can you give me?" And as they're doing that, they are taking your energy. They are energy suckers. Yeah . . . I asked him if there was anything else? He encourages you to read spiritual books and, again, check out "ways to wellness" because you could meet other like-minded people . . . there's all sorts of opportunities for you to step in to that. And he's saying, like, there's a whole different life waiting for you to step into it. And you know that, but you're reluctant. You know that, intuitively, you know that. A different life, all you have to do is just say, "okay, I'm ready for it," and boom, it's going to be right there for you, and it's going to be so much more in tune with who you are and it's, you know, you're going to find your people, you're going to find your path. It's just gonna open up. But, you know, he can't push you, he can only tell you about it. It's really like, all you have to do is say, "Okay, I'm ready." And that's all. That's all you need to do. And boom, boom, boom, things will start to happen. But he's just, he's like, just waiting. Just waiting. Jokingly. Now, you know, this is a joke. He just stepped out to have a cigarette while he's waiting.

Not for real, but . . . so, um, very much waiting for you to accept your path. And a lot of times, he's like, "You're your own worst enemy and belittle yourself about what direction you're supposed to be going and are just real reluctant." He calls you "a reluctant disciple." Because you're a disciple. There's no doubt about it. Reluctant to sort of, there's something about surrender that you think you surrender and wonder if you're ready for your path, but life as you know it, having to give it up, that's really scary to you. But it's not that you have to give it up, it's that you have to allow new things into your life. And he's like, "How bad could that be?" Um, and as soon as you surrender, it will, boom, happen. So yeah, not to preach on that, but he really wants to make it, very adamant that you understand it. Yeah. Because everything to you, even though stuff is starting to fall into place, but it's like, everything is a struggle. Like carrying weights uphill. Yeah. And just surrendering. And it's as simple as saying, "I'm ready, bring it on." And, boom, away you go, and it's all good. It's all good.

Do you have any questions for him [Jessi's spirit guide]?

JESSI: Um, I'm not very good at this question thing.

PSYCHIC: Not a problem. I'm feeling that everything you needed to hear has been shared.

JESSI: Pretty much.

PSYCHIC: But, um, I always leave it open in case there was something you had, and I'm looking at him, and . . . again, a lot of love. A lot of love and support from the other side. And this is not mandatory that you have to do this, but it's an option that you have. It's like sitting on the table. You walk in and pick it up. It's really that simple, but, uh, just wants to remind you, it's on the table.

JESSI

AGE 34

I began attending church again when I was 34-years-old. I met a girl named Sarah and she and I became close friends. I looked forward to seeing Sarah and the other ladies at church every Sunday. It gave me a place to go. I rediscovered my faith within the walls of that sanctuary. The church gave me a sense of peace. A sense of belonging to a group of people who were happy to see me, a place where I fit in; that's something I never really had growing up. It felt like a haven. A place where I could reignite my faith in God. My faith that my life could be okay. My faith that God had a plan for me. Sarah and I spent a lot of time together. It was a relationship which, for me, felt very close and comfortable. It's the type of close connection I craved all my life.

After about two years of going to that church, one day, Sarah told me she was moving away. It's a normal thing to tell another person. "Hey, I'm moving to another state. How exciting!" But for me, it was a launch code for another trip into the darkness. I lived my entire life with a fear of getting too close to people. Being close to a person meant that I could lose them the same way I lost each member of my family. Losing Sarah took me back to the foundation of those feelings I had as a little girl. It made me remember how it felt to live consumed by sorrow, unloved, unwanted, and alone. It took me right back to the loss of my family. I may not have realized it at the time, but I *loved* Sarah. She was a true connection; one of the only ones I ever had, aside from the one I had with Ty. Our friendship was a safe space for me. I allowed her access to that vulnerable space in my heart I never allowed anyone to enter. And I did it without realizing I did. She had breached the walls of protection and I was suffering.

When Sarah moved away, I was devastated. I couldn't go to church anymore. I had anxiety anytime I even thought about it. The church reminded me of Sarah. It reminded me of our relationship that meant so much to me and that I no longer had. The other ladies were still there. Church services were still held every Sunday. I tried to go back once, but I just couldn't do it. I didn't even manage to make it into the building. Being there without Sarah felt wrong to me. I left the church parking lot feeling empty. And I cried . . . a lot.

For a long time, I couldn't view church the same way. It was a turning point for me on my spiritual journey, and not in a good way. I now equated attending church with the death of a friendship that was accompanied by feelings of anxiety and panic. It was a new low I wasn't searching for, was careful to avoid, and never expected.

While I desperately craved a close connection to other people, I also feared it. Because of this, I often pushed people away if I felt like they were getting too close. I still do. I guess it's some type of a defense mechanism based on self-preservation. If I was the one doing the pushing away, I could prevent the potential hurt I would feel, if I ever lost that person. It pretty much became a self-fulfilling prophecy. Get close, get closer, push away, push away farther. Make sure there's enough distance. Lessen the feelings. The problem is you can never get close to people that way. You stay disconnected. You still crave love and friendship, but you also avoid it and make it nearly impossible for others to connect to you by keeping them at bay.

There are times when I realize a relationship in my life has gotten deep enough, and the connection close enough, that I begin to feel physical panic. I love this person. What if I lose this person? What if something happens to her? What would I do then? What if she dies? How would I deal with that? (Uh, the answer is not well at all.) It's a pattern of feeling and thinking that's hard to break free from, like I'm trapped in a circular, never-ending, panic inducing trap. It's a bitch to crave love just as much as you fear it.

I spent years upon years of my life wishing for relationships it seemed I could never have. And sabotaging the ones I did have, at least on some level, whether I wanted to or not.

Every person I'm close to now is forced to deal with this. The push and pull. It's not fair to them. Really, it's not even fair to me. But it is my reality. It's something I'm working on. I have my own family now, my husband and kids. I have Stephanie, whom I now consider to be my sister. I have Mona, my mom's best friend, who is more like an aunt to me. I have Boss Lady from work, my close friend. There are others, but that is the short list.

Do I fear losing these people? Every. Single. Damn. Day. I try not to think about it. But I dread what will happen if I ever get the call. He's gone. She's gone. It's almost like I need death conditioning. (Is that a legit thing? If not, it totally should be.) That's something I'm working on, my ability to deal with death and sorrow, to accept and acknowledge it, and deal with loss.

If life is a battlefield, you can draw me into the plans. I'm still fighting, day by day. I hope one day to conquer my anxiety and fear of loss. I know I'll never be free of the worry and fear completely, but I hope one day to get to the point I stop pushing people away. Until then, I'll be fighting the invisible battle in my own mind and heart. I want close relationships. I want to love people. And I don't want to fear the things I need most: people who love me, and people whom I love. It's a battle worth fighting.

JAMIE

Jessica's Cousin

AGE 37

2014

S ince Jessica and I didn't know one another well during our childhood years, our relationship continued in the same non-intersecting fashion, as we entered our teenage and adolescent years. Like it was for many of us in the family, Jessica was out of sight and out of mind. It's a hard thing to admit, but it's true. I was only 12-years-old when the murders happened. It's not that I ever stopped talking to her. It's that I never really started. We had a fairly large family consisting of a total of twelve cousins on my mom's—and Jessica's dad's—side of the family. I had no idea what had happened to Jessica in the years following the tragedy. Not only was I rarely ever in the same state as Jessica, but for seven years of my childhood, I wasn't even in the same country.

I remember hearing an occasional update from our grandma about how she was doing over the years, when my dad would take me to stay for part of the summer with my grandma and aunts in Michigan. Once, I specifically remember her telling me, "Jessi (the nickname she was going by) is living in a foster home now." Jessica was 13-years-old at the time. You could tell it bothered my grandma to say that about Jessica, that she had ended up living in foster care. For me, it wasn't any easier hearing those words. I felt the same way. How could Jessica end up in foster care? I didn't understand it. We had a big family. People who loved her. Grandma told me that "Jessi seemed to be doing better there than she has anywhere else." That surprised me. Really . . . in foster care? Doing well? It was a difficult thing to comprehend.

I also remember wondering why Jessica had changed her name to Jessi. Grandma told me, "That's what she goes by now, and if you call her Jessica, she'll correct you. She doesn't like it. She prefers to be called Jessi now." Given all she'd been through, I guess she had earned the right to call herself whatever in the heck she wanted to be called.

Our teenage years turned into our adolescent years, and those turned into full-on "adulting" years. We'd lost touch completely. It wasn't intentional. That's just what transpired. We were two cousins, estranged by time, unbuilt relationships, and distance.

One day, in the "people you may know" section of my Facebook feed, up popped a picture of Jessica. This beautiful, vibrant, fierce-looking lady with hot pink hair stared at me from the screen. It was the face of my long-lost cousin, little Jessica, whom I grieved alongside at a funeral in 1989, now grown. I was pretty much stunned, but also excited.

I was now a 37-year-old woman and she was 34. We were both adults. I remember thinking to myself, "She survived. She made it." That was my initial thought. I knew what she had been through. I was incredibly curious to learn more about her life and how everything had gone. I hoped she had a happy upbringing, at least as happy as it could be, given the terribly tragic circumstances that left her pretty much orphaned at an early age.

Bringing up a person's entire family being murdered isn't exactly table talk or fodder for an opening conversation, whether you are related to a person or not. That part was kind of awkward to navigate. I went with the sit-back-and-watch-and-observe-and-don't-mention-it-to-her-until-you-know-how-she'll-be-with-it approach. It's not like Bob, Jeff, or Jacque were related to me, so I had no clue what Jessica's new last name became after Huber.

Since I now knew Jessica's married name from her profile, I got nosey and ran an online search. Various news stories came up. I even came across a true crime book written about the tragedy. I bought it immediately. I had wondered about the details my entire life.

When I read the book, it eviscerated me. Totally and completely. I wasn't just reading the words of some random stranger's story. I was reading the words that comprised my cousin's life, the story of my own family, and it transported me right back into that little white church in 1989. I think the thing that tore me up most was reading it as the mother I now was. My son was nine-years-old at the time, the exact age Jessica was when all this happened. Through his current age, I saw her.

Her age, maturity level, thought process, emotional capacity, and what life would have been like for her, by realizing what life would be like for my son if something like this had happened to him at that age. It poured over me and pulled me under like an emotional tsunami. These people, my deceased aunt and cousins, deserved so much better in life. And they deserved so much more after death than the words on those pages.

When I looked up news articles I saw that the names of my little deceased cousins were often misspelled, or their ages miscalculated. These weren't just names and statistics of violent crime, they were my cousins, and Jessica's immediate family. They were people. Good people who didn't deserve this. It stung. And it chiseled away at me. It wasn't the kind of mental torture that faded over time. The more I thought about it, how wrong it all seemed, and how wrong it all felt, the more it ate away at me. If I was having this type of an experience after seeing and reading all of this now, I could only imagine the way Jessica felt. It had to bother her. It had to.

Again, I came back to my questions about Jessica. Do you mention it to her? Does she want to talk what happened in the past? Is she trying to forget it? Is she, by some miracle, managing to really move on with her life?

After reading that whodunit-style crime book, I felt compelled to send her an e-mail. It was the letter that I, as an adult woman, needed to send to both little Jessica and the grown woman she had become. I know she would remember I was there that day at that terrible funeral all those years ago. I had no idea how she would respond to it, or if she even would. I didn't know if it would upset her. I didn't know if it would make her angry. I wasn't sure if it was okay to bring up her family. But I decided it didn't matter. Her reaction would be whatever it was. I needed to say the words. No matter how they were received by her, I needed to say them.

I wrote and rewrote the words.

I read and reread the words.

Then I hit the "send" button.

And waited, and wondered . . .

From: Jamie Collins
Date: 6/12/2015 9:10 PM
To: Jessica Toronjo
Subject: Re: Hi

Hi Jessi,

Well, I really felt compelled to send you this. Truth is, I think it's been a long time coming, although I didn't realize it. I'm a writer, but finding the right words in a time such as this probably won't come easy, so I'll just speak from the heart and be honest.

We really didn't get to spend all that much time together as kids, given the states between us and various parenting-related issues we each had, but I want you to know I admire you. I know things couldn't have been easy for you. I remember being at the funeral for your family. I was about 12- or 13-years-old at that time. I remember feeling so sad and emotionally distraught inside. Until about 5 years ago, I couldn't bear to hear the song, "Amazing Grace," because that's what it reminded me of. I can't even imagine the way you felt that day, the days prior, and in all the days that would follow. I was about 3 feet away, when I watched each of our aunts, in turn, hug you and tell you they loved you, and would be there for you. I know they each meant it. But the truth is, we all got to leave that day to return to life as we knew it, myself included. We were able to go back to some sense of normal. You didn't get to do that. Your world imploded. Completely. And I can't imagine how hard that must have been (at age 9/10), and still is, although I know you now have a beautiful family of your own.

Anyway, after seeing your post on 4-29, your family was on my mind. I think in that moment, I realized I didn't even know the date it all happened. A date you would never forget. So, I started googling and stumbled across the "Pelley" name (as

I had no clue what the married name for your mom was) and came across the book about it. I saw the pictures of your family online. It brought back a lot of memories. And feelings, too.

As for that bullshit crime book written about the tragedy, the guy who wrote it clearly did an unfathomable amount of research, but took an angle that didn't at all involve telling people about who your family members—our family members—were, as people. It did lay out the story and facts. I always wondered what happened to Jeff, if anything, and when, and why. I had my own gut feelings about him the day of the funeral. But it's not the type of thing you can just ask a family member about, as it dredges up so much pain. But I found it interesting to read what they knew, when they knew it, what ultimately happened, etc.

And reading the book and seeing you on Facebook for the past year made me want to reach out to tell you that while you and I don't really "know" one another well, we're a lot older now, have become who we truly are, and I would LOVE the opportunity to get to know you.

Your dad and my mom were close. They had a special bond. I remember a day when I was about 5 or 6 years old. I was riding in the car with my mom and your dad. Your dad was driving with his hands off the steering wheel, using his knees to steer the car to make me laugh. It's the only clear memory I have of him, my Uncle Eddie. That day in the car.

I don't think I ever realized how close in age you and I really are. We can't rewrite the past. But we have now. We have today. And I'd like to be a part of your life, if you'll allow me to be.

I'm not sure how reading all of this makes you feel, and if it's in any way bad, I'm sorry. But sitting on my couch at 37-years-old and reading that book really hit me hard. I would welcome any relationship you'd like to have with me. I'm sorry you didn't always feel included in the family dynamic. Truth is, I didn't always, either. (Through the fault of no one really—just the situation and distance.) The parent that tied each of us to the core family being gone certainly didn't help things in that regard. As I got older, I found it difficult to be with the family when the piece tying me to that family was gone. It was like a big reminder. I was states away, but I'm sure being in the same state made it hard at the holidays, etc., if you didn't feel included over the years. My heart breaks at the thought of it. It really does.

Anyway, I just wanted to tell you how I feel. I hope your conversation with your son went well. I saw your post on that, you finally telling him about the tragedy, so he'll hear it from you rather than seeing it on TV.

Let me know how you feel about this. :) I swear I won't be a rambling weirdo from this point forward. (Okay, just sometimes . . .)

Jamie
Sent from my iPad

JESSI

My Reaction to Jamie's E-mail

As soon as I read the words of Jamie's e-mail, tears began to fill my eyes. A few made their way down my face, as I thought to myself, "Oh, my God. FINALLY! Another person who *wants* to be a part of my life. Who wants me to be a part of hers." Behind the flow of sentimental tears, a wave of excitement followed. And behind that, the thought lingered: *What made her want to get to reach out and get to know me?* I was intrigued. I wondered why. *Why her? Why now?* That's what I really wanted to know. For me, it was completely unexpected, but totally welcomed.

At this point in my life I had no close family connections to my past, with the exception of the bond I shared with my grandparents—my dad's parents. They had always wanted to be a part of my life, even though they were denied that opportunity. I would describe my relationship with my aunts as "in passing" and somewhat normal, but I didn't need normal. I needed more. As the years passed, there would be no birthday cards, telephone calls, or meet ups. I needed their time, attention, support, and love. While I did still communicate with some of my family members, I felt no true connection, and desperately desired a link to my past. A strong connection to someone who was related to me. Another set of eyes through which to filter my own view of my family, my childhood, and my past. Someone who knew me, the real me.

The moment Jamie's words unexpectedly found me, I felt she was someone who offered that deeper level of connection. It was instantaneous. She was my family. I knew exactly who she was. When Stephanie had reached out to me, I realized that I had blocked the memory of who she was. I hadn't remembered Stephanie until we spoke and I looked at old photographs she sent me. But this was Jamie—my oldest cousin—Marla and Ron's daughter. We shared the same grandparents and aunts and uncles. I knew her. I remembered her. Jamie knew my past. She knew who I was. She was one of the few cousins in the family old enough to truly remember what had happened to me via personal experience, rather than through stories. She was at both of my parents' funerals. She knew what I'd been through. It had been a long time since we'd been in a room together (and it's not like we ever really spoke when we were), but that didn't matter. That's what made it deeper for me. The fact that she knew me—Jessica, the real me—and she wanted to get to know me better.

I was touched that she wanted us to actually get to know one another and learn about each other's lives. To be there for one another as cousins. I hoped that this relationship with her could give me the bond I always wanted. Her words hit me deep.

They were the words I'd waited 26 years of my life to hear from someone. I have a few things to say to her.

Jamie, I had no way of knowing that what we would come to develop in the year that would follow your e-mail is an unbreakable bond, paused only by time and proximity. It's like I knew you all along, and you knew me. As though we were meant to reunite and become intertwined in one another's lives, a place where we each belonged.

I had no idea we would become so close. That we would share darkness, memories, stories, laughter, tears, and dreams. That you would walk through the dark days of the past with me, speaking about it in a normal way, not in broken whispers. I didn't realize talking to you about my entire life would become like a form of therapy for me. I had no way to know that you would find a way to begin to filter light through my broken places. Nor did I know that we would one day write a book together—this book. I had no way to know this e-mail from you would be the start of something special and life-changing. But it was.

You are my cousin. You are my friend. You are my confidante. You are my sounding board. Some days, you are the voice of reason in the back of my head. The lecture I'd rather not hear. The encouragement I need on a dark day. The light shining on a bright one. You are a connection to my past.

Never have I felt more understood.

Never have I felt more at peace.

I am proud to call you my cousin, even happier to call you my friend.

Sincerely,

Your Long-Lost Cousin

Jessica

In Defiant Dignity, We Rise

When we find ourselves standing along the median of hell, we are not always trapped there, in that dark, soulless, desolate place. But there, we were planted. Somehow, to survive. Someway, to find a will to flourish from our mangled roots which now stand in a tragically tangled, chaotically beautiful, unintended display of rebellion upon the rock to which they now cling. There, not just to hold a space for others, but to illuminate a stairway. One that leads out of hell, back to the light. We were not punished, nor intentionally exiled. We are not cursed. We were simply left behind. By people. By circumstances. By life. By time. And from those losses, we became what it is we now are: the chosen ones. A pointer to the stairs of light. Upon tears, heartbreak, laughter, and ashes, from that barren bedrock where roots don't seem to grow, from that place where we were planted to toil and tumble from the things we should never survive, on wings of defiant dignity, we rise.

—Jamie Collins
(for Jessi and all trauma survivors)

JESSI

AGE 36
April 2016

S ince the time my children were toddlers, I would show them a picture of my family and tell them "This is my family. My mom and my sisters, Janel and Jolene. They aren't here anymore; they're in heaven." We would go over the names and faces. I at least wanted my kids to *see* my family and know them in some small way, even if it was only via a visual remembrance on a flat photograph depicted in colored ink. There were times when my son or daughter would ask some follow up questions. "But why aren't they here anymore?" "What happened to them?" "Tell me why." To those questions, I would reply, "They're just gone. There was an accident. They aren't here anymore. They aren't with us now. They died when I was young."

My children pretty much accepted this. It's all they ever knew. From a young age, they stopped asking questions. But I always knew the day would come when I would need to tell them more about what happened, when they'd reached an age where the thought of what happened to my family wouldn't seem utterly terrifying, like a killer could come and kill all of us, too. They had to be mature enough to be ready for a story like the one I needed to tell. This conversation with my daughter, who is one year older than my son, was anticlimactic. She accepted my truth without asking many questions.

Then, when I was 36 and my son was 15, the day to tell him finally came. It was in April, so the anniversary of the murders was drawing near. I knew television networks seemed to like to rerun my family's "special" around that time, and I was worried my son would see it—without me having first explained it—or would hear about it from one of his friends. The time for the telling of some terrible truths had finally come.

So, I just took the direct approach. "Hey, there's something I'd like to talk to you about. I'd like to tell you more about my family, about what happened to them."

"Okay." His demeanor shifted to serious in an instant and he took a seat on the couch in the living room, his full attention on me.

"Well, I know you know my family is gone, that they died. You've always known that, but I've never really told you about what actually happened to them. It was back in 1989, when I was nine. They were all at home, where we lived in Lakeville, Indiana, and they were murdered. It happened at our house, while I was away at a sleepover at my friend's house. They were all shot with a shotgun. The only reason I'm still here is because I wasn't there that day."

In that moment, the look on my son's face told me he finally understood, on some small level, what my life had been like. They weren't just dead, and it wasn't just an accident. Upon hearing this news, he realized how devastating this tragedy would have been for me, as a young girl. It also helped my son to realize why I was the way I was during his childhood years. When he was a young boy, I *never* allowed any guns in our home—I mean, never—none at all, not even toy guns. It was a hard rule. There were no exceptions. Not a plastic gun. Not a BB gun. No guns. I was terrified of guns and wanted them nowhere around me. I equated guns with the death of my family. For the first time in my son's life, he saw my strict antigun rule in a different light. He now had the piece of the puzzle that triggered my gun-fearing craziness. This conversation was the same as the one I had with my daughter a few years before this one.

Both of my children were very accepting of my situation. Our conversations concerning the big reveal went well. It was as though they realized the topic was sacred ground. I love and appreciate them for that. It did make it easier for me to tell them. But it doesn't make the situation suck any less.

It hurts me deeply to know that my children will never meet their grandma, even if we were so different and didn't always get along. It kills me that they will never get to meet their Aunt Janel and Aunt Jolene, the two most beautiful pieces of my childhood. It slays me that we will never have a home to visit for my side of the family. It hurts my heart to know my own children also pay the price for this terrible tragedy that altered my entire life. My lost relationships have now become their own lost relationships. The cycle of loss carries on. It will continue to impact my own life, and the lives of those I love, moving forward. It stops for no one and never ceases to carry on, reverberating into future generations as it moves on, unendingly.

I'm sorry that I don't have a family to share with you. I'm so sorry . . .

JAMIE & JESSI

Telephone Call

JESSICA, AGE 37—JAMIE, AGE 40
May 2016

After Jessi and I initially reconnected on Facebook, we spent time getting to know one another. In the beginning, it was mostly by text exchanges and Facebook messages, but after a while, we began to talk by phone, too. We started to watch television shows together that we both enjoyed (like *Reign*) and would then actively text each other to share our thoughts on the latest episode. We also shared a lot of pictures, decorating ideas, paint color choices for our homes, candid thoughts, and personal musings. I started to send her inspirational quotes that made me think of her, as a survivor, whenever I came across them online. It felt good, for both of us, to acknowledge that reality—her reality—as a survivor.

Almost a year after sending that e-mail to Jessi back in June 2015, we had a collective epiphany and we made the decision to begin working on this story together. I'll candidly admit that immediately following that collective declaration we had, I had a rather colossal who-in-the-hell-am-I-to-think-I-can-write-a-freaking-book moment and immediately fired off a text to Jessi that read, "Um, let me just try to write the first chapter, so I can see if I think I can actually do this thing or not, okay?" Let's just say after I got that first chapter down: It. Was. On.

From the beginning of our chats, one thing became clear to me: Jessi feels a major disconnect from her mother, my Aunt Dawn. It was, and continues to be, a difficult thing for me to reconcile. As I listened to her speak, I could hear it in her voice on several occasions. There was something lurking beneath her words and tone. Finally, I decided I had to figure it out. One day, I asked her about it. (By this point, she had grown accustomed to me prying for information, so I dived right in.)

JAMIE: *Okay, so today, I want to talk to you about your mom.*

JESSI: *Okay.*

JAMIE: *I've noticed any time you talk to me about your mom, no matter what it is we're talking about, your voice changes. It shifts. You use that same tone of voice I hear you using when we talk about you as a child, as Jessica. You disconnect. You feel distant to me, every single time we talk about her. I mean every single time. I've been trying to figure out why that is. Do you think you're just mad about her life choices, you know, meeting and marrying Bob, which ultimately resulted in the tragedy? Is that what it is?*

JESSI: *Oh yeah. I definitely feel that way about it. I never liked Bob. I felt like he was forced on me. I had already lost my dad. And then she met Bob and married him. Then we had to move to his house in Florida. I had to leave all my friends, change schools, move away. I never wanted that. That's what my mom and Bob wanted. I didn't really have a choice. I was just a kid. I just had to do it.*

JAMIE: *That makes sense. I figured you held some resentment toward her for that because of the way things ultimately turned out. It basically resulted in the tragedy happening and you being where you are today, with no family. That makes sense. I think any child would probably feel that way if placed in that situation. But . . . I think it runs deeper than that. Never one time during our discussions have I ever heard you talk about her in a, well, I guess what I would describe as a loving way. And I don't mean that you didn't love her or that you don't now. I know you do. I know you loved her and miss her. But I just mean that you don't talk about her the same way you do when you talk about your sisters. I feel the love radiate off you when you talk about them. I feel the love you have for Janel and Jolene. I can tell how much fun you all had together. How much you love them. But any time we talk about Dawn, your tone shifts completely. Every. Single. Time. I'm trying to figure out why.*

JESSI: *Yeah, I was really angry at her for a long time. For most of my life, actually. I was pissed. Her decisions changed everything. They are what brought me to this place where I am now, with no family, with them all gone. But it's just, I don't know, it's almost like I just never really felt that close to her. I did feel close to my sisters. We played and did things together. We spent all our time together. I mean, my mom did love me and I loved her. I know she took care of us and cooked food for us all the time. But I always just felt different and didn't really feel close to her. I can't remember anything we really did together . . . and I know we did things.*

JAMIE: *Now we're getting somewhere. That makes sense. From what you've told me before, I guess if you always felt kind of different than your mom and sisters, like you were always the loud one running around and getting into things, that maybe you just felt like you and your mom weren't the same.*

JESSI: *Yeah, we definitely were not the same. I'm totally different than she was. I was, even back then.*

JAMIE: *That makes sense.*

JESSI: *I carried a lot of anger and, I guess you could call it a grudge towards her for years. I was so mad at her after they died. I was mad about everything with Bob. Janel should be here with me now. If my mom hadn't said no at the last minute about her going to that sleepover with me, like she was supposed to, Janel would be here. I would have someone. I would at least still have Janel.*

JAMIE: *Oh, my gosh, Jess. I never even thought about it that way. So, basically, you've been carrying this anger over the fact that Janel is gone and you have always viewed that as being your mom's fault. That maybe she couldn't have necessarily seen the murders coming, but not only did that happen, but you feel she robbed you of having someone here with you, Janel.*

JESSI: *Yep. I should have Janel here. I would at least have had one person left. It would have been Janel and me. But I was alone. It was just me.*

JAMIE: *{At this point, my mind and heart are reeling. I cannot even fully comprehend the words as they are being spoken to me, but the profound message sitting beneath them is slowly sinking in. The resentment. The anger. The grudge. Her mom. Her sisters. The choices. Her being left alone. Her having no control over any of it. I think I understand it better now.}*

Wow. It all makes more sense to me now, Jess. I think I get it. Maybe not fully, but everything you said today really helped me to understand it better, the way you feel about everything. It really helped.

JESSI: *Yeah, I mean, I've gotten over the anger I have toward my mom. I know I was angry. But when I went to see the psychic and she told me my mom knew I was different than her and my sisters were but that she knew that is what would help me to survive this, the thing that made me different from them, it kind of helped me to get over it.*

JAMIE: *{I hear her saying those words, but they feel flat. She's not really over it. She just thinks she is. That's what my gut is telling me in this moment.} Yeah, I remember you telling me about that. But I still hear it in your voice when you talk about her. You're still carrying something that relates to your mom. There's still a disconnect. I don't know what it is. It just feels like there's still something there I just can't quite put my finger on. Maybe, over time, I'll be able to.*

JESSI: *{laughing} Yeah, maybe.*

JAMIE & JESSI

Telephone Call

May 2016

essica and I found ourselves talking quite a bit by telephone once we decided to begin writing this book. To be able to tell her story, I first had to learn it. We typically spoke several times per week, often every other day. One such call sticks out for me. By this point in time, we'd regularly chatted for about a month. I had learned a lot about her life's story. We shared a lot about our lives, families, hopes, fears, disappointments, and dreams. This particular call took place in early May 2016. She and I spoke for 45 minutes. The tail end of that conversation went something like this:

JAMIE: *Well, Jess, I guess I should get off of here now. It's 6:25. I better get some dinner going . . .*

JESSI: *Okay, uh, well . . . I know you've probably noticed how I'm kind of weird when you tell me you have to go. I feel like I need to tell you something. {I sense awkwardness in her tone. I've noticed it before at the end of our calls, but not enough to think much of it or bring it up.} I'm sure you've probably noticed it, but every time we get off the phone, I know I probably sound weird or act weird, when we get off the phone. Like I either jump over you with my words, act awkward, or repeat myself to say goodbye more than once. Have you noticed that?*

JAMIE: *Well, now that you mention it, yeah. I don't know that I would have really noticed, but now that you're saying something, yeah, I've noticed . . .*

JESSI: *I just don't like to tell people goodbye. I'm afraid it will be the last time I ever talk to that person and I don't want to say it. I don't* *want to know that it was the last time. Even at work, if someone is leaving and tells me "Bye," I'll just be like, "Okay, I'll SEE YA LATER!" It's always really awkward for me.*

JAMIE: *Interesting. So, is it like that for you all the time? Anytime anyone attempts to tell you goodbye?*

JESSI: *Well, not all the time. I mean, I don't ever like saying goodbye to people. But if it's someone I actually feel close to and love, then I don't want to say it. I just don't. I said goodbye to my sisters back then and never realized when I left the house that day that it would be the last time I would ever see them or that I was actually telling them goodbye for the last time. It really was goodbye with them. I don't ever want to do that again. I don't want to realize it was really goodbye after the fact. I'd rather not say it. I would rather avoid it. I know it sounds silly. Like it won't change anything. Either something will happen to the person or it won't; I know that. But I just can't get myself to say it. And if I do say it, it eats at me after the fact, that I said it. That something could happen to them.*

JAMIE: *I understand. I think that makes sense. I can see why you would feel that way. I mean, you really did say goodbye to Janel and Jolene without realizing you even were. You didn't know it would be the final words to them. It was just bye and then out the door, like it was no big deal. But it was a big deal. I can see why that would haunt you. I get it. So . . . if you don't want to say goodbye to me . . . then I guess that means you really care about me, then, huh? {laughing}*

JESSI: *{laughing} Um, yeah, it does. I just feel like you know me. I'm not really close to anyone. I never had that close connection to anyone, growing up, that I wanted to have. I never did. I mean, I have that with a few people now. But with you, I know I can talk to you, I can tell you anything. I know you'll listen. I guess . . . I feel love.*

JAMIE: *Aww, I love you, too, Jess. I'm so glad you told me that. I know you didn't have to. Well, I don't want it to be weird when we say goodbye on the phone, because we talk all the time, so we'll have to come up with something else. Hmmmm. What if, after we tell each other we have to go, I just count down from three to one, and once I get to one, we both hang up? But we both have to actually hang up, or it won't work. Would that be better for you?*

JESSI: *Yeah. I totally think that would work!*

JAMIE: *Okay. {laughing} That's the new plan then. I'm so glad you told me this. I would hate for it to be awkward for you all the time, when we get off the phone. We talk all the time, so that would be weird. I totally get it. Well, I seriously better get off of here now, I need to start some dinner, but we'll talk again this week, okay? Maybe in a day or so?*

JESSI: *Okay.*

JAMIE: *Okay. Cool. That's what we're gonna do then. I love you.*

JESSI: *I love you, too.*

JAMIE: *I'll talk to you soon. Okay, we're totally gonna do the new thing right now, okay? Three . . . two . . . one." {hangs up phone}*

This was a profound moment for me. It made me wonder how many moments of Jessica's life she'd spent navigating awkward goodbyes. Part of me felt flattered she felt close enough to me for it to bother her; the possibility of a true goodbye. But another part of me ached for her, for the little broken girl who carried this trauma forward in her life in this way. The one who had a hard time getting close to people because she feared losing them. The one who worried about letting people in too close to her because it gave them the power to hurt her. The one who feared she would, once again, say the final, formal goodbye to another person she loved. She'd said it too many times already.

This was one of many conversations where I walked away armed with a better understanding of the person my cousin was, not just the broken little girl, but the fierce, resilient, bubbly young woman she went on to become.

So, from that moment on, Jess and I did not say goodbye to each other. We closed our calls to that verbal countdown on the one. No more formal goodbyes. She had said enough of them.

JAMIE & JESSI

Telephone Call

June 2016

*W*e had already talked about her darkest day during a telephone call that took place a few days prior to this one. It became clear to me that the things Jessica recalled, she recalled vividly. The things she could not recall, were literally irretrievable to her. I could tell she was really trying. She just couldn't. I assumed she probably had repressed memories, so I conducted a bit of research. The following is what transpired during our next telephone call.

JAMIE: *Hey Jess, today, I want to talk to you about your darkest day. I know we talked about that last time and I have most of what I need from you, but I do have a few follow-up questions.*

JESSI: *Okay.*

JAMIE: *Now, I know last time we talked, it seemed like you were able to remember vividly most of what transpired that day you found out about the tragedy. But I know you couldn't recall the name of your childhood friend or her mom. I think that's interesting. You knew this girl pretty well, right? I mean, you were pretty good friends?*

JESSI: *Yeah. We were good friends. I was over at her house all the time.*

JAMIE: *Okay. And I know you spent a lot of time there, but I think it's interesting that you cannot remember her name.*

JESSI: *Nope. I can't. I really can't.*

JAMIE: *Okay. And that's okay. We want to tell your story as authentically as possible. From what you've told me, I'm pretty sure you probably* *have repressed memories. I think the reason you cannot recall her name is because your mind has, literally, repressed it. Because I know you really want to remember it, you just can't, and I'm sure it's driving you crazy.*

JESSI: *Yeah. I think I probably do have repressed memories.*

JAMIE: *Have you ever read about repressed memories or done any research or anything?*

JESSI: *I have not.*

JAMIE: *Wow. Okay. Well, it seems like you probably do have repressed memories. I assumed you probably did, just based on what we've talked about before. But I want to talk to you about that. I did a bit of research on it and it's pretty clear that people who experience trauma or tragic events often do repress memories. It's like a phenomenon. It's a legit thing. It sounds like even someone with a more normal trauma could have that happen to them, like a child losing one parent, for example. And here you are, basically living that type of loss four times over. It makes total sense that you would repress the memories around your darkest day.*

JESSI: *Wow. I did not know that. I guess I just never realized. I mean, I know I can't remember some stuff, but I had no idea why.*

JAMIE: *Well, it's totally normal. I honestly think anyone in your situation probably would have that happen to them. Rarely do you ever hear about someone losing as many people as you've lost, and especially as young as you were. I think it was pretty much something that could be expected, based on what you've been through. Hell, even if you just lost only one person, you may have done it. It's a means of self-preservation. Your body and mind have literally blocked the bad events to keep them away from you because you cannot deal with it. It's to protect you.*

JESSI: *I can see where that would be true. It's weird because some things I totally remember, but others, I just can't.*

JAMIE: *Let me ask you this, you said you were at your friend's house—the one where you had the slumber party—all the time. Do you remember what her room looked like? Do you remember what she looked like?*

JESSI: *I do not. I was in that room all the time and I can't remember anything about it. It's like I was never there. But I know I was. I just can't remember it.*

JAMIE: *Do you remember what her mom's name or what she looked like? Their last name? Anything?*

JESSI: *Nope. And it's crazy because I was there on a regular basis. We had sleepovers. We did things together. But for the life of me, I cannot remember her name, what she looked like, her mom's name, what her mom looked like, or what her room looked like. She even had a little sister who played with Janel—that's why Janel was supposed to go with me that weekend—but I don't remember what the sister's name was, either. Or even their last name.*

JAMIE: *Okay. Well, it is what it is. We have two options. One is for us to try to figure out who this girl was and to track her down. The second option is to just tell the story like it is. You know what? I think that's what we should do. Let's not go try to figure out things we don't know to fill in holes. Those holes are actually a part of your trauma. They're a part of what this tragedy did to you. I think we should tell your story 100% authentically and just make up a pseudonym for her. This really happens to people. Something bad happens to them and then they repress their memories. I think it's so interesting you didn't even realize you did that; that you actually have repressed memories. I think we should tell it like it is. She doesn't get to have a name because, to you, she no longer has one, because this trauma runs so deep and hit you so hard you completely repressed her identity.*

JESSI: *I totally agree. I think that's how we should do it. Other people may have had this happen to them and they may not realize they have repressed memories, too. Maybe this will help them.*

JAMIE: *Yeah. I think that's the way to go. While I've got you on the phone, I also did some research on OCD. I know we talked about that recently, too. How you have your rituals and quirks.*

JESSI: *Yeah.*

JAMIE: *Well, you'll probably be interested to learn that OCD is also very common in people who have experienced trauma. Again, even a single traumatic loss or event. So, I think your OCD is also related to the tragedy; the way you dealt with it. Another way you tried to allow yourself to handle dealing with it.*

JESSI: *Wow. I had no idea. I mean, I know I do all these weird things. I have for years. I always have. I can't help myself. But I had no idea they were because of what happened.*

JAMIE: *Yep. I think so. The therapists and stuff seem to say that it helps a person who had something happen to them that was out of their control to feel like they have more control over their life. They begin to control little things and form routines for them along the way.*

JESSI: *Wow. I don't even know what to say. I mean, my family has to deal with the way I am. I know it's hard on them. It's difficult to be around someone who has all these things that have to be done a certain way all the time. I know it gets on their nerves. I guess it makes me feel better to know that there's probably a reason for it. That I didn't just become this way. That it's because of what happened to me.*

JAMIE: *Yep. I know you were not a fan of your therapist from your childhood. You needed help so badly. I don't know how anyone could deal with this without professional help. And here you are, thirty-seven-years-old and you've carried this on your own all these years, with no real help. I really hope that one day you may be able to find someone to really help you. It may be easier for you to talk to someone now that you've shared all of this with me. You've told the entire story one time already, so I would think it may make it easier for you to share it.*

JESSI: *Yeah, I hated him. That didn't work at all. I don't know, I've just kind of always dealt with it on my own. I mean, it would be nice to have help, but it's just something I've never had. Just talking to you has really helped. I've never told anyone else all of this. I mean, my husband and close friends know parts of my story or about what happened, but they don't know all of the stuff we've talked about. No one does. You're the first person I ever told this to.*

JAMIE: *{At this point, we've made so many connections and reconciled so many loose ends that I am emotionally whirling. I've realized many times over that I am the first person with whom she's ever shared her story. It blows my mind. It seems so profound, like such a gift of trust and reverence.}*

Well, I want you to know that it means a lot to me that you trust me enough to share your story with me. That you are trusting me to tell it the way we think it needs to be told. I'm so happy to do this for you. It's truly an honor for me. I mean, anyone would have written this book for you, even best-selling authors, and the fact that you trusted me to do it. I have no words, really. I know I've told you this before, I'll give this everything I have, Jess. I won't let you down. It feels like a sacred honor and a privilege for me to get to do this for you. We've talked about this a lot, but I truly believe this was meant to happen, at this time, and in this way. That you and I were meant to come together all these years later to do this, together. To tell your story. To help other people.

JESSI: *Yeah. I think so, too. I've thought that the entire time. This was meant to happen. We were meant to do this. I'm glad we're doing it this way. Honestly, I probably would never have done it otherwise. I really wouldn't have. I know I can trust you. It's not weird for me to talk to you about all of this. I know I can tell you anything. You're one of the most important people in my life. You're my connection to my past, from the family. I always wanted that. And now, I have it with you.*

I cannot even articulate how profoundly amazing it was to help Jessi make important connections to her past. To understand herself better, as a person. To see that she wasn't odd and the things she did weren't just unexpected and strange, but that she was simply an individual who fit a normal pattern for a victim of trauma. Her mind repressed the memories because it needed to in order to survive. After everything she'd been through, I was just so happy to be able to do this with her. To get to talk to her and get to know her like this. To learn her life's story. In some ways, I feel I know her on a deeper level than anyone else. This is, without a doubt, one of the most personally gratifying and pivotal things I have ever done in my life. It truly is.

JAMIE

AGE 40
June 2016

*I*s Jessi what you would expect when you meet her? I'm sure this is the one thing you are probably dying to know, after reading her story.

In the summer of 2016, not too long after we started working on this book, she drove the stretch of road that separated us—five and a half hours from Midland, Michigan, to Indiana—to spend four days with me in my home. It was the first time we'd seen one another in more than 20 years. Yes, 20 years, which is a long damn time by any reasonable person's standard. We were two excited cousins finally getting the opportunity to reunite and we had plenty to talk about.

I honestly wasn't sure what to expect. Twenty years is a long time not to see a person, especially a person you never really knew well to begin with. But from the moment we laid eyes on each other—in the gas station parking lot, where I went to rescue her after she got a bit lost on the way to my house—there was not a single moment of awkwardness that hung between us. It was as though the blood that ran through our veins and our family history gave us a commonality that was enough to make us feel we belonged with each other two decades later. I guess you could call it a soul connection. Jessi was one of those people I felt I had known my whole life, even though time and distance had always separated us.

So, what is she like? Is she what you would expect after knowing what happened to her?

Yes, and so much more. As a person who interviewed her for countless hours via telephone seeking answers to deeply probative questions, I already felt like I knew her. I knew more of her story and past darkness than most. Yet one of the things I could never quite understand was the reason for her hot pink hair. She could never tell me why she had it, even though I knew there had to be a reason. She did tell me on more than one occasion that she felt more like herself with the hot pink hair. She began to dye her hair different vivid shades of color in the eighth grade—in my mind, at the beginning of her long transformation out of the darkness and *into Jessi*—although she also made appearances in bleach blond and the sandy original version over the years, too. But looking at her today, it's pink. Bright. Vibrant. You can see it from a mile off.

I believe the pink hair became a symbol for Jessi—the new version of her that grew out of the little girl, Jessica. But I never understood it until she came to visit me. When she showed me old photographs, I saw her with sandy blond hair, like mine, but a bit darker. Then she showed me pictures of her in high school as a platinum blond. The moment I laid eyes upon those pictures, for the first time, I understood.

When Jessi looks at herself with those sandy blond strands, whether it's in the mirror or in a photograph, what she sees is Jessica. She sees the sad, broken girl who crawled across three decades of sadness. That was her reality. She chooses *not* to see that part of herself anymore. So, Jessi has embraced the old Jessica in a new light, one which comes with hot pink hair as an accessory.

When I saw Jessi's face in that photo album or sitting beside me on the couch wearing her glasses, I couldn't help but see "Jessica," too. The same Jessica I left standing in that cemetery back in 1989. After meeting Jessi, the fiery, vibrant lady with the hot pink hair, who is so happy, positive, and full of life, I didn't want to see that old version of her, either. I wanted to see the new version with the pink hair and fierce spirit.

She will always be Jessica. To her. To me. To all who truly *know* her. But because of all she has gone through and all that she has seen, the hard times she's faced, she chooses to live in this form now. And for the first time, I finally got it. She is supposed to have the hot pink hair. It's who she is. It's Jessi, who used to be Jessica. And upon first sight, she is now more happy and alive than nearly any other person I've ever met. I'm not even sure how that's possible. But it is. The pink strands have become an anthem of sorts.

As an adult, Jessi remains the same little girl who worshipped Wonder Woman and once attempted to drive her tricycle down a tall stairway. She is the girl who cried a million tears. She is the girl whose heart nearly did actually break. She is the girl who used to cut herself. She is the one who felt so sad, alone, unloved, and unwanted she had no idea how she could remain here and continue to live. But she figured it out.

And now, she is pink. She is beautiful. She is a streak of light across a black sky.

Is she what you would expect?

No. She is so much more.

She is fiery.

She is a hot pink lesson on living, personified.

She is love.

And she is light.

JESSI & JAMIE

A Telephone Call

June 2016

I'll never forget one conversation I had with Jessi not long after she came to visit me in Indiana. Working on this project, we obviously talked about some deep, dark stuff. But, we also talked about a lot of happy, profound stuff, too. One day she called me to report something that seemed like the smallest of things to remember, but at the time, to both of us, felt monumental. Here's how that particular call went:

JESSI: *Hi. I'm so excited, I wanted to call you. I had a breakthrough today! I remembered something from when I was a kid! A good memory.*

JAMIE: *Oh, my gosh. You did? That's great! What is it?*

JESSI: *Well, I've always been terrified of June bugs but never really had a reason as to why. And today, I saw a June bug and it kind of flew toward me when I was with a friend, and I completely freaked out. It made me remember something from back when I was a kid. My mom had picked us up from the babysitter's house, my sisters and me . . .*

JAMIE: *Ha, ha. The one who made mashed potatoes that tasted like dog food?*

JESSI: *Yep. That's the one! Ha, ha. So, I was riding along in the car with my mom. I was in the front seat, I had the window cracked a bit, and all of a sudden a June bug flew into my hair. I couldn't get it out. I was screaming and freaking out in the car. That's why I hate June bugs!*

JAMIE: *{Dying laughing and so freaking happy she's laughing and telling me a happy story from her childhood of a normal time with her mom and sisters.} Wow, that's great, Jess! I'm so happy to hear that. You remembered that—something happy. See? You do have good memories from your childhood, too, not just bad ones! I hope you can find more of those the longer we do this . . .*

I know it may sound trivial for a person to remember why she hates June bugs, but for Jessi this was a big moment. It showed us that we weren't only opening up a portal to her dark past, but also able to retrieve happy glimmers of memories from the time spent with the family she'd lost. I can't even begin to tell you how exciting this was for both of us. I got off the phone with her and told my husband about it like it was the biggest breakthrough of all time.

I remember another time when Jessica had to visit the emergency room to get stitches in her hand after she accidentally cut it on the top of a chipped glass while she was washing dishes. The next day she told me, "You know, last night at the hospital, when they called out 'Jessica' because it was my turn to go back, for the first time ever I didn't flinch when I heard it. It didn't bother me that someone had called me 'Jessica.' Usually, I cringe whenever I hear that name." It was another seemingly inconsequential yet pivotal shift in her journey to healing.

Jessi and I realized that what we were doing was reopening her memory. I won't lie: I did have a palpable fear sitting directly behind the excitement as to what could happen as a consequence of us trudging through the darkness of repressed memories together. I was no therapist. But it's something we talked about often. We were open about it. We realized the potential risks. We saw the gains. We knew we could stop at any time. Both of us acknowledged all these things.

The more we talked and the more she opened up to me, the more she wanted to do this work. I could tell she was emotionally growing from what we were doing, even over the phone. I could sense the change taking place within her. I was just as excited about learning new things about her as she was. I was just as interested in helping her to free herself from the restrictive chains of her past, as she was. But that flicker of fear continued to burn like an unextinguished ember in the back of my mind. I didn't want anything bad to happen to her. And I certainly didn't want to do anything that could cause her more pain. It's a fear I could not completely shake, even on the best of days. The concerns and potential consequences were real.

That said, we were committed to the project of unraveling her past. We were totally doing this. Us stopping? Not happening. We were carving deep, winding tunnels into the cave of darkness from which she had hidden for three decades. Real progress was being made. And I'm not even talking about progress on the book. *I'm talking about her taking back her story, her words, her power, and her life.* I realized that's what we were really doing together. Nothing was more important than that. Nothing. Every call became a big deal. Every interaction a blessing. Each new memory, a beacon of light streaking across an otherwise dark past.

The book became almost a secondary concern, no longer the driving focus. There was power in what we were doing. Power, and healing, and hope. I cannot even begin to tell you what it feels like to do that with, and for, a person. For some things, there are no words. And there never will be.

I continue to stand in awe.

JAMIE

September 2016

$\mathcal{W}$hen I sat down to begin writing, I thought I had a fairly good idea of how this story would probably end. Something tragic happened in Jessi's life. Somehow, someway, she managed to survive it. I just needed to learn all the intimate details so that I would be able to paint all the light and shadows with the words needed to properly convey it. This was going to be her life's story as a trauma survivor. But as I said in the introductory pages of this book, life doesn't always go the way we think it will. The story I set out to tell would become *so much more* than what we initially believed it to be.

It is important that I tell you that we ceased all efforts to work on this book for a period of at least four consecutive months between October 2016 and January 2017. I guess you could say life threw a few solid sucker punches our way, going for a total knock out in a championship bout entitled, "Shit Just Got Real." Let's just say life reared her pretty head back and cackled in our completely unsuspecting faces. During that time, I was no longer filling the role of being the author who was writing her story. I was simply stepping up to be her cousin, and only that, to help her as best as I could through all that would ultimately transpire. It turns out this wasn't *just* a true crime story after all. It was *so* much more than that.

The second half of this book—it became *the real story,* one people need to read, experience, feel, and hear. It is the one that begged to be told. And we are totally going to tell it.

No shame. No fear. No regrets.

"Triggers are a bitch." —Jessi

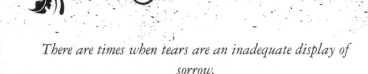

*There are times when tears are an inadequate display of
sorrow.
When invisible holes are left in families,
friendship circles, churches,
and entire communities, cloaked in mourning.
And so begins an endless ripple of loss,
spilling into an ocean of endless tears,
where an undercurrent of suffering lurks
beneath its crushing waves.
But all people see
is that foam that glistens,
floating upon the deceptively calm surface of molten,
aqua-colored glass,
swirling as it laps at the edge of grief,
before pulling everything into its omnipotent wake,
wave after wave,
after the next wave,
down, down, down, always down,
as you struggle for your next breath.
And all people see is that foam,
dancing along the edges.*

—Jamie Collins

JESSI

AGE 37
October 21, 2016

When Lexi died on October 21, 2016, it devastated me. She was a beautiful young woman whom I'd known for 22 years. She passed away at the young age of 24. I used to date her uncle—the boyfriend who lived in the mobile home with me after high school—many years before. Lexi was like a niece to me. She was someone I spoke to often and saw frequently throughout the years, even after her uncle and I broke up. Our social circles often intersected because Ty and I were close friends with Lexi's mom and she's someone we hung out with regularly.

Lexi died of cystic fibrosis, suffering valiantly from a terribly debilitating disease that resulted in her struggling to fill her lungs with the air necessary for her to draw the next breath, and it was like that with every single breath she took. It was torturous to watch another human being suffer the way she did and to know that death was making its way to her. After she died, I was then blindsided by the unexpected, extended hospitalization of my husband, who had developed blood clots in his lungs. Both were triggers for me. I had absolutely *no idea* how to grieve the loss of Lexi without losing what was left of me. The loss of her ate away at me, bit by broken bit, from the inside. The reality was that I had no idea how to grieve a person's death. She was the first person I'd lost since losing my family all those years ago.

I couldn't bring myself to attend her funeral on November 1, 2016. My husband Ty went and served as a pallbearer. I just couldn't do it. I knew the funeral would be an emotional tsunami that would crush me. I would never be able to survive it. I desperately wanted to go, but there was no way I could. I feared what would happen if I did. I ended up writing a poem in memoriam to Lexi, which I gave to her mom to share.

In the weeks after Lexi's death I was afraid if I allowed myself to cry—to really, full on do the ugly, sobbing, soul-crushing cry that lingered within—I wouldn't be able to stop. I'm not saying I didn't cry. I shed a lot of tears in the month after she died. But I also tried to build a dam across my heart to keep the darkness out. I felt like it was coming for me . . . again. It took a lot of effort to rein myself in. But I did.

I basically lived my life on auto-pilot for a month or so after she passed away. The sadness lingered, but I tried really hard to keep myself busy. I took care of my house. Cleaned like an OCD freak. The floors glowed. The dishes were spotless, as were the tabletops, counters, and every piece of furniture or fixture in our home. I prepared the elaborate, gourmet dinners to which my family had become accustomed. At work, I found comfort in my daily routine. If I just kept doing all the things I needed to do and always did, then maybe I could keep the emotions that continued to gnaw at my broken places at bay. I didn't want to let those feelings in. I couldn't. I did *not* want to go back to where I'd been, down that long, dark road of despair and suffering.

Routine, routine, routine. Just stick to the routine, Jessi. Everything is normal. Don't let it in. Keep pressing forward. Just keep doing the normal things. Stay busy. Try not to think about it. Too sad to think about. Avoid. Avoid. Avoid. Divert your thoughts to something else. Deflect. Deflect. Deflect. Stay busy. Focus. Work to stay in the here and now. Don't go to the dark place. Don't shift. Don't fall. Don't crumble.

I battled internally to remain happy, bubbly, vibrant, outgoing, bright, bold Jessi. The woman I'd worked so damn hard over the years to become. I couldn't allow those negative emotions to overwhelm me. They held the power to pull me under. I couldn't survive it. Not again.

JESSI

AGE 37
November 21, 2016

S o, after Lexi died, in the week leading up to Thanksgiving, my husband was admitted to the hospital with blood clots on his lungs. He remained there for an entire week, while they tried to figure out what was wrong with him. If they could get the condition under control, he would be fine. But they explained that blood clots, like the ones he had, were dangerous and could potentially be life-threatening. They had to find the cause and work to medically stabilize him. Ty's hospitalization blindsided us. It was so unexpected, there was no time to plan or prepare.

I was worried about him, so much so I made myself feel physically sick over it. I'd just lost Lexi the month before, and now I could lose my husband, too. (At least that's where my mind went.) It took the doctors several days to figure out what the issue was so they could treat him effectively. During Ty's hospitalization, I took time off from work to spend the entire week with him. At one point, I headed to my best friend Stephanie's house, briefly, to cook a homemade Thanksgiving meal to bring back to the hospital, so that Ty and I could eat it together. It was definitely not one that would go down in the family history books as our finest Thanksgiving ever, but we did the best we could under the circumstances. With Ty in the hospital, bills mounted. Not only hospital bills, but our household bills, too. A man obviously can't do electrical work while confined to a hospital bed. And his wife taking a week off work certainly doesn't help matters, either. But we were both where we needed to be—together—at the hospital, until the doctors got things sorted out.

My absence from work threw off my daily routine in a major way. The rituals of comfort were gone from both places: work and home. While most people would probably enjoy having an entire week off work, for me it made me feel like I had no set purpose. Nothing to do. All those OCD tendencies had no real place to live within my days. I felt off-kilter because of it. I had nothing to channel my energy into, aside from my own thoughts, turned to worries, and that didn't help a damn thing.

It's as though Ty being in the hospital that week triggered something deep within me. It brought back the sad thoughts. The *really dark* ones. Although I'd never visited my deceased family in the hospital, because their deaths were immediate, something about being in that sterile, cold place filled with people who were hurt, sick, worried, or potentially dying took me back to that deep, dark place I'd somehow managed to escape. I felt open and vulnerable to loss again. I started to develop an unhealthy fear of losing either my husband or someone else I loved, the same way I'd just lost Lexi. I began to breathe thoughts of worry like wisps of air while cloaked beneath a thin but ever-present veil of anxiety.

After the doctors figured out what was wrong, they assured me Ty was okay. That he would need to return in six months for a check-up, and maybe some additional testing, but he was going to be fine. Logically, I knew he wasn't going to die at that point. But my mind couldn't stop flitting through hellish hypothetical scenarios. *What if he dies? What if someone else close to me dies? At some point, someone else is going to die. Maybe more than one person in my life. It's inevitable. How am I supposed to deal with that?*

The reality was that someone eventually would die and then I would have to fucking deal with it. I did try to talk myself off the mental ledge where I was perched, gripped in worry, wrapped in self-inflicted emotional terror, and clinging to the edge of darkness. Stephanie and Jamie both tried to tell me things would be okay. That things would get better. That it was okay to be sad over Lexi. That things would get better in time. Ty consistently tried to assure me he was fine and nothing bad was going to happen to him. But their words didn't reach me out on the ledge.

The thoughts swirled. The emotions bubbled just below the surface. I felt myself sliding backward. I tried to plant my feet, but it was to no avail. The darkness was coming. It was headed straight for me. And once it arrived, it was going to have to drag me down. I would not willingly succumb to that hell without leaving claw marks upon the ledge on my way down that dark corridor.

I'm going to try my best to tell the part that comes next, but it's a hard thing to explain. Even for me, and I lived it.

JESSI

AGE 37
Late November 2016

O nce Ty was discharged from the hospital on November 29, 2016, slowly, some of my old habits began to creep back in. While it's not uncommon for me to drink a bottle of wine a night—I admit it, I'm an avid wine lover—I'm the type of person who can drink that much in one evening and not at all be affected by it. I drink to relax. I drink so I can sleep. If I don't drink, my insomnia prevents me from getting any sleep at all. It's a persistent problem I've lived with ever since my family died. I'm lucky if I manage to get a solid four to five hours of sleep on any given night. It's usually less. Nightmares. Memories. Anxiety. Difficulty falling asleep and staying asleep once I do. These issues have been a constant for years.

I began to drink to the point of utter intoxication, with no conscious memory of making the decision to do so and absolutely no regard for my own safety. The odd thing is, it wasn't like it was one of those times where I was pissed off or hell bent on getting wasted, like people sometimes do. It wasn't a choice made in the spirit of having a good time. I didn't have a bad day. I didn't consciously decide to throw the bottle back in a state of celebration or sorrow. I drank, and drank, and drank, and drank some more, and never had a single, identifiable thought about it. No desire to do so. No precursor. I simply awoke in the aftermath, depressed, sad, angry, and nothing short of a hot mess.

I had no memory whatsoever of the stupid decisions I made or the events that transpired *for an entire week of my life.* Just a faint glimmer here or there, or the briefest flash of a memory in the form of a picture in my head. I would only see or realize what I'd done after these potentially catastrophic events unfolded. I felt like

I was going crazy. When you know you *don't want to hurt yourself*, but hear stories about how you tried to, find these crazy rambling notes that you don't remember writing, but did, cast your eyes upon your body and see evidence of self-harm, or other people tell you about things you *do not at all remember* and *cannot possibly explain*, you begin to wonder if you're losing your fucking mind. At this point, it seemed to be a viable possibility. That scared the living shit out of me.

I could see myself spinning out of control. I was making terrible and potentially dangerous choices and putting myself at risk. I was also putting those around me at risk of losing me. It's as though my words, thoughts, and actions were outside my conscious control. I felt like I was just along for the ride. I became fearful for myself. Worried for my family. That's when you know you're out of control. There is nothing and no one that can save you, once you've detached. You're fucked. That's exactly how I felt.

I also began to lose time. There were significant gaps for which I lost all conscious memory. And I don't mean gaps like, when you drink too much one night and can't quite recall all the details of the night before or things seem a bit fuzzy. I mean, I had no memory of them at all. I was doing some strange shit and acting like a person I was not.

I wasn't out of body. I was out of mind. It's like I was outside myself, just watching the sad, fucked-up shit show that I was allowing to turn into my own life. I didn't want any of it. This wasn't who I was. It wasn't me at all. I was happy. I was a survivor. I loved life and embraced every moment of it. I was happy Jessi with the pink hair. But here I was. Lost. Broken. Spinning out of control. It was like watching my life from the outside.

I found myself moving toward that deep, dark place devoid of all light and lacking all hope. The darkness was here. The hell I had feared all along had arrived. I was gripped so tightly in its clutches, I could barely breathe, barely move, barely function. Bad decisions. Bad thoughts. A bad ending. That's what I feared most.

JESSI

AGE 37
Wednesday,
November 30, 2016

I can only tell you what I now know occurred during my "Gap Week" by piecing together information, notes, and the stories told by those who were around me during that time.

One night, I had a knife stashed in my bedroom. I wrapped the knife up in a blanket, tucked it in my arms, and marched out to the living room to where my husband sat. He had no idea what was wrapped up in the blanket.

JESSI: I'm going to go see my dad. (Meaning, my dad's grave, because he's obviously been dead since I was five.)

TY: What? Going to see your dad's grave? No, you're not.

JESSI: Yes, I am.

TY: No, you're not, Jessi. It's late. What are you talking about?

JESSI: I'm going. I have to go.

TY: You've been drinking. You aren't driving anywhere.

JESSI: Yes, I am. You aren't going to stop me. I'm going to be with my dad. I don't care what you say, I'm going.

TY: If you want to go, I'll take you. But I'm the one driving. If you are gonna go, I'm the one taking you.

JESSI: Just forget it!

I'm told I then turned around and stomped my ass back down the hall with the blanket. Pissed.

Apparently, I then I took the steel blade and etched it across the flesh of my leg, until the blood began to flow freely, trickling down my leg in warm, red lines. I then grabbed a notebook and wrote these words. I would see them the next day, along with the new cut on my leg:

I see nothing.

Nothing.

Blood, that's it.

Maybe that's all there is.

Born, living, dying.

Blood.

One cut, one sting, no feeling, numbing.

Wishing it would end.

Idle, still feeling, wishing it would just end.

JESSI

AGE 37
Thursday,
December 1, 2016

The next morning, I woke up with a laceration across my lower leg. *What the fuck did I do? What did I do? Why would I do this?* I did not intend to cut myself. I have no memory of making the decision to do so. And I do not recall writing those sad, cryptic words that constitute a blood poem on those pages. Yet they are in my writing, in my notebook. I can't make any sense of it, but I'm scared. And confused. *What the fuck is wrong with me? I don't know what's going on. I'm scared.* I'm worried about the things I did. I feel ashamed. I haven't cut myself since junior high. Why would I do that again? WHY? A lot of questions began to taunt me, with no clear answers to follow.

It's a hard thing to explain, the time/reality jumping. I guess that's the best way to put it. There were periods of hours, turned into days, where my conscious memory seemingly disappeared. I couldn't account for it and sure as hell couldn't make sense of it. It wasn't like people told me about the things I had done and then I was like, "Oh, yeah, I remember wanting to do that and making that terrible choice last night." "I remember drinking far too much and cutting myself." "I remember wanting to kill myself." It was quite the opposite. I had no conscious memory of it at all, aside from one brief but vivid mental snapshot of me staring down at the blanket and knife sitting on the floor and wrapping the knife up in the blanket. One mental image. That's it. That terrified me. It would be one thing to be pulled low and want to do these things. But it felt like I wasn't the one making the decisions anymore. I had no desire to do the things I had done. None at all. Yet I was doing it, these terrible, dangerous things. It freaked me the hell out to hear about it. I felt out of control.

The real me wouldn't want to die. I'm a happy person. I have a good job. I have a home. I have a husband and children I love dearly. *I would never do that! Never!* Hell, if I really wanted to, I'm pretty sure I would have ended it all somewhere along the way by now. I'm 37-years-old. If I'd wanted to kill myself, I would've already done so.

It's as though I had stepped outside of my normal self, into this darker version of me. The one who was over it all. The one who was okay with dying. The one who wanted to end the fucking pain. The one who drank to excess. The one who cut herself. The one who lashed out at the people she loved. The one who was tired of struggling. The one who took risks. The one who did things Jessi would never do. A person who bore no concern for the consequences of her actions. The one who was falling apart before everyone's eyes, including my own. The one who had no fucking clue why she was doing any of these things, because she had no memory of it at all.

How did I fight so hard to end up like this? What the fuck happened? I felt detached. Deranged. Mentally checked out. And as the week went on, more shit just kept happening. I had no clue what was going to happen next, but I feared it.

TYSON

Friday,
December 2, 2016

I've been with Jessi at the house all week trying to keep a close eye on her after they let me out of the hospital. I could tell she was having a tough time dealing with everything and seemed to be emotionally down. I could see she was struggling to keep it together, so I'd intentionally hovered. I figured she probably needed a break from me, so I decide to stop by my buddy's house tonight to hang out and give her some space.

After I arrived, Lexi's mom stops over. She'd just lost her daughter—the girl who was like a niece to me and Jessi—not long ago, so young. She had to watch her suffer. She had to watch her die. Cystic fibrosis was a bitch. It's hard to imagine any parent having to go through that.

After she shows up, we get to talkin' and she asks me how Jessi is doing. I tell her that Jessi is having a really hard time dealing with Lexi's death and everything that had happened with me being in the hospital. Jessi couldn't attend Lexi's funeral because she can't handle dealing with death or funerals because of what happened to her family when she was just a kid. Jessi had written a poem for them to read aloud at her funeral. I know it killed Jessi not to be able to go to her funeral, like everyone else who loved her did. Jessi did love her. She just couldn't handle it. We all understood why.

For the past two weeks or so, I've watched Jessi struggle. She's been crying all the time over Lexi dying. The past week has been worse, more like how Jessi always gets around the anniversary date of the deaths of her family. I've worried about her all week because of it. I have watched her struggling. But I figured she'd be okay if I just step out for a bit tonight.

Jessi texts me a few times while I'm at my buddy's. I respond, "I'll be home soon," but kind of lose track of time, talkin' to people. You know how that goes. You drink the beer, you shoot the shit. You mean what you say, then look up, and before you know it, way more time has passed. I tell everyone I'm leaving, get up, and head home. Lexi's mom wants to come along so she can see Jessi and check in on her. Lexi's mom is like family to us, so it's no big deal for her to tag along. She is welcome at our house any time.

We pull into the driveway. I open the door and walk into the house. It looks like a tornado struck. There is stuff spread all over the kitchen counters and onto the floor. "Jessi," I call out.

I don't see her in the living room or kitchen, so I keep walking through our house toward the bathroom. And that's when I see Jessi lying on the floor, curled up in a fetal position, completely hysterical. I notice she is wearing the purple, button-down shirt I'd recently worn as a pallbearer at Lexi's funeral. The moment I see that purple shirt, I realize what this is all about. I bend down and scoop Jessi up in my arms and pull her up off the floor. "Are you okay, Jessi? Look at me. Are you okay? What happened? Are you okay? Talk to me." Her eyes flit open and shut, then she looks up at me. It looks like she's in a daze. I can tell she's out of it.

Jessi then looks and sees Lexi's mom standing in the bathroom beside me. She immediately begins sobbing, gut-wracking sobs, and reaches her arms out towards Lexi's mom, the same way a small child would when they want to be picked up. I realize this is what she needs in this moment; she needs her, so I set her down next to Lexi's mom, who extends her arms out, then wraps them around Jessi, and Jessi just clings to her. Like a lifeline. Jessi is sobbing and clutched to her tightly. It tears me up inside to see my wife like this. It kills me to know there isn't anything I can do to fix it. I hate this for her. No one should have to feel like this. I walk out of the bathroom because I know she needs this time with Lexi's mom. I can see that's what she needs right now. It will probably help her. I know it is Lexi's loss she's grieving. That's what drove her into being this upset. Seeing her in that purple shirt. Curled up in a fetal position on our bathroom floor, it slays me. It makes me feel so helpless.

Lexi's mom manages to get Jessi calmed down. But within minutes of her leaving our house, Jessi flies into a rage. She pulled down our movie stand, breaking it. She then begins to sling movies across the room, every which way, in an angry, violent manner, like she's lost her damn mind. I assume Lexi's loss has triggered this. All her feelings are coming out in the form of anger. Movies end up strewn all over the living room, kitchen, and anywhere else that was within pitching distance. I'm talking hundreds of movies, big piles of them, everywhere. She then storms back into the bathroom and begins to bawl. I can hear her sobbing from the living room. We did exchange some heated words. But I know I can't get through to her in this moment. Not right now. She is too angry. Too emotionally messed up. Fighting the inner demons of her past. Yelling. She just keeps telling me, "YOU DON'T UNDERSTAND . . ." "You'll NEVER understand . . ."

Damn it. That's what she always tells me. That I don't understand. She's right, I don't. But I really wish she would let me try to. I want to know more about the past that seems to haunt her. I've been here with her for eighteen years. Eighteen damn years! Her past is like a divide that stands between us. I only know what little she's told me. It isn't much. Her past is something that stands between us, invisible, but always there.

She's back in the bathroom. I know better than to try to talk to her right now. She's too pissed off. There is only crying. Only yelling. She wants to wage a war. I walk into the living room, sit down on the couch, and cry. That's the only thing I can do.

A few minutes later, our teenage daughter arrives home and is standing on the porch with a few friends. *What bad timing. I don't want her to see any of this. It's the worst possible time for her to be home, much less bring her friends over.* She opens the door and sees me sitting on the couch upset. She doesn't know what happened, but realizes it probably has something to do with her mom. She quickly senses it's not a good time to have company over. "Are you okay?" she asks me.

I reply, "I'm okay. It's just your mom. She's having a hard time right now."

"Okay," she softly replies, turns her back to me, pulls the door closed behind her, as I hear her tell her friends, "Okay, let's just go ahead and go now . . ."

It kills me that my wife is in the bathroom falling apart right now. The tears falling down my face aren't for me. I cry them for her. I feel so helpless. Like there's nothing at all I can do to help her. I'm on the outside. Always on the outside. She won't let me in. Maybe I could help her, if she'd allow me to try. But she won't. I worry about what could happen if she doesn't pull herself together. I've never seen her like this before. Not like this. She's falling apart. She's out of control. It's like she's losing it completely. I'm not sure she'll be able to pull herself together. And that scares the living hell out of me . . .

STEPHANIE

Jessica's Best Friend:

Saturday,
December 3, 2016

J ess and I talk on the phone all the time, typically a few times per week, if not every day. We've gotten so close over the years, since reconnectin', we consider ourselves sisters and refer to one another as "my sister" more often than we call one other by name. We are sisters. Not by blood, but by choice. One afternoon, I was cleanin' my kitchen, when the phone rang. I looked down at the screen of my phone and saw that it was Jess. Not an unusual occurrence. I always look forward to chattin' with her.

STEPHANIE: *Hey, Jess.*

(Inaudible sounds, sobbing, gasping for air, I can barely make out anything she is saying.)

JESSI: *I need you . . . I need you . . . I need you. (Followed by more inaudible gasps and sobbing.)*

STEPHANIE: *(It immediately becomes clear that she is bawling. Her voice sounds different. Not normal. She sounds hysterical. I know immediately something isn't right. Something is wrong and it jolts me into a state of focused attention and worry.)*

Jess, what's wrong? Tell me what's wrong. I can barely understand you.

(More inaudible sounds. I cannot make out the words. At this point, I strain to hear anything she attempts to say to me, but it is muffled by soul-wracking sobs.)

JESSI: *{gasping} . . . my mom . . . my sisters . . . I can't . . .*

STEPHANIE: *(Oh no. Oh no. Oh no. I realize something is really wrong. I pretty much instantaneously take on the calm and collected persona of a 9-1-1 dispatcher because I know the situation is serious. I have to get her back in reality with me, not where she is in her head right now. I realize this is not at all a normal call, but a potentially catastrophic one. I have to handle this right.)*

Jess, I need you to calm down. I'm right here with you. Take some deep breaths. Just breathe. I'm right here. I don't know what's goin' on, but I'm right here. Just take some deep breaths in and out. It's okay. I'm right here with you. It's okay. Whatever it is. You need to calm down. Tell me what's goin' on . . .

JESSI: *{Sobbing hysterically}*

STEPHANIE: *(Nearly every word she says, broken by sobs and inaudible. I strain to hear her, completely gripped in worry and fear. She doesn't sound like herself right now. Her voice sounds different. Distant. She is slurring her words to the point it concerns me. Some of the things she says sound off, like she is not with it right now. It's really hard to make out anything from what she's saying to me. I can't understand her. I can't. I'm trying. But I can't.)*

JESSI: *{sobbing hysterically} I wrote it down. {sobbing and gasping} And I gotta find my pad of paper. I wrote it all down.*

STEPHANIE: *Yes, find the pad of paper. I want you to find it and read it to me. Go find it. Read me what you wrote.*

JESSI: *{frantically searching for the notepad} I just {sobbing} . . .
I wrote notes . . . to my kids . . . to tell them goodbye . . . or
whatever . . .*

STEPHANIE: *(Her slurred words disturb me. I become worried this is
more than just sadness and sobbing. She may have had too
much to drink or taken something.)*

*Goodbye? Why would you tell them goodbye? Jess, have
you been drinking?*

JESSI: *Yes.*

STEPHANIE: *Okay. Well, I think maybe you should take an anxiety pill.*

JESSI: *I took all of them.*

STEPHANIE: *(Fuck. This is bad. This is really fuckin' bad. I can tell
she is in a bad place right now. I want to jump through the
phone. I'm too far away to be able to do anything. I have
no idea how bad off she really is right now, but based on
the way she is slurrin' her words and sounds so out of it,
I think she may be in danger. Fuck. I've got to try to snap
her out of this place she's in right now. I need to get her back
in to the present moment with me. Back to reality. That's
what I need to do.)*

*Okay, you need to . . . whoa . . . you need to concentrate
on somethin' else right now. Okay. You need to focus on
somethin' else. (If I can get her to enter one of her OCD
cleaning/sorting rituals, perhaps that will help pull her
out of this dark moment and back to the present.) Okay,
I want you to listen to me. Here's what I want you to do.
I want you to go into the kitchen. Let's go into the kitchen
right now. I know how you like to organize your cupboards.
I want you to pick one cupboard and to organize it better,
so it's the way you like it. How about the spice cupboard?*

	Let's do the spice cupboard. Let's start with that. I want you to put me on speakerphone, so you can still talk to me while you do it.
JESSI:	*Okay.*
STEPHANIE:	*Now, I want you to open the door to the spice cupboard and to take everything out of it. Put all the spices out on the counter.*
JESSI:	*Okay. {sniffing}*
STEPHANIE:	*(I hear her open the cupboard and it sounds like she's taking everything out, that's a good sign. I need to keep her going, to keep doing this. It's working.)*
JESSI:	*{sobbing.} Alone . . . {gasping} No friends . . . No one around . . .*
STEPHANIE:	*(I try to calm her down numerous times but every time I get her to enter a calmer state, she goes right back into it. She is completely hysterical. I've never heard her like this before. She's been upset before, but never like this. I have no idea what's going on, but I know it's bad. I hear her moving things around. Thank God, she's playing along. She's going to organize the spices.*
	And then, I hear a shuffling sound, followed by a loud, chaotic sound, followed by silence. Complete silence. It was like she was there with me and now she's not.)
STEPHANIE:	*JESSI. JESSI. ANSWER ME. CAN YOU HEAR ME? JESSI. ARE YOU OKAY? WHAT HAPPENED? ARE YOU STILL THERE? I NEED YOU TO ANSWER ME. ARE YOU THERE? PLEASE ANSWER ME.*
	(The fear hits me. I realize I have no idea what just happened. She may be hurt. I have no fucking idea what

just happened. Is she okay? I don't know. Oh, my God, this could be really bad. So bad. Something could really be wrong. Oh, my God. I'll call Ty. I decide to leave the phone line open with her on my phone, so I can hear if she responds. I pick up my son's phone, look through my own phone to find Ty's number and call him.)

STEPHANIE: *Ty, it's Stephanie. I was just talkin' to Jessi and she was freaking out. She was completely hysterical and then she was just gone off the phone. She was in the kitchen. I can't get her to answer me. I don't know what happened to her. You need you to get your ass home now! Somethin' is wrong with her. GO CHECK ON HER RIGHT NOW!*

TY: *WHAT? I knew I shouldn't have left her alone. I'm leaving right now . . . {hangs up}*

STEPHANIE: *(On the open line where I had the connection with Jess, I begin to scream into the phone at her) JESSI, ARE YOU THERE? CAN YOU HEAR ME? WHERE ARE YOU? WHAT ARE YOU DOING? ARE YOU OKAY? I NEED YOU TO FUCKING ANSWER ME. PLEASE ANSWER ME. TY IS ON HIS WAY THERE. HE'LL BE THERE ANY MINUTE. PLEASE ANSWER ME, IF YOU CAN HEAR ME.*

(By this point, I'm filled with fear. Every minute that ticks by feels like an eternity. I'm shaking and have a bad feeling in the pit of my gut. I need to see how close Ty is to the house, because the waiting is killing me, so I call him again.)

STEPHANIE: *Ty, it's me.*

TY: *I'm pulling onto the street now. I've got Lexi's mom with me. We're almost there . . .*

STEPHANIE: *Okay. Look in the kitchen. That's where she was. She has me on speaker phone. Let me know how she is. Let me know when you find her. I'm still on the phone with her.*

(I hear the door open and Ty and Lexi's mom running into the house to look for Jessi. I am screaming into the phone) TY, DO YOU SEE HER? SHE WAS IN THE KITCHEN. FIND HER! DO YOU SEE HER?

Never have I been more scared. I went from a normal day to the feelin' like I was about to lose someone I love deeply. I found myself wonderin' if this call she made to me was her goodbye. I did not want to say goodbye. Not to Jessi. Not this way. Not like this. Not now. Really, not ever. But, especially, not like this.

Please let her be okay. Please let her be okay. Pleeeeease. She has to be okay. Please be okay.

The time between the loud sound and them walkin' into the door of the house seemed like forever to me. I was so scared. I honestly felt like I was having an out-of-body experience. I was so full of fear, shaking something terrible, my hairs standin' on end. It felt like I was floating above myself. In reality, I know I wasn't. But that's how it felt at the time. Immersed in fear. Gripped in panic. Consumed by worry. And waitin' for them to find her and tell me how she was . . .

God, please let her be okay. Pleeeeease don't let this be it. Not like this. Not this way. She's come too far for shit to go down this way. Please be okay. Please be okay. Pleeeease.

TYSON

That Same Day

Saturday,
December 3, 2016

ince being discharged from the hospital, I saw my wife spiraling out of control. She was emotionally overwhelmed, too sad, too hurt. She cried a lot. There wasn't anything I could do to help her. Trust me, I tried. When she's pulled low like this, there's not much I can do. I try to be there for her. I try to spend time with her, when I'm not on the road working. I try not to leave her alone. Hell, by this point, I'd hovered over her all week at the house. The doctor told me to stay off work for a week, so I was around the house *way more* than usual, since I was typically gone working out of town six days a week. I wanted to give her a little space and time to herself.

I was hanging out at a friend's place to watch a UFC fight on TV not too far from our house, when my cell phone rang.

TY: *Hello.*

STEPHANIE: *Ty, it's Stephanie. I was just talking to Jessi and she was freaking out. She was completely hysterical and then she was just gone off the phone. I can't get her to answer me. I don't know what happened to her. It sounded like she fell or something. You need you to get your ass home now! Something is wrong with her. GO CHECK ON HER RIGHT NOW!*

TY: *WHAT? I knew I shouldn't have left her alone. I'm leaving right now . . . {hangs up}*

Coincidentally, Lexi's mom had just shown up at my friend's place. We run into each other often because we know the same people. She had just gotten Jessi calmed down the night before by holding her, and ironically, we found ourselves in pretty much the exact same situation. I told her, "Something is wrong with Jessi. I need you to come with me right now. To the house, to check on her." She immediately agreed to go with me to check on Jessi again, since she knew how bad things were.

We hopped into my truck and sped down the street toward the house. Every minute seemed to take forever. Stephanie sounded scared on the phone, panicked even. I wasn't sure what I was going to find. I didn't even want to think of what she could have done. *I shouldn't have left her alone. Damn it!*

We jump out of the truck and run up the driveway. We run into the house. There are spices and kitchen items all over the counter and floor. The place is a mess. I don't see Jessi anywhere. I can hear Stephanie screaming through the house because she's still on speakerphone with the line open to Jessi's phone.

STEPHANIE: *TY, FIND HER. WHERE IS SHE? DO YOU SEE HER? SHE WAS IN THE KITCHEN. FIND HER! Tyson, Tyson—did you find her? Is she okay?*

TY: *We found her. She's in the kitchen. She's on the floor. We gotta go. We're calling 9-1-1.*

STEPHANIE: *Oh, THANK GOD. Keep me posted on how she's doing. Call me . . .*

The paramedics show up and start working on Jessi. They cut her pajama shirt open, put her on a stretcher, and wheel her out the front door of our house. Our daughter wakes up and sees them wheeling her mom out of our house on a stretcher. *Damn, I wish she didn't see that.*

Man, this could have been bad. I mean really fucking bad. She could have died. I shouldn't have left her. Damn it. I was with her all week, watching over her. I thought she'd be okay. I didn't know. I wish she didn't have to struggle like this. It sucks to see your wife falling apart and to know there isn't a damn thing you can do about it. Not a damn thing.

JESSI

AGE 37
December 4, 2016

I woke up in the hospital with very little memory of what had transpired, what was wrong with me, or why I ended up in a hospital bed hooked to IVs. What I do remember is one vivid mental image of paramedics cutting off my Victoria's Secret pajama top. That's it. I was pissed about that because it was my favorite pajama top. I also remember talking to Stephanie on the phone, but I couldn't tell you what we talked about. Beyond that, I cannot recall anything. *Why am I here? What happened? What did I do?*

The doctor walks into my room to talk to me, once he knows I'm awake.

DOCTOR: Did you try to kill yourself?

JESSI: I don't even know. I don't remember any of it.

That was the truth. I had no idea what had happened, much less why. I don't remember. I just don't. That is the beginning and end of my explanation.

JESSI

AGE 37
December 4, 2016

I evidently wrote this letter in the pages of a notebook on the night I ended up in the emergency room. I found it after I got home. Oddly (or interestingly, depending on how you look at it), I have no memory of writing it. When I look down upon the words, it's as though I'm reading the words of someone else. The beginning paragraphs appear to be written in my handwriting but then it morphs into a frenzy of scrawled words that don't look like my handwriting at all. Yet, I know they were written by me. I'm going to share it with you verbatim. I wrote these words on the day I ended up taking an entire bottle of prescription anxiety pills and drinking heavily, before ending up unconscious on the kitchen floor. I'm not hiding the reality of my lowest low. I'm done hiding. I'm done pretending. I'm done cowering to circumstances I never chose. It's important that you see it. All of it. Exactly as it sits tucked between the pages of a spiral notebook in my home.

I know in my heart it's selfish. I miss having the what if moments with my mom, dad, sisters, Janel and Jolene. My own children whom I love dearly are grown and have no time for me anymore. My hubs is busy with work and his own life. I get it. He IS thinking of his family and where we can live and keep power, have running vehicles, and food in our house. He is doing his best, and I know he is doing his best. I think, honestly, I am hindering it.

Work I absolutely love. I feel safe there. But even my crazy is reaching there. Seeping very slowly. Jessica! Why did you return!

I was doing fine. Yes, I know we are the same person from different times. I hoped we would never cross paths again, but here we are. Who wins—you, the lost, hurt, bitterful, hateful little child or me—(Jessi) who has moved on to become successful, loving, happy, making a difference in every life I come in contact with! I am so confused and lost. I seriously want to end this battle. I am tired. Don't know if I can carry on. I love everyone: my husband, daughter, son, boss/best friend, Cass, Mike, Cuzzo Jamie, Steph—my amazing sister, and all those who attempted to love me.

Lexi Sue Martin, Your death fucked me like no other. You were so young and didn't deserve it. I know you were ready and that's okay. You left an impression on me forever. I love you! You were so strong, amazing, and great!

To those who did love me, which were very few, I love you and will be watching over you every moment.

My children, I know I did you wrong and I am sorry for that. Remember our good times. Please. I am not a bad person, just a person with deep-rooted issues which you will never get, and hope you never do!

Wonder woman was my hero. She was amazing.

Anyone reading those words realizes they were intended to be my last. They go a long way in explaining my splintered, distorted frame of mind in that moment. Following the two major life events, I was pulled so low that I didn't want to live anymore. So completely out of it, mentally, I don't remember writing those words, much less any of the other bizarre shit I did that week. I was drowning in the darkness. Suffocating within my own flesh. I was there, but I wasn't there. I was breathing, walking, and talking, but

I wasn't. I was alive, but not really, not deep down inside. I was on functional autopilot.

Those two events—both major triggers—occurring so close together perpetuated the avalanche that ultimately broke little Jessica. The events that caused her to emerge within me at the age of 37 to claim Jessi, the lady who had survived the hell that had consumed her life, as a victim of the dark past she tried so valiantly to move past. I was broken. I was lost. I was falling apart. I was tormented beyond measure. I was fucking dying on the inside. I was breaking on the outside. I saw no way out of the darkness. Any hope I had was gone, sucked up, torn away, replaced by sorrow, grief, and profound sadness that threatened to consume me fully. I was spiraling.

This moment would mark my breaking point. My life was at stake. The place I held in the lives of those close to me was threatened. And I had no idea how fucked up I was, nor any idea of how to try to fix any of it. My broken places were splintering. I was falling apart and crumbling into ruins right before my own eyes. I was breaking apart in front of my husband and children. I was falling the fuck apart. And all they could do was watch, and wait, and wish I wouldn't. But I had no control over it. None at all. I was a fucking mess.

I had no clue how to lift myself out the darkness. I wasn't sure it was even possible. Maybe this was it. The breaking point. The endgame. I'd done all I could to try to survive.

Jessica was here now. She was making her presence known within me. And there wasn't a damn thing I could do to escape her reality, because it was also my own.

JAMIE

Jessica's Cousin
December 4, 2016

I knew Jessi had recoiled into a dark place in her mind, but I didn't realize the full extent of it. I only knew bits and pieces. While I knew she was in a downward spiral, she didn't share all her lowest moments with me. There were a few times when she admitted certain things to me or would send me pictures of the damage she had inflicted upon herself. It emotionally slayed me. I was glad she felt she could confide in me, but at the same time, I was at a total loss for what to do. The only thing I could do was try to be there for her, love her, and support her, to help her try to find her way back to the light.

Anytime Jessi was in a downward dive, I could sense it. It was palpable in her tone, clipped words, and the flat effect of her voice that was so incredibly different from the bubbly persona she normally exuded. I could sense how distant or sad she was when we spoke. It was as though her emotions carried over to me. Like we had an unexplainable connection through the work we were doing together, maybe like actual transference, empathic blending, or something. Therapists claim that to be a potential consequence for them when dealing with trauma victims. I believe it and can see why. When she was sad, I felt her sadness. When she was hurting, I could feel the hurt she expressed like it was my own. I could hear the shame in her voice. I felt the shame. I'm pretty sure it was sadness, hurt, and shame over not being able to just continue to carry the load on her own. She'd proven she could walk life's path alone for almost three freaking decades, but once Lexi passed away and Ty was hospitalized, her time dragging that burdensome load of trauma behind her was up. Consider it done. Her time hanging on in emotional solitude as a means of survival was over. This was her breaking point.

When Jessi worried about herself or her own thoughts and actions, that carried over to me, too. I would worry myself sick over it. *What if something happens to her? What if this is too much for her to handle? What if this breaks her?* While I knew her telling me her story was therapeutic and helped to lighten her load in a monumental way, it also brought all those thoughts and feelings back to the surface, those dark, terrible feelings she felt as a little girl. I used to lay in bed at night and pray to God. I would ask him to guide her on the path she needed to walk for healing. *Please be with her. Please carry her. Please help her through this. She's been through so much already. Help her through this dark, dark time.* I would then talk to her family and ask them to surround her, hold her up, lift her spirit and help to bring her some sense of peace, and allow her to finally get the help she so desperately deserved and needed all along. *Please be with her. Please hold her. Carry her through this. She's hit the lowest of lows right now. I'm not sure she can do this again. I'm not sure she'll get through it. Not again. She needs you. Anything you can do to help her. Please surround her with your love and carry her.* I asked this of God—Dawn, Janel, and Jolene—every single night. I felt helpless. I'm pretty sure all of us involved in her life did. You may think I'm crazy for talking to dead people, but there wasn't much else for me to do.

I was consumed by worry and plagued by Jessi's sorrow. I wondered if us talking about the past had reopened a portal she had sealed over and sworn she would never again trespass through. I know in some regards, it definitely had. I never wanted to go back to that little white church. And here we were, writing a damn book to tell her life's story. Talking about all of it candidly and completely on the phone every other day. We were dredging deep down into the tragedy and all the emotions it carried, which felt like being swept under by a fierce current.

Once I realized she had repressed memories and did a bit of research on it, I was worried that she needed professional help to try to fully understand and grasp her dark past and the emotionally burdensome baggage that came along with it. Of course, she needed professional help. No doubt about it. Who in the hell wouldn't after going through what she had endured? While I knew that from the beginning, her repressed memories presented yet another layer of potential issues for her as a trauma victim, heavy satchels she continued to drag along behind her over all these years, locked up tight, never opened. They still existed. She was still carrying them. Every single damn day. Everywhere she went. Those heavy bags. With every breath, and every step she took. I so desperately wanted to help her unpack those damn bags and finally put them away, perhaps under the bed, where she knew they still existed, but wasn't still afflicted by their oppressive weight at every waking moment.

I only hoped she could survive this . . .

JESSI

AGE 37
Monday,
December 5, 2016

"The human mind is a fucked-up thing."
—Jessi

O
n Monday, I went back to work. We needed the money, since Ty and I had both been off work for a week or more and our household bills were piling up. On top of that, we knew hospital bills would soon begin to fill our mailbox, even with health insurance covering a portion of it, and that didn't even take the upcoming Christmas holiday into account. Not only did we need the money, but I needed to get back to normal. Surely, work would help to get myself and my life moving back down the tracks of normalcy. I could immerse myself in my daily routine to bring myself back to that safe space, or so I hoped.

By the accounts of those around me, including Boss Lady, my behavior on Monday was strange, to put it politely. I wasn't my usual bubbly self. I walked out to the front of the daycare center or into Boss Lady's office to cry several times throughout the day.

I have no memory of this. Perhaps I should just let her tell you about it.

BOSS LADY

I've worked with Jessi for the past 15 years at the two daycare centers I own and operate. Not only am I her boss, but I also consider Jessi to be a close friend of mine. I've noticed she always has a hard time holding herself together, emotionally, during the last week of April each year. Knowing what I do about her history, I totally understand why. I usually just tell her to take as much time off as she needs to that week, even if that means the entire week, because I know she has a hard time making it through it. She cries a lot. She has a hard time dealing with those past losses she still grieves. Every April, it's like it hits her full-force and she's in the throes of emotional torment and suffering.

In the month following the death of Jessi's friend, Lexi, and in the weeks after her husband's unexpected hospitalization I began to notice Jessi shifting back to that dark space she always falls into every April because it's the anniversary of her family being murdered. It's something anyone who knows her can't miss. When this happens, it's like she becomes an entirely different person. She looks different. She sounds different. She even acts like a different person. Her voice becomes distant and flat. Her responses are always short and clipped, often consisting of only one word. Her tone sounds robotic. It's like she's standing there talking to you, physically, and you're looking right at her, but it's like she's not really there with you at all. It's a hard thing to explain. It's almost like there's a clone of Jessi occupying her space or something, like a physical stand in for the person she normally was. Whenever this happens, the light is gone from her eyes. She is expressionless and devoid of all emotion. It's as though she's seemingly detached, removed, and barely there. Not only do I see and sense this change in her, but all the parents and kids at the center do, too. At the beginning of December, I had moms walking up to me asking, "What's going on with Miss. Jessi?" "Is she okay?" With her like that, there was no way I could put her in a classroom, so I decided to have her spend the days in the office to assist me instead. That way, she would still be able to work and receive her paycheck. I knew she needed the money. I could see she was having a hard time coping with the death and hospitalization. It's like they triggered something in her.

Jessi knew the daycare center and its policies and procedures forward and backward and was meticulous in the performance of her job duties, but during that first week of December, it was like she was a tourist at her own job who didn't know all the things she knew before. I remember one day Jessi handed me an attendance sheet to use for the day for one of the classrooms—the paper the parents would sign their kids in and out on when they came and left—but when I looked down at that attendance sheet, I saw that it was one that had already been filled out from being used for the week before, so it wasn't blank and ready to be used. (This is OCD Jessi we're talking about here.) This struck me as odd. She was the one who never broke a rule or missed a procedure. Ever. And here she was, handing me a completely filled out, used attendance sheet as though we could use it. One look at it should have told her otherwise. I could tell she was just trying to help me out and do what she could, but it was like she was a visitor at the center, not a seasoned employee, much less my OCD assistant director and a star employee.

On Monday, December 5, 2016, Jessi was assisting me in the office yet again. I had noticed I hadn't really seen her eating much the week prior, so when I ran to McDonald's to pick up my lunch that day, I ordered two cheeseburger meals, so I could bring one back to Jessi. As soon as I got back, I told her that I had bought her some food. I sat down at my desk, pulled the cheeseburgers and fries out of the sack to set them out on my desk for us. Jessi pulled her chair over to the corner of my desk, as she often did, to eat with me. She immediately began scarfing down the food. She looked like a starving person who hadn't seen a bite of food in days. She was shoveling in fries like she was the poster child for the famished. She ate every bite of that meal I bought her. I didn't really think anything more about it, until about 45 minutes later, when Jessi looked over at me and said, "I really need to eat lunch. I can't keep food down lately and I haven't had anything to eat today."

But she had just scarfed down an entire cheeseburger meal from McDonald's 45 minutes prior. It's as though she didn't remember it. It's like she never ate lunch at the corner of my desk. If I didn't know better, I'd think I was losing my mind or something, but I was there, I saw her, and she ate every bite of it.

I was already concerned about Jessi based on how she'd been acting for the past week at work, but in that moment, I became even more worried about her state of mind, ability to function, and her safety. I told her, "Jess, I know you're having a hard time. I really think you need to go to see a doctor." I then called Tyson and told him, "I really think you should come get Jessi, Tyson. I don't think she should be driving herself anywhere right now." She was too out of it. It was like she was there physically, but mentally she wasn't herself at all. I told Jessi that Ty was on his way and was going to go with her to the doctor. She was accepting of it. While her replies were still one word and robotic, she seemed to understand that she needed help.

Jessi stood up, gathered her belongings, said, "I'm going to go ahead and just wait outside for him." She then turned and began to walk in the opposite direction of the exit, although it was clear to me that the exit was where she was attempting to go. Instead, she walked into a back office. I saw her turn around with a look of utter confusion plastered across her face, like she was lost. Jessi had worked in this building for four years, yet she seemed to suddenly have no idea where the exit was located. The same exit we walk out of to do our routine fire drills with the kids on a regular basis. The same exit doors she walks through every morning and walks back out of every night. This was a building Jessi had walked out of hundreds of times. It was truly bizarre. I didn't know what to make of it. All I know is that I was happy Tyson was going to make sure she was going to see someone to try to get herself some help.

JESSI

AGE 37
Monday,
December 5, 2016

*H*ow in the hell is it possible to not realize where the exit is located to a building you've worked in for four years? I couldn't tell you. But it happened. Boss Lady told me about it. One more thing to add to the pile of problems that began to mount in my life. By this point, I was amassing a mountain from which I could not crawl out from beneath, despite my best efforts to do so. People undoubtedly thought I was losing my mind.

While I didn't realize a lot of what I was doing, saying, or the way in which I was acting around those who knew me best, what I did realize was I could not reconcile the things they told me in the moments when I was actually mentally checked in and present. I was doing weird things. *Why?* I didn't mean to do them. I didn't remember doing them. Hell, I didn't even want to do them. Yet there I was, doing weird things. It was not only embarrassing and scary, but bizarre as hell. I had worked the entire week before and had no memory of it. *None.*

I needed help. I had no clue what was happening to me, but it was clear that I was no longer in control of my own thoughts, words, and actions, at least not all the time, anyway. Not anymore. There was a disconnect within me or something. I was completely losing it. My issues had even made their way to my happy place—work, where I get to be with the children who need me—and that left me no safe place to exist. I was surrounded by the darkness and the confusion that accompanied it everywhere I went. I was falling the fuck apart. Fast. I had no explanations. No answers. Just gaps in time. Blurry moments. Words leaving my mouth. Bizarre actions not intended. Things I could not reconcile. And I was reeling in the aftermath.

I called Tyson while sitting in my truck in the parking lot in front of the daycare center and told him, "I need to get help." I then drove to a nearby medical clinic, where Ty met me in the parking lot. My hope was to walk in and be able to find a new doctor—a family doctor—who could help me with my issues. I didn't like to take pills, but given my current situation, I was willing to do anything. We walked in and I explained the situation and the lady at the front desk told me, "It will be at least two weeks before we can get you in to see a doctor." *Two freaking weeks.* Upon being told this, I turned to Ty and said, "I don't have two weeks."

Walking out of the building, I began to cry, telling him, "Ty, I don't have two weeks. I have to go to the hospital."

He said, "Let me make some calls." Ty called around to find a suitable place I could go where they would accept me as a patient. I remember him saying, "Are you sure you want to do this?"

I replied, "I have to. I know I won't make it." They were the truest words I have ever spoken.

My life was on the line. I was living life way too far outside any reasonable person's boundaries. I had no control over what I was thinking, saying, or doing. This was it. Figure it out so you can survive, or don't and die. I had to find help. I fucking had to. I wanted to live. I knew I needed fucking help. No doubt about it, I need to save myself. I needed to keep my kids' mom safe. I needed to save my husband's wife. But could I?

Because the other option was looming. The other option would, undoubtedly, lead to my own death. While I didn't know a lot of what went on that week, that much, I did know.

JAMIE

Monday,
December 5, 2016

I spoke to Jessi the night she ended up checking herself into
the psychiatric ward of the hospital. She sounded so monotone
and emotionally flat, it was almost like there was nothing left of
her. It was the voice of a downtrodden person who was vacant and
hollow and felt nothing but empty. It killed me to hear her like
that. I honestly wasn't sure she was going to make it. Of all the
times I'd ever heard her sound like this, this was the worst. Her
clipped responses held a space for the chatty, vibrant woman my
cousin used to be before Lexi's death consumed her and the triggers
took her.

She told me she was putting herself in the hospital because
she was scared for her own safety. Truth be told, I was scared, too.
Really scared. She didn't want me to freak out if I wasn't able
to reach her because she and I typically spoke every other day.
She knew they would probably take her phone from her once she
checked herself in.

I understood why Jessi had admitted herself to the hospital.
I encouraged it. I tried to help her feel good about the decision. I
told her it wasn't her fault she felt like this. It was because of what
happened to her. These losses were triggering her past. I knew that
she would likely be in there for a while. I felt good about it. I could
tell she wanted to go. She was ready to at least *try* to get the help
that, for the first time in her life she realized she needed. It was so
obvious to anyone else that a little girl who'd been through what
she had would need professional guidance to deal with what all the
turmoil this tragedy had heaped upon her. To her, it came as a total
shock. But she did, finally, see things for what they truly were and
understood she had no choice other than to rely upon another human

being, a professional, for help. I prayed she would get that help. She needed it. She deserved it. Surely, a person checking herself into the psychiatric wing of a hospital with an endless past of suffering like hers would be given the resources she so desperately needed.

I texted Tyson several times while Jessi was in the hospital to check on her. It was making me crazy to be so concerned for her and not to have any idea how she was doing. *Was it okay in there? Did she hate it? What was it like for her in there?* I didn't have a clue.

It baffled me that out of our entire family—Jessi's remaining extended family—I was the only one who actually spoke to her in any meaningful way who knew that she was in the hospital to begin with, much less, the reason why. The only one of many. If I hadn't circled back to reclaim a relationship with her, she wouldn't even have had that, not even me. If our family had *known* about this, they would have cared. They are good people. But how it is that no one bothered to get to know Jessi during her teenage and adult years, much less to send her meaningful messages, calls, voice mails, cards, or birthday gifts, I cannot say. Here Jessica is, Ed and Dawn's daughter, with a family of her own, but otherwise, feeling very much alone in this world. For me, it was a messed-up thing to bear witness to and internally ponder. It made me angry. But it wasn't my place to tell anyone else about what was going on. If they were truly involved in her life, they would have known. The only people aware of Jessi's hospitalization were her husband and children, Stephanie, me, Boss Lady, and I told Mona the bare bones, just enough to let her know Jessi was in the hospital and I thought it good she was there, because Mona was worried sick and messaging to ask me about her. It was one of those moments where I just had to hold it, as people often do—this emotionally torturous information—and deal with the reality of it as best I could. The same way Jessi typically always did: pretty much alone.

I do think us talking about what had happened to her helped her. For her to have someone acknowledge her reality. The feelings. The aloneness. The sadness. The path that her life had taken. The way she felt cut off from the world on April 29, 1989, and in all the days that would follow it. It helped her to talk about it, to share it, but it sure didn't fix anything. Nothing would. I hoped that in that hospital room, surrounded by medical professionals, she would finally find a way to lessen her life's load.

Only time would tell . . .

MY JOURNAL

Written While I Was Hospitalized
[Exactly as it appears in Jessi's journal.]

December 5, 2016–December 12, 2016

Feeling afraid, feeling despair. Trying to get the help I need, but getting nowhere. Tears, uncontrollable, knowing what I had done and had to do. Tyson, so helpful and trying so hard to do as much as he can do. So, this was it. I have to be safe. At work, at home, just crying. Thoughts I don't want to be having. Though more frequent. The <u>end</u>. The cutting. I feel relief with cutting, but know it's not okay, physically letting out a sigh of relief. Relief for an instant as the blade glides across my skin and the warm blood turns cold as it drips from the fresh wound. I just want to stop, but I can't. Scared. I've come so far since the horrible tragedy my former child self "Jessica" endured so long ago. The cutting is back, back after 22 years. With no sign or thought of it, just sprung upon me. And Lexi, your death was so hard on me. We knew it was coming, but still hit me like a ton of bricks. I guess this should have been my first sign something was changing in me. I withdrew from the world. Crying and crying. My emotions were everywhere, sad, mad, confused. I didn't know what or how to feel. Everything I thought about came back to you. I feel so guilty not going to your funeral. But my last funeral was the biggest tragedy of my life and I couldn't bear the thought of facing that or the emotions that came with it ever again. I feel cut off from it all. An outsider looking in. 22 years I knew and loved you and I felt distant still. My behavior came out as anger to everyone around me. But it wasn't about or directed at them. I just wasn't sure how to feel. I didn't like feeling that way, it was unsettling to me. I am normally in control of myself, my emotions, but this moment in time, I wasn't. Spiraling out of control, not knowing how to grab the reins and be in control again. My second sign was Ty being in the hospital. He wasn't even going to tell me. [He worked out of town for weeks on end, at times, so I wouldn't have necessarily known if he didn't tell me.] I held it together for a minute or so. But when my good friend [Boss Lady] hugged me (after she had just covered my shift for work), I broke down. Uncontrollable tears, thoughts running through my head. I knew I couldn't lose him. Losing him would mean my breaking point. And that wasn't good. I gained my composure again and drove 2 ½ hours to him. Seeing him so vulnerable was scary to me.

November 23, 2016

[Jessi reflecting back]

It was the day before Thanksgiving and I planned to go with Stephanie to make sure Ty had a somewhat real Thanksgiving dinner. A plan that started with Ty & Steph. A whole chicken, homemade mashed potatoes, corn, pumpkin pie, and some rolls & mac and cheese. We drove back to surprise him. Well, a surprise that ended not as planned. He was mad. [Mad that I'd left him at the hospital by himself and went with Stephanie to go cook all this food.] I just kept thinking how much time and effort it took to pull this together. He told me "You can't surprise people in the hospital." [Like they should just be miserable because they're in the hospital, instead.] I lost it! I grabbed my purse, started crying, and made my way out to my truck. Stephanie followed me and tried to calm me. I was hysterical! Death, done, end, it's now not worth it, it's over, but how?

Ty called me and I just kept telling him I couldn't do it anymore. My pulse was racing, the tears streaming down my face, hysteria had taken over. I needed to soothe the pain and quick. I just kept punching myself in the face, until I felt the inner calmness starting to take hold. [I'd never done that before. I'm not saying I'd never hit myself once or something, but never like that.]

I went back in. Tension. The thoughts still there. I still wanted to end it. I couldn't eat for days. I wanted to be there for Ty, but my thoughts were elsewhere. A week we were there. We came home and I just got worse. The thoughts were constant, the cutting, and now the drinking more than ever. I was withdrawing from everything. I didn't want to cook, clean, go to work, or talk to anyone. I just wanted to fade away into the abyss where I could feel nothing. The darkness was taking a hold of me, faster than I had ever seen. There was no turning back, no escaping its clutch. It had me. Sadness, despair, enveloped me. Planning, thoughts, and more cutting, then Lexi's mom and Lexi's daughter came over to save me. I was happy for an instant. This was the first time I had seen her since Lexi's passing. We hugged, cried, and I even made dinner. Then they left. And the darkness, like a black cloud, came over me as quickly as it had left me. This should have been the sign. I drank and drank and drank myself into oblivion. Not sure what happened, but ended up in the E.R. Everything so fuzzy, not being able to remember any of it. Well, besides waking up in the hospital bed dazed and definitely confused. Depression. That word set in black and white on the paper they sent with me. What? That thought never crossed my mind. No, that can't be right. Anxiety? Check. OCD? Check. Depression? No, not me. I couldn't have been more wrong . . .

I tried to return to work on Monday, that was my safe place. But for some reason it didn't feel that way for me anymore. I kept leaving the room to cry. Then pulled myself back together the best I could and went back in the room. The children knew. Not exactly what, but they knew something was amiss, wrong with me. A few wouldn't leave my side and seemed sad. They just kept repeating "I want you . . . " With my heart breaking for them because they could sense my doom, I knew I couldn't stay. Meanwhile, my boss had looked up psychiatrists for me to call. All had to have a referral, which I didn't have. I called doctor's offices to see if they were taking new patients, a few were, so I went there, feeling a bit hopeful and anxious . . .

Deep in my heart, I knew what was going to have to happen for me to survive this . . . I realized "Jessica" was back, along with the stuff I was already dealing with. She had so much baggage that never was dealt with so long ago. So double the load, double the feelings. No wonder I am feeling out of control! We drove to the E.R. where they checked me out. Nervous, anxious, sad, and scared all of which I felt at that very moment. Hours later, I checked into the ward. OCD and anxiety in overdrive! I had nothing of my own and felt helpless. The room was crisp and neat. I still felt lonely and out of place. I paced for about 2 hours rubbing my thumbnails, the right thumbnail one direction, and the left thumbnail the other direction. "He [Ty] forgot about me. He forgot about me." Those were the thoughts racing through my head as the tears started to fall. Feeling out of place, sad, lost, and still the feelings of despair. Still pacing and pacing. Finally, a knock on my door. Ty had brought me my comfort items: Ellie Funk [a stuffed elephant with beads inside of it that you can put in the microwave to warm it up. I bought it several years ago and have been obsessed with it ever since], my two red pillows, and my gray and white blanket. I felt a little relieved he remembered. All I wanted to do was cuddle up in my blanket and hold Ellie Funk tight. I still felt the darkness, but my familiar stuff was like a small flickering candle which brought a little light and hope to my future.

They have group sessions, which I go to. But the stuff they are learning and working on, I already do. I am still in a funk, but am forcing myself to eat, since it had been days.

December 8, 2016

I have been feeling a bit depressed, don't want to leave my room. I finally did go color for a bit, then got to <u>finally</u> shave my armpits. My anxiety was crazy because I couldn't. I did 1st group then came back to my room. I looked over, and on the board, someone <u>finally</u> took the time to write on it fully! I started crying. It was very touching that Cindy, my counselor, would take the time to tell me to "Have a wonderful day!"

Kota [my daughter] came to see me today and I was excited and relieved to see her. Though we didn't talk much, she sat with me as I ate, and we watched one of the "Ice Age" movies. After she left, I was feeling genuinely happy. I actually stayed out of my room and watched some more movies with others who were here also.

December 9, 2016

I forced myself to stay out of my room most of the day, which is a daily struggle at the moment. Austi [my son] and Kota [my daughter] came to see me. Austi always knows how to make me feel better. He, of course, was his funny/silly self . . .

December 10, 2016

My anxiety was pretty high. I didn't get much sleep again. 2nd group was so much fun and I felt normal for a few. We played Wii Bowling and Sword Fighting. It was pretty fun. We were all laughing and relaxed! I came back to my room and Kota had dropped off my shampoo/conditioner, mousse, my deodorant, brush, and Chap Stick! Having my own stuff felt amazing. Ty surprised me with a visit! That made my night. He did ask if they knew when I would be coming home. Monday was the possible day. Thinking of being in the real world scares the shit out of me. Wondering if I can still function like I used to. I'm trying so hard to get back to where. I was, no, better than where I was. Trying to deal with my emotional baggage that spreads throughout the past 27 years of my life. I did take their advice on one thing. When I feel like I want to cut, I have a bright pink ponytail [holder] I put on my right wrist to snap. The physical pain is still there, but it's not dangerous.

December 11, 2016

I actually got six hours of sleep! I woke up feeling more refreshed than I had been. It's easier for me to keep myself busy and not just lay in bed all day.

JAMIE & JESSI

Telephone Call

December 13, 2016

Once I learned Jessi was finally discharged from the hospital, I called her on my way home from work the next day. I wanted to give her a day to acclimate, but I was *dying* to talk to her. I was excited, but slightly nervous, too. It had been a week and a half. I wanted to know how she was doing, what her stay was like, if it was weird being there, how the experience was, what the other people were like—patients and doctors—and whether she had gotten the help she so desperately needed when she admitted herself.

JAMIE: *Hi, Jess. I just wanted to call to check on you. Ty said you were getting out today. How are you?*

JESSI: *Okay. {her voice was flat and lacked affect}*

JAMIE: *I know it probably sucked being in there, but I'm really proud of you for realizing you needed to do that—to check yourself in. I know it wasn't an easy thing for you to do that.*

JESSI: *Yeah. It was okay. I mean, I would have rather been at home, but I knew I needed to be there. It was hard for me to leave. I was kind of scared to leave, even once they said I was ready. {same solemn tone, no spirit}*

JAMIE: *So did you get to talk to anyone?*

JESSI: *No. Not really. I mean, I got to talk in a group, you know, with other people, but I didn't get to talk to anyone by myself. That's what I wanted.*

[Now, in this moment, it becomes clear to me that she did *not* get the help she needed, despite the fact she stayed in the hospital for a week and a half. While they may have helped to stabilize her, she wanted *real* help.]

She didn't get any help at all? No individual counseling? Are you freaking kidding me? How is that even possible? A girl who had become an unfortunate casualty of tragedy—one of the worst types imaginable had now also became a casualty of the mental health care system. For God's sake, this was Jessica Pelley, who had her entire family murdered. If she can't get help for *that*, how in the hell is anyone, anywhere, supposed to get help for *anything*? I was almost choking with anger, but I had to suck it up and pretend I wasn't totally pissed off that this had happened to her.

JESSI: *Well, they did refer me to a psychologist. They said I need to call; it would take me probably, like, a month to get in.*

So, let me get this straight—my cousin, Jessica-fucking-Pelley—who needs help and formally walked herself into a hospital in an emotional state to plead for it, with a past like hers, as dark as they come—cannot get the help she needs for at least a month? Are you fucking kidding me? How is that even possible? If she thought she had a month, she wouldn't have checked herself into the hospital in the first place.

Anyone who doesn't think we need to offer more services to those in need of psychological assistance in this country is out of their freaking minds. Truly. When people want help and reach out, they cannot always get it. That defies all logic. It defies human decency. But, for her, I try to rein in my disgust.

JAMIE: *Well, that's good, at least. You know, maybe you'll get a good person and it will really help you. It's not your fault you're having a hard time dealing with all this, Jess. At all. It's to be expected. No one could go through everything you've been through and not have these types of issues. Everything you are dealing with is totally normal, given that situation. It really is.*

JESSI: *They said I was depressed.*

JAMIE: *{Jessi's tone tells me she can't believe they would assign that word to her. It bothers her. I sense shame lingering beneath the word when she says it.} They did? Well, I'm honestly not surprised they would say that, given the situation, Jess. You do feel really sad and are having a hard time dealing with Lexi's death. You don't feel like you're in control anymore, like you're being pulled too low and don't know how to cope with it. It makes sense that you would be depressed with all that going on, given your past. You've had a lot of bad things happen right in a row.*

JESSI: *Yeah. I guess.*

[Her tone remains flat and devoid of all emotion, aside from the shame associated with the "D" word: depression.] I don't recall much else transpiring during that call.

I hung up the phone feeling worried. Maybe when she got to talk to someone in a month, it will be the beginning of healing for her. *If she could make it a month.* It's hard to reconcile the fact that a person like *her cannot* get help when she tries to get it, even after spending a week and a half in the hospital to seek it. It just seems so wrong. I can't even wrap my mind around how messed up that is. What I now know on a personal level is that the mental healthcare system is tragically broken, perhaps more so than the broken people who actually need it.

I sincerely hoped she could find her way back to the light because she was broken. She was shattering in the few places that remained unbroken. And there wasn't a damn thing any of us could do to stop it. Not a damn thing, but to helplessly bow our heads, pray, worry, and hope like hell.

Please let her get the help she needs. Dear God, please, please help her. Don't let this be the way she goes out after all of this. She wants the help. She needs it now. Pleeeeease help her get it. Surround her in your loving arms, hold her up, and let her make it through this. Please. Please. Please help her.

Looking back, I now realize she sounded to me on the phone the way she sounded to Stephanie when they attended summer camp together all those years ago when she was ten. Flat. Distant. Gone. That dark place takes her there. She's here, but she's not, all over again.

Will she be able to eclipse this darkness?

I didn't know . . .

JESSI

AGE 37

Early December 2016

*I*t feels as though I am dangling by a single frayed thread. One that could snap at any moment. I pray to God for help. I am devoid of all hope. I have no energy left to rage, rebel, or pretend to be okay for one fucking minute more. I feel like I'm on a death march, my stay at the hospital was only a temporary respite.

I now realize that I have been in denial about so many things: my past, my feelings, the way the tragedy reshaped me. Over the years, I became a brightly colored façade of a person who appeared happy most of the time—and for the most part, was—but a person cannot walk barefoot across a thousand acres of thorns without wounds being inflicted upon her flesh. It wasn't until now that I *finally* looked back and saw all these thorns I walked across over the years. It wasn't until now that I saw things as they really were, and myself as what I truly am. I have absolutely no fucking idea how to move forward from here.

I'd like to say that the hospital's doctors and psychologists really helped me pull myself together. That they hooked me up with an amazing therapist who shook my soul to its broken core and helped me to begin to rebuild the tragic pieces of my life. But that didn't happen. Instead, I was offered group therapy sessions with a room full of other people in the psych ward. I guess it helped me to see I wasn't the only one drowning in darkness, but it sure as hell wasn't the treatment that I desperately needed. The gaping hole in my soul was filled with surface talk. The group therapist attempted to anesthetize the pain I had with general suggestions to meditate, write in my journal, draw pictures of a safe place, and flick a hair tie against my wrist when I feel like I want to hurt myself. Those bullshit suggestions are not going to help me to survive this. I was

still dangling by that frayed thread—the only thing holding me—
and waiting to fall.

When I finally checked myself out of the hospital, I was referred
to a therapist. I have no idea if this guy was going to be able to help
me, but he is my last lifeline. He was all that I had left now. One
man, one broken girl, and one last hope. I guess we'll see how it
goes . . .

"Death is at my door.
It sits upon the stoop, calling my name.
It is coming for me.
Looming over me.
Attempting to grasp me in its unrelenting clutches.
It lurks.
Waits.
But I dare not answer.
It taunts,
longing to welcome me into its cold, outstretched arms in
surrender.
But I do not want to die.
I do not want to die.
I do not want to die.
I dig my heels into the dirt,
brush my hair back from my face,
and raise my hand,
as a final act of defiance
for what is about to happen.
And somehow,
on the barest dangling thread of courage,
weakly
but boldly,
I whisper in reply,
'Fuck you. I won't let you take me. I will not go.
I want to live.'"

—Jamie Collins (for Jessi)

JESSI

AGE 37
December 13, 2016

*T*his is the week that I realize I am going to die, if nothing changes. My weeklong stint at the psychiatric unit of the hospital only carried me so far. The fortress I'd built to defend myself from all life's tragic bullshit had come tumbling down and now my sorrow lay like broken bricks at my feet. It feels like I'm seated at a terminal in life's airport with no connecting flight, no ticket, no reservation, no plan. I am not suicidal. I have no desire to die. It's more like I'm trapped in an emotional prison, as if I'm being dragged, hour by hour, day by day, to my own grave. If this therapist I am on my way to see right now cannot help me, my children are no longer going to have a mother. My husband will no longer have a wife. It's not like I don't love my family enough. I do. So, why can't I just get better for them? Because for the first time in my life, I realized I have to get better for *myself*. I have *to do this for me*. Not for anyone else. If I don't learn to heal the broken places within me, I have nothing to offer to anyone else. I can no longer hide from all that I truly am. The time has come for me to march straight into the darkest trenches of hell, look death's looming shadow in its wicked, obsidian colored eyes, to finally see and acknowledge my own pain, my own past, and my own reality. To really fucking see and acknowledge it. This is my live or die moment.

I'm riding along as a passenger in the front seat of Tyson's truck. I pull my coat around me to steal its warmth, as I shiver and stare out the window. Aside from the bitter cold air that fills my lungs and the heat blowing from the vents, I feel nothing. It's almost like being dead inside. I am barely here. I am hanging on, minute by minute, breath by breath, barely present but holding a physical space. Ty is driving me to my therapist's office—the guy to whom I was referred by the hospital during my stay—for my first appointment. Ty knows I'm nervous about it. He also knows that I now know I need the help.

As we pull up to the address it becomes clear that the doctor runs his therapy practice out of his house. Granted, it's a nice two-story home, but still. I was expecting an office building and a woman seated behind a sterile reception desk who greets me and asks me to fill out papers or something. It seems odd, like I'll be ringing the doorbell to announce the arrival of the broken girl, his next appointment, instead of a delivered pizza. Instead, I stand holding a space on his front porch, a screwed-up-little-girl-turned-trauma-survivor, wallowing in the darkness and clinging to what little is left of herself. So little. Barely anything at all. Each breath now stolen by memories. A future now a mere flicker, threatened to be consumed by the pain. I have no idea how to deliver myself from this pathetic existence. My inner desperation brings me here, to this professional therapist's place, in search of what, I don't know, exactly. But there has got to be *something* to help me. There must be: something, *anything*, words, medication. Hell, I'll take anything. I can't do this alone anymore. This is what it feels like when a person's soul is splintering. I know it is. I am fucking dying slowly, bit by bit. *I'll do anything. Anything. I just need help. Please let me get help I need. Let him be good at his job. Please God, please. Please help me. I can't do this anymore. I can't . . .*

I nervously step out of the car, make my way up the driveway, step up onto the porch, and ring the doorbell. Tyson is sitting in the driveway, waiting to make sure that I make it in okay. A man answers the door. He seems nice enough and he invites me in. I wave goodbye to Tyson and pull the door closed behind me. I follow the man up a nearby stairway that leads to his office, which is apparently located on the second floor of the house. When we walk in he points me toward a recliner chair with a mat on the floor in front of it. I immediately notice that the mat is crooked. *Why is it crooked? Why doesn't someone fix it? Why would anyone leave it like that? Don't they notice it?* It bugs me. *It's not like it should be.* I pull my shoes off, neatly line them up on top of the mat in front of the recliner and pull on the mat to straighten it up perfectly, the way that it belongs. *There. I feel better now.* The doctor (who I've began inwardly referring to as "the Man") then takes a seat. I pull my legs up onto the chair and cross them in front of me. *It feels better this way. I feel safer. More protected.* I feel nervous energy flowing through my body. With both of my legs still up on the chair, I tilt forward and begin to nervously rock forward and backward in the recliner. I keep rocking. Up and back. Up and back. Up and back. It gives me something to do, physically, to channel my inner-anxiety outward.

This guy seems nice. He really does. He speaks to me in a respectful, kind tone. I can tell he's trying to make me feel comfortable, because I'm pretty sure he knows that I'm not comfortable here with him, doing this right now.

We fill out a lot of paperwork together. He asks me a bunch of general questions about myself, my situation, and what brought me here today. I explain that I checked myself into the hospital for my own good to keep myself safe. I tell him about my friend Lexi's death. I tell him that my family died a long time ago. That they were murdered in my childhood home. That I never went back home after that. I tell him that Jeff killed them. That Lexi's death took me back there, to that dark place, to that time. That I'd always felt abandoned by those around me. That I couldn't seem to escape the sadness and sorrow. I was right back there, in that hell, like I was back when they left me. He isn't digging deeper. He's listening to everything I tell him. I feel heard, like he's actually *listening* to me. This isn't as weird as I thought it might be.

He then leads me through several psychological tests, including that one with those strange ink blots, where you say what it is you see in each picture. I wasn't sure what to expect, but so far this guy seems legit. I like that he actually has a background in Post-Traumatic Stress Disorder (PTSD). I'm pretty sure I probably have that. Jamie talked to me about it after we started working on this book. She went over the list with me and I had every single identifier on it.

I'm doing my best to answer all his questions. I'm trying to be honest and direct. It's the only way I know how to be. The things I have to tell him aren't easy for me to own, much less say aloud. I think he's staying on the surface level with me to help make me more comfortable. I appreciate it. I'm guessing he has to do all this psychological testing to try to figure out what's wrong with me. I'll take all the damn tests. I'll tell him everything. Every. Last. Fucking. Thing. Anything. All of it. Whatever he needs me to do. I'll say it all. I'll do it. I'll tell him every last detail. *Am I really fucked up? Salvageable? Can we find a way to make it through this? Am I what he expects someone like me to be? Will he be able to help me? To save me?*

Is there any hope—even the barest frayed thread of hope—left for me?

JESSI

AGE 37
December 2016

"*T*he wound is the place where the light enters you." That's what the famous philosopher Rumi once said. Before I started talking to The Man, I would have told you that quote is bullshit. Complete and utter bullshit. Who wants to be wounded or broken? No one, that's who. And who wants to actually admit that they are? Also, no one. In order for the light to enter your life following a tragedy, you must first be willing to acknowledge that you're actually broken to begin with, and why. It requires you to take a long, hard look at those underlying cracks in your resilient armor to see it all for what it truly is. For any person, much less a survivor of trauma, that is not an easy thing to do.

As time went on what I learned is that therapy is hard. It's easy to feel like an inferior human being because you need to ask for help. The associated stigmas of embarrassment, helplessness, and a greater level of self-screwed-upness (yeah, we just made that a word) are totally real. You *do* feel like a loser because you *need* help. You *do* feel weak, because you realize you *can't* just help yourself. And therapy requires you to *actually share* all that sad stuff you'd prefer to lock away and pretend never even existed. It's not easy to sit in a room with a stranger and to dredge up all your deepest, darkest shit to relive it. But it does help. It's as though it sets a small piece of your soul free each time you do it. That's what I learned from the sessions I had with The Man.

By the time I started talking to The Man, I'd already shared my life's story with my cousin over the course of six months of phone interviews, so this felt more like the rehashing of a story I'd already told. That made it a bit easier for me. And for the first time in my life, I not only wanted to remember the repressed memories I'd buried inside myself, I craved the details. Each new fragment that surfaced through therapy became a pebble that would form the bedrock for the new foundation of my life. We started to make connections, where I'd realized, *I do this because of the trauma from the tragedy. Not just because I'm fucking weird or broken or something.* The formal diagnosis words didn't matter to me. The reason I had them did. Beneath it all, there was a reason. I felt relieved as we began to uncover more pieces. I knew there were things that I could work on. I knew I could try to get better.

Guided meditation became the main vehicle we used to retrieve repressed memories during our sessions together. It helped me to dig deep inside myself to access the lingering fears, feelings, resentments, and regrets I held. And by this point, there were a lot of them. Session by session, I gained a lot of insight about myself— as a survivor of childhood trauma—in the process.

I would sit in The Man's office with my eyes closed as he told me to breathe deeply in, to relax my body, and allow my mind to enter a plane of tranquility. He spoke in a calm and reassuring tone in order to immerse me into a state of deep relaxation. During our first guided meditation session, The Man told me to think of a safe place in my mind and anytime anything happened in my thoughts that made me feel unsafe, to go to that safe place.

I immediately found myself seated in the corner of a bedroom, sitting on the floor with my back pressed up to the wall and my legs pulled up to my chest in a protective posture, next to an old-school radiator, the kind that sits on the floor next to the wall. I was in the little house in Toledo Ohio, that was yellow like the sun, in my old childhood bedroom, where I lived with my daddy, sitting in a corner I'd long forgotten existed. But I saw it in my mind. That's where I took myself. That was my safe place. The memories were there to be found.

During one of our sessions fairly early on, I connected with my seven-year-old self, Jessica. The man verbally talked me through it.

THE MAN: What are you feeling?

JESSICA: Scared.

THE MAN: Where are you?

JESSICA: Outside. I don't want to come in from outside.

THE MAN: Why?

JESSICA: I like to play in the woods.

THE MAN: Okay. Why don't you want to go in?

JESSICA: Jeff is in there. I don't like him. He makes me do things I don't want to do.

THE MAN: Like what? What does he make you do?

JESSICA: He threatens my sisters and uses them against me. I feel like it's my fault. My fault that they died. I was supposed to protect them, like I always did, but I wasn't there.

The Man brought me out of guided meditation. When I consciously reentered his office, tears I did not realize I was crying were streaming down my face.

The Man recapped everything I'd said during our session. That he was talking to me, to Jessica, at age seven. That she was afraid of Jeff and the reason why. He then asked, "What do you think of that, now, as Jessi, hearing that?" I replied, "I'm not sure what to think. I feel sad for her. I understand how *she* felt . . . how *I* felt. I remember . . . "

The Man said, "If you had been there, you could have died, too. That's what would have happened. Your nine-year-old mind may *think* that you could save them. But *you couldn't*. You would be dead, too. That's what would have happened." I knew everything he said to be true. I just never allowed myself to actually feel or believe it.

I think I needed to hear him say those words. To tell me that it wasn't my fault. To tell me that there's not anything I could have done. He continued, "You are bearing the cross for your sisters, protecting them, by letting Jeff do whatever he wanted to you." Until he spoke those words, it's something I never realized. That I was bearing the cross for my sisters. I was carrying that guilt with me across the years. It was a burdensome load. And inside me, I carried a lingering fear of Jeff ever since the day that cold case team arrived on my door step to confirm for me that he was my family's killer.

JESSI

AGE 37
January 2017

I entered my counseling sessions broken in more ways than I even realized. I didn't give myself the deference I would have given to any other person who wasn't me who had lived through my circumstances. Being told what was wrong with me didn't fix me, but it did help me to understand that I'm not just some weird or fucked up person who does bizarre shit. I had no idea this tragedy controlled nearly every aspect of every waking day that followed it. Let me count the ways:

» I don't know how to be alone. Ever. It instantaneously shifts my mind to a dark place.

» I developed a deep love for animals, especially dogs, because they accept me unconditionally and don't expect anything from me.

» I grieve on an endless loop internally, even when try to I deny myself the feelings externally.

» I don't allow myself to truly feel love. I hold love from afar.

» I crave attention and affection from others, but I won't allow myself to actually have it.

» I worry about losing anyone I care about, so I constantly push people away.

» I fear going into stores or other public places. When I do go out, I go at the oddest times of day or night when I know there will be very few people out.

» When I go anywhere in public, in my head I always come up with an escape plan.

» I fear that a stranger may snap and harm me or others around me. Always have.

» I have difficulty breathing in crowds and often must flee due to an anxiety attack.

» I hide the deepest part of my identity from everyone around me, denying the depths of who I am.

» I continue to suffer from insomnia, which has plagued me *every single night* for the past three decades.

» I used to have flashbacks about what happened to my family and the hellish way they died.

» I have vivid nightmares about death that cause me to awaken gripped in terror, experiencing a full-on panic attack, often veiled in a layer of sweat with tears streaming down my face.

» I fear guns, even toy guns, and want them nowhere around me. Ever. I don't even want to see a gun.

» I control nearly every element of my life with habits and rituals, too many to list.

» I have no idea how to function if my daily routine or my scheduled plans are disrupted.

» I like things to be predictable and to follow an expected pattern at all times. I don't like surprises.

» I came to hate the name "Jessica" and began to cringe any time I heard it.

» I hated the way I looked growing up, so pathetic and sad.

» I get anxiety any time I attend social gatherings. Many times, I don't go, because my anxiety holds me prisoner from the things I would like to do.

» I feel trapped in closed spaces.

» I like things to be well-organized, in patterns, meeting my own standards, and perfect.

» If I think others are pointing at me or whispering about me, it shifts me back to that little girl I was in the fourth grade, standing on the playground alone, while the other kids whispered and kept their distance.

» I am afraid to answer the phone when it rings. I like to be in control of when I talk to someone.

» I am afraid to answer my door when someone knocks.

» I have to clean the house and wash all dirty dishes myself, my way.

» I cannot ask others for help.

» If I do ask others for help, I have a hard time accepting it.

» I made my kids self-reliant from a young age.

» I can't leave my house sometimes.

» I cut myself to seek physical relief from my emotional pain.

» I fail to acknowledge what happened to me.

» I fail to acknowledge the pain that it caused me.

» I fail to acknowledge all the ways this tragedy has uprooted my life.

» I fail to acknowledge the broken little girl in me. I push her back, always back.

» I fail to acknowledge the way this tragedy broke every single part of me.

» I fail to acknowledge that I used to be Jessica Fucking Pelley and the totality of what that statement actually means.

» I fail to acknowledge the essence of my existence, who I am, my own reality.

I wish I didn't do *any* of these things. I wish I *didn't want* to count stairs and ceiling tiles. I wish I *didn't* give a damn how many ounces are in a bottle or that I could stop myself from only grabbing the second item back on a shelf, never the first. I *wish* my television volume didn't have to be in a number that ended in a multiple of five. I *wish* I *didn't* have to mourn dates on an annual basis. These things, they control my life and rob me of freedom and happiness. These habits, rituals, feelings, and triggers control me. And yet, to some degree, they saved me. In the end, I guess that's all that matters.

JESSI & JESSICA

February 2017

*A*bout a month after we started our sessions together, The Man shared a profound piece of information with me.

THE MAN: . . . Given all of the things you've been through, the tragedy and trauma, a dual personality can emerge. It's referred to as "Dissociative Identity Disorder."

Dissociative Identity Disorder? Holy fuck. To hear a psychologist say the words aloud helps it all click in to place. There really is a Jessi and a Jessica. The two inside of one: co-existing in me.

THE MAN: It's not like a split personality. They aren't separate. It's us attempting to merge Jessica and Jessi into one person. You've separated the emotions and thoughts between the two over the years and compartmentalized them to protect yourself. To survive what happened to you. What we're trying to do is to get all the feelings and thoughts to connect and coincide in one place— of both Jessica and Jessi—in you. Together. Without the walls of emotional separation.

Mind blown. It appeared my cousin Jamie had cracked the code on this separation of identities long before The Man even came into the picture. I had managed to separate them within myself to make my life easier. Jessica was the sad, hurting, bitter, angry, little girl from the past. Jessi was who I became. The happy, vibrant, spirited, resilient girl I long ago glanced down upon in that first photograph of me with hot pink hair. That was Jessi. That's who I wanted to be. The problem was, I tucked Jessica deep inside myself and didn't merge her with Jessi, the new me. In fact, I despised her. I felt sorry for her. She was sad and pitiful. I pushed her down. I loathed her existence. She was the past. She was pain. She was everything I no longer wanted to see, feel or be. Yet, she still *was me*. Cognitively, I realized it. I still do. But emotionally, I still can't reconcile all the thoughts and feelings together because I've kept them separated for so long. Hell, I still talk about my childhood self in third person even today.

That initial therapy session was about nine months ago and since then, I've learned there is no easy way to merge the old me with the new. According to The Man, this is something we're going to have to work toward in deep psychotherapy. And it could take years.

It's emotionally exhausting to contemplate allowing Jessica to become a true part of my new identity. I fought against her for so long. I treated her the same way everyone else in her life did. I failed to acknowledge her hurt, her isolation, and her pain. It kills me to know I did that, but it's true. I denied her thoughts and feelings. I needed her to pretend they did not exist, so that I could carry on. But I realize now that without her I wouldn't be here. So, I must now try to integrate the two in order to find a place of peace and understanding upon which we can coexist. I'm working on that. At least now I see that it's possible. The road is long, but a beacon of light and hope shines in the distance. Today, I have far more answers. I understand myself better than I ever have before.

Am I healed? Not fully. Am I whole? Not totally. The reality is that I probably never will be. But for the first time in forever, I see a luminous path of light standing before me, if only I choose to do the work, to take the steps firmly upon that bright path, to walk forward in life with my head held high and my heart open. Open to vulnerability. Open to new feelings and memories. Open to the potential of being hurt. Love was a feeling I had packed safely away in my old emotional baggage. But for the first time in my life, I wanted it—that feeling, love—more than I feared it. And that, for me, was a reawakening.

DISSOCIATIVE IDENTITY DISORDER

JESSICA + JESSI
2017

While we all experience dissociation at times, for example, when driving to the store on mental autopilot and not consciously thinking through the route we drive or our specific actions, dissociative identity disorder (DID) is a severe form of dissociation that surpasses the norm.

DID is defined as being a severe condition in which two or more distinct identities, or personality states, are present in—and alternately take control of—an individual. Some people describe this as an experience of possession. The person also experiences memory loss that is too extensive to be explained by ordinary forgetfulness.

DID is a disorder characterized by identity fragmentation rather than a proliferation of separate personalities. The disturbance is not due to the direct psychological effects of a substance or of a general medical condition. DID was called multiple personality disorder until 1994, when the name was changed to reflect a better understanding of the condition—namely, that it is characterized by a fragmentation, or splintering, of identity rather than by a proliferation, or growth, of separate identities. As this once rarely reported disorder has become more common, the diagnosis has become controversial.

The *Diagnostic and Statistical Manual of Mental Disorder, Fifth Edition* (DSM-5) criteria is:

1. Two or more distinct identities or personality states are present, each with its own relatively enduring pattern of perceiving, relating to and thinking about environment and self.

2. Amnesia must occur, defined as gaps in the recall of everyday events, important personal information and/or traumatic events.

3. The person must be distressed by the disorder or have trouble functioning in one or more major life areas because of the disorder.

4. The disturbance is not part of normal cultural or religious practices.

5. The symptoms are not due to the direct psychological effects of a substance (such as blackouts or chaotic behavior during alcohol intoxication) or a general medical condition (such as complex partial seizures).

While the cause of DID is not entirely understood, individuals diagnosed with the condition often report having endured severe physical or sexual abuse, particularly during childhood. For those with PTSD, the younger the person was at the time of the trauma, the more drastically they can be affected by the trauma. The lack of a primary caregiver who can be relied upon is another key factor affecting the development of and severity of PTSD as it relates to people who endure childhood trauma. For those under age ten, it can be more severe. Children with ADHD (or undiagnosed ADHD) can also be more deeply affected by tragedy or childhood trauma.

People with DID often describe feeling like they have become either unaware of or outside observers of their own speech and actions. Some hear voices. Others look different when they assume an alter state.

DID can manifest at any age.

DID is characterized by a failure to integrate various aspects, including memory, consciousness, and identity into a single multidimensional self. The individual may assign certain thoughts and feelings to an alter to protect herself/himself from experiencing or dealing with those issues and the feelings that stem from them. Sadness often becomes an overwhelming feeling that an individual with DID will attempt to avoid at all costs. An alter state may step in to hold the feelings, thoughts, memories, and pain. This protects "the system" (person).

The identities/alters can emerge at any time, but especially in situations where the person is under psychosocial stress.

Alternate personalities/alters are often visibly obvious to those around the person with DID.

Amnestic symptoms and lapses in memory are common and may be noticed by those around the individual.

At times, those with DID can experience states of fugue, where the individual has physically traveled but has no conscious memory of doing so.

A person with DID may experience sudden impulses or strong emotions that do not feel like their own.

It is common for those with DID to self-medicate with alcohol or drugs in an effort to maintain control of and to protect the system (themselves), although they often do not consciously realize the reason they are doing so.

More than 70% of individuals diagnosed with DID have attempted suicide and self-harm is common.

Individuals diagnosed with DID typically see an average of at least seven therapists before being properly diagnosed with the condition.

The best course of treatment is typically psychotherapy. Because of the suicidal and self-harming tendencies, treatment of DID is crucial.

DID is a controversial diagnosis within the mental health community.

JESSICA

(Yeah, you read that right.)

AGE 36

Early December 2017

*N*ow I understand why I am left with merely two brief but vivid mental flashes in my mind out of the 168 total hours that comprised the entire first week of December. I truly was outside of myself. I was still occupying the physical space, but not the conscious mind.

Jessica was the one who took herself into work each day during that last week of November. From the accounts of others, she looked and sounded different than me. She was the one working in the office with Boss Lady because she was out of it. She didn't know all the things I knew.

Jessica was the one who drank to excess in an attempt to numb and protect her body and mind, more commonly referred to by therapists who treat DID as the system. For all intents and purposes, I was "out" of mind.

Jessica was the one who wrapped a knife up in a blanket on the floor of her bedroom. She was the one who carried it to the living room because she apparently wanted to visit her daddy's grave to kill herself.

Jessica is the one who wrote a blood poem. She is also the one who wrote cryptic letters to her kids.

Jessica was the one who etched cuts into her arm or leg to relieve some of the pain she felt.

Jessica was the one who got shitfaced drunk and ended up on the bathroom floor, huddled in a fetal position, wearing that purple shirt. She is also the one who ended up slinging DVDs at Tyson while screaming like a person off the rails in a fit of rage.

Jessica was the one who took an entire bottle of anxiety pills, drank to excess, called Stephanie, and was found unconscious on the kitchen floor. But she isn't the one who woke up in a hospital bed at the emergency room. That was me, Jessi.

Jessica is the one who wrote a suicide note. She is also the one who wrote Post-It notes which she placed on Dakota's and Austin's bedroom walls and doors as a final message from their mother.

Jessica is the one who wanted to die. Not Jessi. Jessi wanted to L-I-V-E.

Jessica is the one who scarfed down that cheeseburger meal from McDonald's beside Boss Lady's desk that Monday afternoon. (Jessi is the one who wanted to eat lunch an hour later.) Jessica is also the one who was handing Boss Lady used attendance sheets because that's something that OCD Jessi would *never* do. Like, ever.

Jessica is the one who kept walking to the front of the building or into Boss Lady's office to cry every day that week.

Jessica is the one who didn't know how to find the exit to a building Jessi had worked in for four straight years. (Jessi knew the way out of that building.)

And I'm really damn proud to tell you that Jessi is the one who ended up checking herself into the psychiatric ward that Monday night after that crazy ass week that she barely remembers at all. She knew she couldn't handle that overwhelming feeling stemming from a totally normal emotion for humans called sadness. Jessi stepped in to protect herself, her children, and her family. She resumed control over the chaotic mess made by my nine-year-old self who was using her nine-year-old mind to analyze an adult's problems and attempt to come up with her best nine-year-old solutions to them. Jessica's solutions were life-threatening. They weren't logical at all. She just wanted to end the pain. She wanted to put a stop to the suffering. She had experienced enough of it. She did the only thing she knew how to do. She stepped in to protect me, Jessi, from the things which I *could not bear*.

The reality is that I am both of these people: Jessica and Jessi. I was and always will be. But during that particular span of time, each of them held specific conscious mental pieces of my life that were separate from the other. Two halves not diverging. Two halves not always sharing information, ideas, and memories. Two halves still suffering and attempting to survive, each in their own way. Jessi was on the outside wondering what in the hell was happening to her. Jessica was on the inside making decisions and walking through my life.

It makes me feel better knowing that there is a reason I was again inflicting self-harm. There was a reason I was drinking to the point of blacking out. There was a reason I seemed suicidal when I *didn't* feel that way *at all*. There is a reason I had *no idea* what I was doing, saying, or *didn't have control* over how I was acting. It's because I didn't know. I couldn't remember. And I wasn't in control. Not at all. As Jessi, I had no clue that Jessica was holding a space for me, as well as holding some secrets. It's something I'll never fully understand or comprehend—I'm not sure anyone will, aside from therapists who specialize in DID—but at least I can make *some* sense of it now. I am two distinct halves of a whole person.

One day, with a lot of help in therapy, some intense soul-searching, and a whole lot of work, I hope to fuse the ugly edges of the little broken girl and the vibrant survivor into a beautiful whole person with some vividly colored cracks and a far better understanding of herself. One day . . .

JESSI

May 2017

*W*hen you're a survivor of trauma, as I am, the trauma is always present and fills the air that surrounds you in the normal moments of life, much like confetti tossed into the wind. Even if you can't see it—the trauma—it's there. It swirls, it saturates the air you breathe.

My daughter will graduate from high school this year, in May 2017. She's a senior, about to head off to college soon. I feel the same way any normal mom would feel. I'm happy for her and excited about the prospect of her future, but one thing that is *not* normal is the way I've been planning things in my mind for the past four to five weeks, the things I'll need to do to get through her graduation ceremony next Friday. As a trauma survivor, I'm forced to do a whole lot more than buy decorations and find the perfect gift. Any gathering at a public place is now an incredibly stressful endeavor. It's a perpetual struggle for me to attend events with my children or others. I want to be there. But it's hard for me.

The anxiety I experience around crowds of people is real. I fear that something bad could happen. I feel like the space is closing in on me. There are too many people around. I feel like I need to be able to escape. I need to have a plan in place.

So, I intend to arrive at the venue for her graduation at 5:00 P.M., even though the ceremony doesn't start until 7:00. I must arrive two hours early to ensure that I can select a seat near the outer perimeter. That way, if (more like when) I need to escape, I can easily slip out. This type of mental planning has become a way of life. It's a requirement for me to deal with the soul-shaking anxiety that robs me of many normal moments and denies me of many happy ones. It breaks my heart, but there isn't a whole lot I can do about it.

I live my life encumbered by a fear of the unknown. A fear of danger. I fear that a random person could snap or go crazy and do something unexpected to harm other people. While this is now a mainstream fear lurking in the back of many people's minds due to the present-day violence occurring in society, this is a fear I have carried deep inside me every damn day since I was nine years old in 1989. I now know that, as a trauma survivor, it is totally normal for someone like me to feel like this. Someone in my life *did* snap and he robbed me of everything I ever had in life.

My daughter plays the cello in the orchestra. Last year, there was a concert, *Phantom of the Opera*. For her, this was a big deal. I was excited and happy for her. But the moment an event is announced, the worries begin to swirl in my head. The anxiety begins to course through my veins. I'm gripped in panic weeks prior to the event.

As always, I arrived early to the venue. I got a seat near the outer perimeter, where I knew I could escape once the fear overtook me. I had to get up and leave the room for a few minutes several times during the concert. I had to give myself the pep talk. *You can do this, Jessi. You can do this. This means a lot to her. You want to be here. You can do it. Now let's go back in there and sit back down.* And I did manage to always make it back after these little departures.

Once the concert ended, they served snacks for the orchestra members and their families. I had mentally talked myself into participating in this part of the event. I wanted to convince myself I could do it, even when I felt like I couldn't. I had my camera with me, so I could take some pictures. I was going to do this. I was going in there. It would be great. Not a problem at all. I just walk in, eat a cookie, snap a few pictures, and we'll be out of there.

I took two steps into the room and realized I could not be there. I could not eat the cookies. I could not drink the punch. I could not sit with my family. I could not talk to the other moms. I could not take the pictures I so desperately wanted to take of my daughter.

I ran out to my truck and sat in it while the remainder of my family attended the event. They enjoyed that moment in my daughter's life, while I was seated in a truck in the parking lot with anxiety overwhelming me, fear pressing down on me, and tears streaming down my face. Like a loser. Like a failure. Like a mom who couldn't even sit through a freaking high school band's after party.

It makes you feel less than adequate when you're not capable of being there for the people you love at an event, like any normal person could be. I wonder why I can't hold it together. Why I can't just talk myself through it. Why I fail at being a mom, or a wife, or a friend, or a coworker in the important moments. It doesn't matter what I think to myself the reality is that *I just can't do it.*

After this event, Boss Lady told me she saw me when I walked into the cafeteria that day. She had a son in the orchestra. She said, "I saw you, when you walked in. Oh, my God, you looked like a wild animal. What happened?" I knew her description was accurate. In these moments, there isn't a thing I can do but flee. Once the anxiety, fear and panic hit my eyes begin to dart quickly from side to side as the need to flee overtakes me. And I can't be with the people I love, when they sometimes need me to be. *I just can't.*

And that, as a childhood trauma survivor, is now my reality. It's another thing I hope to work through. But as of now, please don't invite me to any social gatherings. If you do, we'll see how that goes. All I can do is laugh. It is what it is.

I have a lot of goals. I have a lot of aspirations. For the first time in a really long time, I see the possibilities of healing, hope, and a happy life. The chance to be whole, in spite of my holes.

JESSI

AGE 38
Present Day, 2018

I'd love to tell you that since I found The Man, I'm cured. That I'm fixed. But that isn't true, and it never will be. I continue to carry the burden of trauma and its lingering loose ends everywhere I go. At the grocery store, I continue to obsess with something as simple as buying a pack of chicken, peanuts with the shell on, hamburger, or anything else sold by weight. The price must end in five or zero—as the self-proclaimed Jessi rule dictates—or be as close as possible to it. If a package of chicken costs $2.19, I think to myself, *"Oh man, why can't they just have one that's $2.20?"* I stand there for as long as it takes and look at every single package available on my five-zero-number-finding-mission. There are times when my daughter is with me and she's like, "Mom, will you pleeeease just pick some freaking chicken?!" I really wish I could, but I can't override the need to fixate on the numbers. So, it's pretty damn clear, even to me, that I need therapy.

Even with health insurance, therapy isn't cheap. It's a difficult thing to afford on a weekly basis. The Man made it clear to me that I would need to attend therapy twice a week for years to work toward finally merging the two selves cohabitating within me—Jessica and Jessi—and deal with all the emotional trauma I repressed for years. I would go every single week, as suggested by The Man, if I could. I simply can't afford it. It's a shitty position to be in when you're choosing between paying for utility bills or therapy. With insurance, it's $25.00 a session. At two (2) times per week, that's $50.00. In a month, that adds up to $200.00. And when Ty, who works as an electrician, is laid off from work as he is each year in winter, we lose our health insurance. Then that cost skyrockets to $150.00 per session. That'll get you to $300.00 per week and $1,200.00 per month. I desperately want the help, but I find myself stuck in the same paradigm as so many other people in this country are, in need of mental healthcare, wanting it, and needing a damn money tree to cover it. Milk and bread or therapy? That is always the question.

So many of the bizarre things I do, my quirks, are directly related to the trauma that befell me as a young child. Apparently, if you're age nine and under, the trauma affects you on a deeper level. If you have ADHD, which The Man and me now both believe I probably did as a kid, then trauma also affects a child more deeply. So, given my circumstances, I was screwed. I'm grateful that I managed to wade through the difficult years of my childhood and my rebellious teenage years, but I did spend the past nearly three decades thinking I did some weird shit without a clue why. However, OCD is common in childhood trauma survivors, as is dissociative amnesia, along with a fear of guns and violence, being in public, and a heightened level of anxiety. Knowing that makes it easier to understand *why* I experienced those things. But it doesn't really make it any easier for me and my family to deal with them.

I want to be normal. I don't want to constantly battle recurring thoughts. I can't believe my family accepts my crazy tendencies. I love them for that, knowing it's not easy to deal with me. I have conflicting thoughts and emotions nearly every waking moment. I want to stop trying to control everything and to stop doing things a certain way, but I can't. My OCD developed to help me feel like I had control because there were so many years of my life during which I felt I had no control. While the OCD helps me to a certain extent, it has become the dictator of my days and drives those around me bonkers. It's not normal to need the television volume to end in a multiple of five. No one else has to have bottles of liquid that contain an even number of ounces. (I prefer them with a two.) No one else can dust, vacuum, or do dishes the way I feel they need to be done. If anyone else attempts to wash my dishes, I will pull those clean dishes out of the dish rack and rewash every single one of them my way.

Whenever I make the valiant effort to suppress some of these tendencies, the mental stream of thoughts that replace that form of control are almost too much to bear. *"Oh my God, did she try to wash my dishes? I know she means well, but that's not gonna work. Look at how they aren't sitting in the right order, even in the rack. They aren't clean."* I know they technically are clean, but they don't feel clean when someone else washes them. It has to be me.

So, when people ask why I don't just stop doing the weird things I do, it's because the impulse to do them is *so strong* and the thoughts that follow if I don't are overwhelming. When I visit someone's house, I'm all right, until I see them turn the volume on the TV up or down. Then, if it's not on a number that ends in five or zero, I will have to ask the person if they can turn it up or down a bit to comply with my self-created rule.

I definitely do much better if the person I'm visiting is neat and orderly, and everything has its place. Then I attempt to learn their rules, so I can comply with them. For instance, my cousin Jamie likes the throw pillows to be alternated on her couch and I know the exact spots. I also know it drives her crazy when people hang towels over the shower bar. I pay attention to things. I watch. I learn. I mimic those preferences, so I don't drive other people crazy the way other people drive me crazy in my own home with those types of things.

Work has always been my safe place and where I feel most at ease. That said, my OCD tendencies don't get checked at the door. They envelop parts of my life there, too. It's just not as noticeable. Granted, my coworkers know I have strong preferences with regard to the way things are done. Rules aren't to be broken. But at the center, my routines and rituals blend right into the structured environment. "Miss Jessi likes things a certain way!" You better believe it to be true. Not only do my coworkers know this, but the kids do, too.

As for my home life, I spend hours each night after work preparing what most people would consider to be elaborate gourmet dinners for my family. Not only do I cook everything from scratch, but I don't believe in buying store-bought sauces, spice blends, gravy, or other mixes, either. I make my own. Several years ago, I began eating clean which means cutting preservatives from my diet. It has helped me immensely to feel better and lose a bit of weight. The best way to ensure that I eat clean is to make everything myself. I find my time spent in the kitchen to be therapeutic. All the preparing, purchasing, pulling, sorting, washing, dicing, spicing, and cooking of items, for me, is a healthy ritual that occupies my time, keeps me busy, and makes my family pretty darn happy, at least most nights.

I'm constantly cleaning. Everything has to be sanitized, wiped down, or scrubbed a certain way. If the spice bottle is sitting weird in the cabinet, I adjust it. If the paper towels are hanging off the roll a little crooked, I have to fix it. If I see dirt anywhere, at any time, it must . . . be . . . cleaned . . . immediately.

I clean when I'm happy. I clean when I'm sad. And if I'm angry, well, that involves a deeper level of exhaustive cleaning. I'm pretty sure my cleaning tendencies drive everyone in my household freaking insane. That said, they're welcome for living in such a clean place 24/7, like a hotel, because it totally is. The maid's name is Jessi. Even when she's tired, the cleaning doesn't stop.

I also constantly take pictures. I take selfies pretty much every day of my life. Whether it's of me drinking a glass of wine or sitting in a chair outside. It may seem like a typical Millennial thing to do, but for me, those pictures are taken with a true purpose. I never want my children to be left with a small, plastic tub of far too few photographs, the way I was. I had so few images to cling to of my family. I possess only *one* picture of my dad. It's of him in his military blues. And the ones I have of my little sisters and our whole family, as we were growing up, are few and far between. It's a sad thing to look down at a handful of photographs and to realize it's all you get to have. I refuse to allow that to happen to my children. I don't ever want them to feel like there aren't enough photographs or memories to ease their suffering and hold the memories, when I'm gone. I ensure they'll have what they need for comfort, reflection, and closure. That's something I never had. I still don't. *But they will*.

As for my departure from life, when the time comes, I've preplanned my funeral and burial, down to what will be read, by whom, the urn, and what photographs will be included on it. Those are decisions my children will never have to make. It's a burden I will *never* place upon my family.

I know my children are self-sufficient and would be okay if I died. I made sure of it. From the time they were little, I raised them to be okay in the event I was gone, because it was a reality I lived for half of my own childhood and I was not equipped to deal with it. That said, there's a downside to making your children almost completely self-reliant. They don't need your help. They can do it on their own—all of it. Hell, my own daughter was accepted to college before I even knew she had applied. That stung a bit. I admit it. But she did it on her own. I am proud of her.

As a mother, their self-sufficiency has wounded me in the past. Sometimes I've wanted to give the good advice or be the sounding board. But at least I know that if I die, they will be okay. In the end, I think it was worth the price. That still doesn't make it any easier to realize your kids could carry on without you. It still hurts a bit, at times.

Let's face it, I'm not an easy person to love. My family knows that. If I'm being entirely honest, my past robbed me of the ability to feel as though I really love people the way I'd like to. I *know* I *love* my husband. I *know* I *love* my kids. But I keep my emotions at bay all the time. I don't do it intentionally. It's like I was stripped of the ability to freely feel or give love. I'm hoping that's something I'll be able to work myself through one day with the help of The Man in therapy.

What can I say? I'm a work in progress. I probably always will be. But, aren't we all?

JESSI

AGE 37
Present Day, 2018

$\mathcal{W}$hen it comes to counseling, it is imperative that you find the right person. Any counselor, therapist, psychologist, or psychiatrist won't suffice. I realize that now. I don't care what degrees he has, or where she went to school. You have to find the right person, with the right specialty, a person with whom you click, who actually gives a damn, and whose methods work for you. The Man is now one of the most important people in my life. The one who accepts me. The person who guides me. He is truly vested in helping me to heal, grow, remember, and live my life out loud.

The people you put around you matter, more than almost any other choice you make in life. Don't allow one bad experience, or one less-than-stellar person to poison your view. As a little girl who suffered alone for 27 years, before being forced by circumstances to find it, I'm here to tell you that it is real—the possibility of help—and there is hope. There is healing. There is progress. And most importantly, there is a better life waiting for you.

I thank God every single day for bringing The Man into my life. As my therapist, he helped me to lift the darkness. He taught me new ways to carry it. He made the bad parts far more tolerable. He helped me to see that asking for help isn't weakness, it's the ultimate display of strength in a person.

"Actions hold the power to imprison a person.
And words, the power to set them free."
—Jamie Collins

That leads me to all the things I never got the chance to say.
I'm going to say them now.
—Jessi

Present day, Age 38
The letter Jessi never wrote.

Dear Jacque,

I had to dig deep to try to figure out what I wanted to say to you in this letter. We both lost what we held dearly in life through the fault of neither one of us. In this situation, we both lose. Completely. There is no contest between us. Loss is loss, and we each suffered our own. The type of loss no person should ever have to bear: not me, not you, not anyone. We were left to dangle in the frayed remains of our former family; a shell of what we had "before" all of this happened. We were left to stand in the "after." That's where we still are now. The place we will remain forever.

You spoke to the press often and freely throughout the years; that is your right. Just as it is my right to now step forward, nearly 30 years later, to say what I think and feel as a result of this horrific tragedy. We both were left in its unimaginable wake. I realize that fully.

As your former step-sister, I felt abandoned by you after the murders. Forgotten about. We were supposed to be "a family." It became clear over the years that what existed between us, once no longer held together by the parsonage walls and our parents, was nothing. Nothing at all. In the eyes of a confused nine-year-old, you left me. I know you may not see it that way. I know there was an age difference between us, with me being nine at the time this happened, and you being 14. You had Jeff. But you knew I had no one, Jacque. No one. I've been pretty much out of sight and out of mind for almost 30 years, with the exception of the few times you reached out to me on Facebook via private messages which consisted of a few well-intentioned sentences. It almost hurt me worse to hear from you on those rare occasions. It made me realize what little there was between us. Not much, aside from a shattered past, faded memories, and broken remains. Sadly, any relationship we had died when our parents each drew their last breaths.

The only time you and Jeff seemed to speak about my mom or sisters to the media over the years was when it served to further magnify Jeff's "loss" or personal interests with regards to his ridiculous claims of innocence. These types of statements helped to paint Jeff more as a victim with the mentions of him "losing his step-mother" (the one he could not stand and was never halfway nice to on a single occasion) along with my precious little sisters, whom Jeff was seemingly decent to, in stark contrast to the way he treated me over the years. I'll give you that. Seeing my mom's and sisters' pictures on a site you set up to proclaim Jeff's innocence is not only ridiculous and distasteful, it is offensive.

I know you saw a different version of Jeff than I did. He was different with you. He was kind to you. I know that now, just as I knew it back then. I'm sure that fact, coupled with the love you feel for him as your brother, and the last living member of your immediate family, make it nearly impossible for you to even fathom the thought of him killing our entire family in cold blood. But he did, Jacque. He did. He killed them. He killed your dad. He killed my mom, and he killed my little sisters, too. Out of rage. As the result of one horrible teenage decision. That doesn't make him Jeffrey Dahmer. But it does make him a murderer, all the same. Somewhere deep in your heart, I believe there exists one tiny speck of "why" or "what if" within you; a small particle of speculation you choose to push far, far away from your conscious stream of thought and always will. You will never indulge that possibility. I understand why. I get it. He is all you have left. But if you saw Jeff through the same eyes through which I saw him over the years, it wouldn't be such a stretch, Jacque. Your brother terrorized me. Regularly. Our parents didn't believe me for the longest time. I was an easy target for a manipulative, fast-talking teenager, such as Jeff: little Jessica, who never sat still, talked too much, and annoyed our parents on an ongoing basis.

I will never see your brother the way you saw him, Jacque. And that's his fault, not mine. He earned that place in my eyes long before the day of April 29, 1989, came and went. These weren't just teenage pranks. He threw a blow dryer in the freaking bathtub with me once. Who does that? Something like that takes a gigantic stride outside the realm of normal and into the questionable territory of "what the fuck" by any reasonable person's standard. How could it not? I want you to imagine for a moment that a teenage boy, ages 13–17, did the types of things I described him doing to me to one of your own children, when they were six, seven, eight, and nine years of age. Would it be an innocent prank then?

It seems every person accused or convicted of a crime has someone who believes he is innocent. For Jeff, that person is you.

You are Jeff's ultimate champion—his sister. You stepped forward on many occasions to declare Jeff's innocence, and even founded an innocence campaign on his behalf. You want to know what hurt me most, Jacque? It was the interview I read following Jeff's trial: the one where you were quoted saying something to the effect you had always viewed yourself as a survivor following this tragedy, up until the day he was convicted, and then, for the first time ever, you felt like a victim. Now flip that around, Jacque. From you to me. I felt more like the victim of an unimaginable tragedy throughout my entire childhood, where I wandered from home to home, place to place where I didn't fit in, pretending to be someone who hadn't lived through the hell I'd lived through. I didn't even want to "survive." I didn't see the point. I was left with nothing. And no one. The day your brother was convicted by a jury of his peers was the first day I felt some small sense of justice and redemption for what happened to my mom, Janel, and Jolene.

I do have a few questions for you to ask yourself.

Why was Jeff telling his friends a week prior to the prom that he would be driving his Mustang—the one with the cancelled insurance that was mechanically disabled by Bob—to prom and attending all the after-prom events: the ones they knew he was grounded from? Your dad was adamant that Jeff was grounded. That never changed. Bob was planning to drive Jeff and Darla to the prom that day. That fact is confirmed by a church member as late as that Saturday afternoon.

Why was Jeff driving a Mustang that your dad had intentionally cancelled the insurance on for a period of six months? Do you honestly think your dad would ever have allowed Jeff to drive an uninsured car, anywhere? This point defies all logic. I know you knew your dad better than I did, and there is no way in hell he would have waved goodbye from the parsonage, while his son jumped into his uninsured Mustang to drive to the prom.

Why did Jeff lie about going to two gas stations that night after leaving the parsonage? Because his car was not running right, because Bob had altered a part on it, and that necessitated the need to stop to get a screwdriver to fix it on his way to Darla's house. The place where he arrived 20 minutes late, not dressed in his tux, and not wearing the jeans and pink shirt he was last seen wearing at the house when my mom, Bob, Janel, and Jolene were last seen alive.

Why would your dad (and even my mom, for that matter) never have planned to take pictures of Jeff in his tuxedo on the day/night of his senior prom? Even if your dad was mad at him, it defies all logic. Why would Jeff have left the parsonage, with them still alive, without ever putting his tux on? Without a single picture ever being taken?

Did Jeff suddenly gain psychic abilities at Great America, when he turned to his girlfriend, Darla, to tell her he felt like, "something was wrong," right about the time he knew the bodies would be discovered on the following Sunday?

If the mob—one of your alternative versions for what could have happened—killed our family, then why was the last outfit Jeff was seen wearing while they were all still alive, the light denim jeans, pink shirt, and two socks, placed into the washer to spin, with nothing else on the night he was going to the prom? It makes no sense Jacque. None. And I'm pretty sure hitmen would bring their own guns, likely with silencers attached to the them, not shuffle through a nightstand in our parents' bedroom for a handful of random shotgun shells.

And lastly, why was the shotgun your dad used for deer hunting still in the gun rack that hung above our parents' bed on Friday night, when I left, but no longer there after the murders? On that point, we will never agree, Jacque. I am totally okay with that.

I am not saying your brother is the spawn of Satan, Jacque. He made a bad choice. One really twisted, fucked up, bad choice for which a lot of people, including you and me, had to pay the price. But I must say that any time I hear Jeff being painted as a model citizen during his many "years of freedom" prior to his arrest, I find myself wondering who could utter those words about a person who lied about having cancer in an attempt to defraud his own trust for $20,000 early; the one that was set up for him (each of us) following his father's death? A model citizen? I think not. But we each get to think what we want, Jacque. I don't expect to ever change your mind, just as you will never change mine. These things are hard to reconcile. They are difficult to understand. And they are even harder to face. We are forever tied by the choices our parents made for us. We are forever bound by this senseless tragedy. We are left with lingering memories of what used to be, what happened to us, and the people we are today because of it.

There are no winners here, Jacque. Not you. Not me. Not Jeff. And certainly not your dad, my mom, Janel, and Jolene. There is only emptiness. There is only sorrow. There is only a past filled with darkness. There is only an unfillable void. There is only what we each are left with, and all that each of us left behind on that day in 1989.

I wish nothing but the best for you, Jacque. I wish you every happiness. I wish you a life filled with love. You didn't deserve this any more than I did.

We will never agree on many things, Jacque. Your brother's guilt or innocence will always remain at the top of that list. Forever. And I'm okay with that. To you, he is innocent. To me, he is guilty. But one day, Jeff will face his final judgment, when he stands before the face of God. I know that makes each of us feel better, for entirely different reasons.

Sincerely,
Jessica

I said to myself, "God will bring into judgment both the righteous and the wicked, for there will be a time for every activity, a time to judge every deed."

- Ecclesiastes 3:17

Present day—Age 38
What Jessi never told you.

Dear Jeff,

This is the letter I never sat down to write. I am choosing to address you with a proper salutation because I feel that says a whole lot more about me as a person than it does you. It's sure as hell not because you deserve it.

I spent more than a decade of my life—ten long, torturous years—misplacing my feelings for you onto your father, Bob, whom I believed to be the killer of my family; the person who took everything from me. It wasn't until I got that knock on the front door of my home in 2002 that I was told, for the very first time, by a cold case detective, that my family's deaths could not possibly have been a murder/suicide at the hands of your father, as I had always believed. But I guess you knew that all along. You are the one person who always knew. That's a whole lot of days, weeks, months, and years to carry that reality.

When I learned that Bob could not have killed my family, you were the first person who came to mind. And not because I wanted you to be. But because that is the place you had earned by the way you treated me over the years. My second thought was "Holy shit, because I actually came by myself, all alone at the time I was living in a foster home, to visit you in Florida, when I was 15 years old, after you extended me an invitation." I had just arrived at your house from the airport and was standing next to the bed, unpacking items from my suitcase, when you entered the room and asked me, "So who do you think really did it?" I immediately replied, "I think it was your dad."

I sure am glad I believed it to be Bob at that time and responded as I did, or I have no idea how that may have ended. Fortunately, when I told you I thought it was your dad, you liked my answer, so we had fun that week. It scares me to think of what could have happened to me had I said anything different. The jet-ski ride and new outfits don't make up for a damn thing in my life. But thank you for the third time I ever actually saw you as a decent human being, Jeff. The third time in my entire life. I think that says a lot about you. I did not really hear from you again after that. You had what you needed from me.

You singled me out. I'm not sure if it's because I was the oldest in my family or what. That is something I will never know. I'm not sure the reason even matters, because the truth is, I never deserved to be treated that way, no child does. I was scared of you almost the entire time we lived together under the same roof, but in a way, found myself torn, because I was grateful you left my sisters alone, only inflicting that type of mean-spirited treatment upon me. And if that laser focus on me meant that they would be spared of your mistreatment, I would take it. But not without invisible scars. I was terrified of you. I hated being left alone with you. I was gripped in panic at the mere mention of you "babysitting" us. You were mean to me, you were a manipulator, and you were a liar. There were only a few glimmering moments when I saw in you what, perhaps, Jacque got to see in you all along. The kind Jeff. The funny Jeff. The Jeff who could be fun to be around. The side of Jeff I did not know.

In reality, we were going through the same shit. What you did to me only further added to my shit. You took your anger issues stemming from your mom's early death and the feelings of resentment you bore toward your dad out on me. I was a kid at ages six, seven, eight, and nine years old. There is no excuse for the things you did to me and the way you treated me. I was a little girl, Jeff. And you were a teenager; one who seemed to get his rocks off manipulating and mentally torturing me because he could, and did, get away with it.

What you took from me on April 29, 1989, was everything. Every single fucking thing I had left. I have no immediate familial connections now. My children will never know their grandma or their aunts. They will never know that part of me, hear stories about my childhood, what a pain in the ass I may have been, or learn more about me growing up as a kid. All my children were left with is a big void. The same void I lived with all the years of my life, from the age of nine to now. Thirty years with no fucking family; that's what you left me with.

You will sit alone in prison because your actions brought you there. I will sit alone behind invisible bars in the real world for the rest of my life, without my former family, because you brought me here. You had one moment of selfishness. One stupid teenage moment of rage. You didn't think—you just acted. You made one extreme choice that changed my entire life—and yours, too. It changed the lives of a lot of people. Your sister. Your entire family and what is left of mine, not to mention all the people who knew us. This was the worst thing you could have done. My loved ones became casualties of your harbored teenage angst and heat-of-the-moment decision, which forever altered everything, for everyone. How was the prom? Was it worth the price you paid? Was it worth the price we both still continue to pay? Was it worth Jacque's daily emotional suffering? Was it worth all the days I no longer wanted to live? You took us all down with you, Jeff. We lingered at the bottom of the lowest, rawest emotional depths of hell on earth at your hands. We still do. And that's on you. It always will be.

I wish you would have looked at me at the trial—even one time. I wanted to look you in the eyes and for you to know that you and I both know what you did to our family—to my family. I'm not even sure if you heard the words I spoke. It bothered me at the time. I admit that I longed for the moment of acknowledgement. The moment when you took one iota of accountability for what you did. A look to let me know you were sorry. You cared. You didn't mean it. You wish you'd never done it. You knew me and wanted to see how I turned out. To wonder why in the hell your former step-sister, 50 times removed, has bright pink hair. Hell, anything. Anything at all. Just a look. But now I realize you hold no power over me; you never did. You are a monster. You have no regard for life or the consequences of your actions. You never fail to proffer your innocence. You even made a mention of trying to emulate your own life after the life of your father. If you want to know what your dad, the pastor, would do in this situation: He would own up to what he did, and ask for forgiveness. That's what he would do. That is something you did not do. I don't know that you ever will. The fact you claim you are innocent is not only ridiculous, it is offensive.. It's as though you and Jacque forget that I'm still here. I lived there. The parsonage was my home, too. I saw what I saw. I heard what I heard. I lived the life I lived. I spent four years alongside the two of you in the same damn household, although I've been treated as though I never did.

When it comes to you, Jeff, I saw who you were. I saw the things you did. My silence over the years has only helped to add speculation to your constant claims of innocence. But I will be silent no more. And you will now face the reality as it sits. The way it all really was. Yourself for who you really are. I'm not sure if the "real" you is the person you showed to me, or the one you chose to show to Jacque and some others, but you can no longer hide behind your false claims of innocence without the world knowing what I have to tell. I will no longer allow you to float in a sea of untold stories I possess. You can no longer hide who and what you are.

I saw you then.

I see you now.

You are my family's killer.

You murdered your dad, my mom, my sister Janel, and my sister Jolene in cold blood.

You want to hear the really fucked up part, Jeff? What kills me just as much, if not more than this horrific tragedy that I lived through, is during your years of proclaimed bullshit innocence, you chose to bring a son into this world, during your days of freedom. Your rash choices not only forever altered my life, and yours—they have forever altered his: your precious, innocent, beautiful son's. Forever. Believe me when I tell you I know what this will do to him. I know. I lived it. He will be the one to pay the ultimate price for what you have done. There is no darkness so dark as the darkness he will enter because of you. I am glad he has your wife to care for him. That's more than I was ever left with in your wake. I hope she is enough to see him through the dark hours. The dark days. The weeks, months, and years without a key piece of his family and a hole that pierces through his soul forever. But at least you are still alive. He can still hear your voice. He can still see your face. He can read your words on a page. That's something I never had. It is something I will never have again. I do not tell you this to hurt you. I tell you this because it hurts me to know this. Deeply. I ache for your son. It nearly brings me to my knees to think about it. When I speak of it, it levels me to tears. I am him. And he is me, in so many ways. I know it's fucked up to sit here and feel so much sadness for a little boy, now turned man, who was born of my family's murderer, but we share a common bond; more than one actually—you and what you've done. You have forever altered my life, and his. And neither of us deserved it. We never will. I know what this will do to him. It emotionally crushes me to know the reality of it. It is a sadness for which there are no words.

I want you to know that I hate you because of the shit you did to me as a kid. It was not okay. I'm pissed off that you killed my family. It hurts. It's an ache I've lived with every single day. It's a hole I will carry with me until the day I die: the loss of my entire family. The loss of closeness. The loss of love. The loss of connection. The loss of a bond. The loss of a common history. The loss of fun, tears, memories, and laughter. The loss of the life I had.

I still have some of your old pictures in a plastic bin stored along with the few photos I have left to cling to of my family. Pictures of us at Christmastime. Pictures of you at your junior prom in a gray tux and pink cummerbund. For years, I saw them as "pictures of my estranged step-brother," but today, I see them for what they truly are: pictures of my family's killer. The face of Jeff, my former step-brother, who was mean to me over the years, then killed my mom, Janel, and Jolene at ages six and eight. That is so incredibly fucked up. It truly is. There is no way to explain the way that makes me feel inside. That the killer lived among us, ate breakfast with us, slept in our home upstairs, and my mom washed his dirty clothes each week. That he, my step-brother, gunned down his own father, in cold blood, in the hallway, next to the kitchen table where we all ate breakfast growing up. Dysfunction at its darkest hour. That's what it became. Pictures of my former life, frayed ugly edges and all, with you at the center of it all.

For the longest time, I didn't think you were the killer. Not because I didn't see you as a person who could be one, based upon the way you treated me over the years, but as a little kid I didn't see how anyone beside an adult could have done something so fucking bad. Back then, murders weren't as common and when there was one, it was typically committed by a grown man. How could I have thought anything different? How could I have known you were the one to do this, until the day I did?

If you would have just looked me in the eye one time during trial, just once. That's all the redemption I sought from you. That's all I wanted. You denied me that. But what I want you to know is that I'm looking at you now, Jeff. We all are. We see you.

Imagine someone doing this to your own son—killing his entire family. Leaving him with nothing. No one. Maybe now, for the first time ever, you realize what you did to me, way back when.

You became a "respectable" person, or so you claim. You claim to never have done anything else "violent" in the years leading up to your arrest and multiple murder conviction, which is arguable. But know this: You are forever stained by what you did. Your soul is permanently stained a dark shade of crimson with the blood of your dad, my mom, and my two beautiful, precious little sisters, Janel and Jolene. Bloodred. That's on you. Forever.

You get to live with that.

That's all I have to say. Don't worry about looking at me, Jeff. I'm looking at you now. I see you for what you truly are. We all do . . .

Your former step-sister,

Jessica

UPDATE

October 2018

S ince Jeff lost the appeal regarding his conviction, his only option is to seek post-conviction relief, which is basically a legal brief asking the original trial court—the St. Joseph Superior Court 1—to reduce his sentence or grant him a "new" trial.

On March 22, 2010, Jeff Pelley filed a Petition for Post-Conviction Relief.

Five years later, on April 22, 2015, it was denied.

On February 22, 2013, Jeff Pelley filed a Petition for Post-Conviction Relief.

As of the time this book was published, his petition remains pending.

Today, She Will Rise.

Some lose all they possess to the merciless grasp of tragedy.
It steals every breath, every tear, every moment.
Taking with it all the people and things they hold dear.
They hide their scars.
Turn their downcast faces away from the light.
Run from a past they can never outrun.
And never will.
One day, a woman arises bearing those same deep scars, somehow
emboldened.
Somehow, able to find the light.
Extending her outstretched arm back to others.
To hold a place for them in the light.
And the truth rings out like a fiery anthem across the hollow
white pages of a loud book.
Echoing from the past of a broken little girl.
Into the light of day.
To reclaim all that was stolen or lost.
To reclaim that which is now hers to claim.
Her voice. Her words.
Her truth. Her story.
And right along with it,
HER LIFE.

—Jamie Collins
(for Jessi)

JAMIE

Present day–October 2018

Redemption is born from vulnerability.
Beauty, from the scars we carry.
And strength, from the darkest of places.
If only, we don't turn away.

—Jamie Collins

*W*hen we began the journey to tell this story, I had no way to know the profound ways in which it would alter the two of us and deeply affect our lives. I honestly hoped it would help Jessica and not damage her in some way. She deserved to feel loved and whole, or at least as close to it as possible, given all she had been through. I hoped that sharing her life's story would allow her to feel some sense of liberation, even if only in some small, positive way. What actually happened surpassed my wildest hopes.

Jessi found herself, for the first time in nearly three decades following this tragedy, on the true path to healing. Through her counseling sessions with The Man, she learned things she'd repressed and pushed deep inside herself away from everyone, including herself. She saw the clear division she had created between herself, as a child, the broken little girl she would carry within her in the decades and herself as Jessi, the survivor, who would find a way to walk out the other side of this tragedy. She learned a lot about her own life, the driving force behind many of her quirks, compulsions, and the power of moving back into her own skin. It was beautiful to witness the transformation. (And that's not to say she's done healing or transforming her life by any means, but it's been incredible to watch.) I often found myself thinking she never probably would have freely accepted help or felt the need to heal the scars of the past if it wasn't for this project. I fear that we would have lost her in December 2016 if not for this pivotal project. I know it to be true. And, for that, we are both eternally grateful.

As for me, I found myself on a curious quest to learn every vivid detail of my cousin's sordid past. The one other people didn't feel comfortable talking about with her, ever. From the moment we reconnected, I knew that no person deserved to carry the weight of the heavy past she carried and definitely not alone. I wanted to help her carry the load, to share the burden. I guess you could say I wanted to help her unpack. We wept together. We laughed together. And most importantly, we grew together. Together, our initial goal of telling her story blossomed into a mission of also writing to honor her—our—family, acknowledge her past, and do what we could to spread hope and healing into the world beyond the bounds of our own words to those people walking amongst us in need of hope, understanding, compassion, love, and some hope of healing. No one else deserves to carry the load alone, any more than my cousin did. Trauma victims do not deserve the things that happen to them. They are left broken and forced to find a way to pick up the pieces.

It wasn't until I began speaking with Jessica about the funeral that I realized I had what I now know to be undiagnosed Post-Traumatic Stress Disorder (PTSD) related to death and funerals. Anything related to a funeral, the ceremonious 21-gun-salute, or the singing of the song "Amazing Grace" throughout my life caused me to experience an immediate visceral reaction. I remember sitting in the wooden pew of a large Catholic church, filled to capacity, for the death of my grandmother—my dad's mom—when I was in my early thirties. That moment transported me back to that crowded little white church in Lakeville, Indiana, in 1989. Back to the events that would long ago precipitate this project, back to where Jessica's tragic story began. The people all around, the sadness, the honoring of life, the sense of loss. Emotion overtook me, and I remember audibly sobbing, nearly unable to catch my breath in the throes of grief at my Grandma Albertina's funeral.

At the funeral for my husband's grandmother, when they went outside to do the 21-gun-salute in her honor, I stayed inside the funeral home. I just couldn't witness it. Even in the building, with each shot fired, I found myself struggling through emotions that had a whole lot more to do with the past than the present. It took me back to my Uncle Eddie—Jessica's dad's—funeral, when I was just seven years old. What I saw in that moment was my Aunt Dawn all dressed in black, being handed a folded flag to signify the death of her young husband, now gone. These things change us. They alter the way we experience life. And maybe they're supposed to. The sting of death does not leave us untouched. It shouldn't.

When I interviewed Stephanie and Mona for this book, I quickly realized they each bore some level of undiagnosed PTSD, just like I did. Undoubtedly, anyone in attendance at the Pelley funeral all those years ago probably did. As humans, we experience trauma, we push it behind us, and seal it over, much like a scab on an emotional wound, as a coping mechanism. It allows us to go on, to pick up the broken pieces and move forward. It works for us most of the time, until we hear, see, taste, or remember something that transports us right back to the past and reconnects us to that wound. Then the scab is off, the pain reemerges, and we are emotionally hemorrhaging from the inside, unbeknownst to those around us.

I wonder if the school photographer ever realized that he or she would be the last person to ever take a school photo of little Janel and Jolene. The trauma would cast a series of invisible ripples throughout the lives of every single person who knew them. For their classmates, the empty desks where Janel and Jolene once sat now lay empty. The place in all future yearbooks for the little "Pelley" girls would be skipped over for the rest of time. And each person who knew Dawn Hayes-Huber-Pelley or Bob Pelley would now have a space in their life once held by them. The ripples would run as deep as fault lines in the earth through the lives of those who knew them, those who loved them, all who remembered them, and those who would miss them. We would bury them, bury the pain, and move on, the way we all did.

I learned a lot from my cousin in the nearly two years we spent working on this book. One thing that stands out prominently for me is the observation that trauma victims are a walking contradiction. They desperately want love and acceptance, yet they rebel and rage against the world, much like those little broken children Jessi tries to help at the daycare center. As Jessi so eloquently tells it, "Being a survivor of trauma is a lot like being an alcoholic. Once you're an alcoholic, you're always going to be an alcoholic. It's the same with people who've suffered trauma. Those people will always be trauma survivors. Forever. Nothing will ever change that." Adult trauma survivors may eventually begin to heal, lift their heads back up, and move on, but then something happens that swiftly pulls them back to the dwelling grounds of sorrow. I saw it happen a few times along the way.

In July 2017, Jessi's dog of 13 years, K.O., was diagnosed with fatal cancer. For the remaining weeks she had left to love him—knowing all too well that death was on its way—she had to watch him stop eating, cease nearly all activity, and eventually die. For her, K.O. was a family member, like having another child. That loss devastated her in much the same way that Lexi's death had. I hated every minute of her suffering. Then in March 2018, I received a phone call from Jessi advising me that there had been a shooting at her daughter's college. Her daughter wasn't harmed or involved, but I cannot even begin to articulate how difficult it is to try to find the right words to assure a former trauma survivor that "it's okay" and "don't worry," when there's absolutely *nothing okay* about the fact that this beautiful person, my cousin, is now perpetually forced to relive the unlivable and to endure the unendurable with each and every triggering event for the rest of her life.

Of all the things I learned from Jessica, the most profound I learned at age 12, was to never proffer hollow words, even if societally appropriate and well-intended to a person in grief. The little girl standing on the grass outside that little white tent in 1989 became a permanent reminder of that particular lesson over the years. I still see her standing there, off to my right, in her little dress and thick glasses, her entire life obliterated and gone.

Actions are what help people in those moments, not words. Rather than saying you'll be there for a person, actually make the effort to be. The most commonly uttered words at any funeral are always, "Let me know if you need anything at all." Let's all spare the words and show up with a casserole, a kind gesture, or better yet, simply our time and attention, instead. Let's listen to the stories. Let's be there to give a damn. It's a lesson I've carried with me for nearly 30 years following this tragedy and one I now believe even more deeply after working with my cousin to tell this story.

It's never too late to make amends.

It's not too late to show you care.

Sometimes uncomfortable conversations must be had.

It's okay to ask the questions. To be unsure. To try to figure it out.

Sometimes we need to own up to the things we did, or those we failed to do.

And it's never too late to tell someone you care, will be there for them, and that you love them.

It's being there for people and loving them that matters most.

It is something they will never forget.

Actions and love have the power to change things.

To alter futures. To transform lives. To give roots to love.

And to change the face of humanity in some small way.

The power to change EVERYTHING.

If only, you find the words. If only, you follow through with actions.

My dear cousin, Jessica Pelley, taught me that.

JESSI

AGE 37
April 2018

A candle doesn't shine as brightly in the light of day because its glow is consumed by the day's light. But in the darkness, that same candle blazes like a luminous torch. Because of the darkness, that one tiny flame has the power to illuminate an entire room. It holds the ability to light the path for others who are lost and stumbling. Because of the darkness, people not only see it, but are drawn to it. They turn toward the light, and they feel its true power. One light in a whole lot of darkness.

I'm the same as other people in most regards. As humans, we are each alike in so many ways. Yet I will *always* be different than most of the people around me because of what I have lived through. Much like people who survive alcoholism, I am a survivor of trauma. I will never escape that. It is a title I will always bear. But today, I realize what makes me different is that I have proven I possess the ability to shine my light from the darkest of places. My light defies the darkness, and there isn't a damn thing the darkness can do about it but watch it shine.

What I want you to know is this: If you were mistreated in life, it wasn't your fault. If your fate was determined by the hands of someone else, as mine was in 1989, you can find a way to carve your own path. If you feel you will never be the same person you once were because the darkness came into your life, you're right, and that's okay. I've been there. You still have power. You can light a candle and walk alongside me: into the darkness, through the darkness, and out the other side of hell, toward the light.

That's the power I have today because of what happened to me. The power to tell my own story. The power to pull others back toward the light. To remind them it's still there. They are not alone. We can stand in the power of our own choices. We can walk with our own light. It is the darkness that gave us this power. Even if the *only* light around us is our own, that faint glimmer shining from deep within, it is enough.

When the darkness surrounds you at every angle, keep pushing.

Walking forward, even when you no longer see the way.

You must survive the darkness, to seek the light.

It's still there.

After all these years of sorrow and suffering, that's what I learned.

The light is still there.

You just have to find it.

What if I had killed myself? Well, then I wouldn't be here to make new memories with my husband and two beautiful children, to create new traditions and have a home with my own family, filled with love. I wouldn't be here to tell this story today. I wouldn't be here to prove to others that you can survive tragedy and darkness, no matter how tragic, or how dark. If I had ended my life, I wouldn't be able today to tell all the people who feel like they are defined by the cracks within them, created by the things that happened to them, that they are not. The cracks in us do not define us. What we choose to do, in spite of those cracks does. We have power over what we choose to do now, the people we are and where we go from here.

What if I find a way to drop all this heavy baggage I've endlessly carried for 29 years?

What if I find a way to create a new normal that sets me a little freer?

What if I surround myself with people who make me feel whole and not broken?

What if I turn back to laugh in the face of darkness? It's stolen enough of my life already.

What if I hold my head high, rise up, and make the most of each of the days I have left?

What if this single choice alone writes my next chapter in light? Because I'm pretty sure it will.

For my final "what if": What if I choose to take what happened to me 29 years ago, and to help others gripped by debilitating darkness? What if I help some others to find *the hope to live*? I think I like *that* what if the most.

So maybe the what ifs aren't so bad, at least not if you ask the right ones. I refuse to live in the past anymore. We don't get to go back. We only get to move forward. Those cracks don't define me. Not anymore.

Today, I'm unpacking. I will never forget the dark roads I traveled on the way here, but today, I am moving forward. Lighter. Happier. More resilient than before. I hope every person sitting in the darkness finds a way to join me. What if they do? What if we *really* find a way to be *happier*, and *lighter*, and *free*?

What if . . .

JESSI

April 2018
Present Day

*T*elling my life story aloud to my cousin felt therapeutic. I was finally able to set it all free. In the nearly three decades I spent with this story living silently within me, it had unintentionally become my prison. In telling it, I had to reclaim every piece of me. Every shattered bit. Every shiny one, too. I had to own every memory and every scar. I had to be willing to look at every moment of my life in order to see it for what it was and what it could be now.

As I spilled the words aloud on the phone and Jamie etched them onto these pages, I wondered how I would feel when we got to the end, and then that day finally came.

Today, 29 years later, when I walked up to the mirror hanging in my bathroom and looked at myself as a 38-year-old woman, what I saw staring back at me for the first time, in a long time, was Jessica. That damn girl. The girl who fought to remain alive. The girl I tried to suppress. The girl who hurt so deeply, I had to tuck her wounded spirit away. I had planned to keep her hidden, but I don't think I realized I ever did this as the years passed. I know that now. I tried to kill Jessica along the way. I had to. It was the only way I could survive.

Jessica was the girl I tried to convince to take her own life on more than one occasion. The girl who fought against me and the one who angered me. The one who made me feel the deepest sorrow and grief. The one who made me feel desperate, left behind, and alone. The one I no longer listened to, felt like, or wanted to be any longer. The little girl who lost everything and everyone. She was the one who was left behind to tell stories and finally get the words down on a page, nearly 30 years later. She was me.

Today, I finally see her staring back at me. Perhaps, she really was here all along. But now I don't want to look away. I don't want to run and hide. I don't want to lash out at her. I don't want to try to bury her below the layers of my carefully constructed life. Instead, I want to hug her tightly, like I do all the precious, broken little children in my life. I want to fight my way through her flailing arms and enraged spirit, even if it means harm might come to myself, to let her know I'm here for her. I want to whisper the words "I love you" in a pure, true way. I want to tell her, "You may feel different or broken, but you aren't bad. You never were. You just made some bad choices along the way. We all do. But you are good. You aren't alone. I am here for you. I love you. And I will always be here for you. You are not alone anymore. You have me."

More than anything else I want to tell her I'm proud of her. I want to thank her for fighting for me, despite my unrelenting desire to kill her off. I want to thank her for the memories she refused to let go of. I want to tell her that I'm so glad I am still here, though I never thought I would be: glad or here. I want to tell her that she is strong, and bold, and fierce, and different, and brave, and courageous, and crazy, and daring, and beautiful. I want to tell her that her mom would hate the pink hair. I mean *really freaking* hate it. I want to tell her that she shouldn't care if her mom hates it or not. It's her. And she should be exactly who she was born to be.

I want to tell her not to be afraid anymore. She made it. She's here to tell her own story.

For the first time in almost 30 years, the thing I want to say most to the girl staring back at me in the mirror today—the one who has been here unbeknownst to me all along—is, "Hi Jessica." I will not turn away. I will not run. I am no longer scared of you. I will stand tall and look you in the eyes today. I'm glad you finally made it out the other side of the darkness. Past the tragedy. Back in to my life. Jessica was the warrior within me all along. The storm inside me that wouldn't be silenced. The little girl who refused to give up. She was never the weak one, always the strong. I just didn't realize it while I walked the path in front of you all these years. You were the one they could all leave behind, even forget about, but not undo, not completely. The girl who would not fall. The girl who did not die. The one who felt it all, remembered it all, tucked it all away, and made it out the other side of the barren ashes to tell this story. You are still here. And you matter.

Hello, Jessica. For the first time in a long time . . . Hello. Please allow me to introduce you to Jessi. It's been a long damn time coming. As of today, I am officially setting you free . . .

To live.
To love.
To be.

JESSICA & JESSI

The Final Chapter

I AM JESSICA HUBER.

I AM JESSICA PELLEY.

I AM JESSI TORONJO.

My mother was Dawn Hayes.
She was also known as Dawn Huber.
And Dawn Pelley.

Janel Huber was my little sister, my childhood sidekick, my constant companion.
As was the little girl known as Janel "Pelley."

And Jolene Huber was my baby sister.
As was the ever-curious and incredibly messy Jolene "Pelley."

We each became what we were through the things that happened to us.
The decisions made for us.
The life thrust upon us.
The tragedy that claimed us each, in one way or another.
Inalterably changing everything.
Our lives unknowingly altered between two fleeting slivers of time.

We are more than the stories on these pages.
We are more than the memories now left behind.
We are people.
We were a family.
And today, in telling this story, I stand in truth and light.
As does my family.

May the embers continue to burn bright long after the last page is turned.

Long after the last breath was drawn.

Long after I gave up, many, many times, then stood tall, forged by the losses that claimed everything I had in this world, besides me.

Over time, what I realized is this: We get to become the people we choose to be.

When we rise up to reclaim the essence of who we are, we not only direct our own path, but empower others drowning in darkness to do the same. To rise up. To seek the light. It's still there.

Today, I am Jessica.

Every version of her you met in this book.

The one I continue to become day-by-day moving past this tragedy.

The one owning every single word of her own story.

I am Jessica.

Unapologetically.

Set free.

AFTERWORD

I intentionally omitted this page on the final version of the manuscript I gave to Jessi prior to publication. She will read these words for the first time when she holds this book, her story, in her hands for the first time.

Jessi,

I feel it is finally time that I share one last important piece of information and one last truth with you. It is the one detail that I intentionally withheld from you during our journey.

It's about that little girl you used to play with.

The one you stayed with.

The little girl who was with you on your darkest day.

The one whose name you no longer remember.

The Nameless Girl, she is no longer nameless.

Her name is Holly.

And Jess, more than anything, what I want you to know is this:

I SEE YOU.
We all do.

We Remember...

My daddy,

EDWARD J. HUBER

1957–1985

We Remember...

My mom,

DAWN (HAYES HUBER) PELLEY

1957–1989

We Remember...

My little sister,

JANEL (HUBER) PELLEY

1980–1989

We Remember...

My little sister,

JOLENE (HUBER) PELLEY

1982–1989

For you,
I SURVIVED TO TELL OUR STORY.

Ed, Dawn, Jessica, Jolene, and Janel Huber

Dawn and Ed Huber, Jessica's mom and dad

Jessica, age 5

Jolene and Jessica

Dawn, Ed, Janel, and Jessica Huber

Jessica, age 5

Janel and Jessica

Jolene, Janel, and Jessica

The parsonage

Dawn, Jacque, "Jeff," Jessica, Jolene, "Bob," and Janel Pelley

Olive Branch United Brethern Church, Lakeville, Indiana

Graves of "Bob," Dawn, Jolene, and Janel Pelley

Jessi, senior year

Jessi, talent show, senior year

Jessi, senior year

Jessi, eighth grade

Tyson and Jessi

Jessi, Tyson, and Dakota

Austin, Jessi, Tyson, and Dakota
(In her mom's wedding dress)

Jessi and Tyson

Tyson, Austin, Dakota, Jessi, and K.O.

Tyson, Dakota, Austin, and Jessi

Dakota and Austin

Stephanie and Jessi

Jessi and Jamie   *Mona and Jessi*

NATIONAL RESOURCES:

National Suicide Hotline (800) 273-TALK
If you are contemplating harming yourself, **text** 741741 at any time.

National Domestic Violence Hotline (800) 799-SAFE

National Child Abuse Hotline (800) 4-A-CHILD

Rape, Abuse, and Incest National Network (800) 656-4673

To find mental health services and support in your area, contact:
National Mental Health Association Information Center,
nmha.org

If you need help, the way I once did, consider checking
yourself into a local hospital.
It may save your life.
It saved mine.

If you need help, reach out.
Talk to one person you trust.
Text the number above.
Make the call.
Send the text.
Get help.
Seek the light.

—Jessi

WE NEED YOUR HELP!

If you enjoyed this book, we implore (yep, we're pretty much begging) you to:

» Post an online review.

» Share a link to this book on social media.

» Tell your friends about it.

We intentionally indie published this book to maintain full control of it. (Much love and a virtual high five to those who step up to help us out.)

To inquire about speaking engagements or share feedback with us, e-mail: contact@boldwhisperbooks.com

Follow us!
www.jessicabook.com
Facebook: I AM JESSICA BOOK
Twitter: @IAmJessicaBook

DO YOU HAVE AN IDEA FOR THE NEXT BOLD WHISPER BOOK?

» Would you like Jamie Collins to write *your* story?

» Bold Whisper Books is actively seeking its next story!

» We are interested in sharing the raw, real stories of survivors on the topics of human trafficking, rape, and school shootings, but are open to all ideas.

Write a summary of 3,000 words or less.
Include your name, telephone number, and e-mail.
Put "Story idea" in the subject line.
Send it to: ideas@boldwhisperbooks

BOLD WHISPER BOOKS
P.O. Box 854
Carmel, IN 46082
www.boldwhisperbooks.com

BOLD WHISPER BOOKS

Where stories breathe on paper. ™

Follow us on Twitter:
@iamjessicabook

Join us in the #IAm movement.
#Iam Jessica.
#Iam a survivor.
#Iam one of tragedy's daughters.
#Iam the face of PTSD.
#Iam owning my story.
#SheIsHope

What about you?
Tag us on Twitter.

ACKNOWLEDGEMENTS

TO CHOIR GIRL'S MOM:

Thank you for giving me a home; and not just a home, but the right kind of home. A place where I fit in and could exist as the girl who, at that time, I was. I appreciate everything you did for me. Thank you for giving me a stable place to live. For that and all you did to help me during those years, I am grateful.

TO ALL WHO HELPED TO CONVICT JEFF PELLEY:

I'd like to extend a warm shout out to each of the detectives who worked on my family's case in the early years, the entire cold case team who made the arrest and conviction of Jeff Pelley possible, the prosecutor who had the balls to bring this case to trial (as a cold case, eighteen years after the murders), the Supreme Court Justices who upheld Jeff's convictions, granting me some small semblance of peace, and every single person who thought of or prayed for me and my family over the years. Justice does not change the past, but it does help to make the steps one walks in the wake of tragedy lighter. For that, I am eternally grateful to all these individuals for their steadfast dedication, the incredible gift of their efforts and time, and this small gift I continue to carry as a result of their admirable actions. The gift of justice. For Jeff. And for that broken little girl I continue to carry inside me. Your work mattered. Your personal sacrifices mattered. And for all of it, every single moment you spent thinking about or working on this case on behalf of my family, I am forever grateful.

With great reverence, admiration, and respect.

TO THE MAN:

Thank you for shining a bright light upon my darkest days. For helping me to learn to understand myself better and realize that I can find a new way to live a happier, healthier, more peaceful life. One filled with light, and hope, and love. Thank you for helping me to search for the memories I deserve to remember. Thank you for helping me to realize my triggers, assisting me with finding new ways to cope with my issues, and helping me to learn how to create the type of life that I, as a grown woman—carrying a broken little girl inside her—deserve to live.

I already have four angels looking down on me now, but to me, you are a fifth. An angel in the form of a man—"The Man"—that I now have here on this earth. Thank you for helping me. Thank you for seeing me, the real me. Thank you for going out of your way to help me find myself, even when I didn't have the funds to pay you, and for giving so freely of your time to see me at ridiculously early morning hours, when you knew I needed it. And most importantly, thank you for giving a damn. My head is held high. And my heart is lighter. Thank you for showing me how to walk in the light.

TO OUR CREATIVE TEAM:

A big shout-out to our incredibly talented creative team: Lauren Sapala, Adrian James, Josh Humble, Alex Bird, and Najdan Mancic. Thank you to attorneys Joseph Dages and Teresa Todd for their legal expertise. We are forever grateful to our amazing publicists, Emi Battaglia and Jennifer Musico. And lastly, a special thank you to our families, friends, and awesome Beta Readers for their candid feedback, steadfast support, and unwavering belief in us and our ability to tell this story. We couldn't have done this without you. And we wouldn't want to. Thank you one thousand times.

BIBLIOGRAPHY

The Committee on Nomenclature and Statistics of the American Psychiatric Association. *Diagnostic and Statistical Manual of Mental Disorders*. India: CBS Publishers & Distributors, 5th edition 2017.

Haddock, Deborah. *The Dissociative Identity Disorder Sourcebook*. New York: McGraw-Hill Education, 2001.

"Dissociative Identity Disorder (Multiple Personality Disorder)" *Psychology Today* (New York, Reviewed 2019) https://www.psychologytoday.com/us/conditions/dissociative-identity-disorder-multiple-personality-disorder#definition

State v. Pelley, 828 N.E.2d 915 (Ind.2005).

Pelley v. State, 883 N.E.2d 874 (Ind.Ct.App.2008).

Pelley v. State, 901 N.E.2d 494 (Ind.2009), *reh'g denied.*

9 780960 086795